As American
As Apple Pie

As American As Apple Pie

BY PHILLIP STEPHEN SCHULZ

WINGS BOOKS

NEW YORK · AVENEL, NEW JERSEY

This 1996 edition is published by Wings Books,
a division of Random House Value Publishing, Inc.,
40 Engelhard Avenue, Avenel, New Jersey 07001,
by arrangement with the author.

Wings Books and colophon are registered trademarks of
Random House Value Publishing, Inc.

Random House
New York • Toronto • London • Sydney • Auckland
http://www.randomhouse.com/

Printed and bound in the United States of America

Library of Congress Cataloging-in-Publication Data
Schulz, Phillip Stephen.
As American as apple pie / by Phillip Stephen Schulz.
p.   cm.
Reprint. Originally published: New York : Simon & Schuster, 1990.
Includes bibliographical references and index.
ISBN 0-517-15034-4
1. Cookery, American. I. Title.
TX715.S299   1996
641.5973—dc20   96-34255
CIP

8 7 6 5 4 3 2 1

Dedication

*T*HIS BOOK is dedicated to the memory of Bert Greene. He guided my life and encouraged my talents in a much-too-short seventeen-year association. We worked well together. His death made the world a sadder place not just for me but for his family of friends and fans—and two cats, Dinah and Punch, and a dog named Lulu. We will meet again; sometime, someplace.

Contents

Introduction

DESPITE ANY doomsayers' thoughts on the subject, Americans still love to eat. And cook, too! It also is increasingly obvious that, as a nation, what we choose to prepare for ourselves most often are the homely and familiar dishes on which we were raised long, long before microwaves or macrobiotics came into our lives.

What I am speaking of are well-remembered comforting foods. And while the dishes that gave us emotional security as kids do not necessarily make us feel better as adults—particularly when we lose jobs, spouses, or big bucks in the stock market—there is a real measure of contentment in eating what we know best. Because familiar foods remind us of who we are, as well as who we once were.

When I left home (over twenty years ago), I would, on occasion, have an urge for my mother's cooking, and simply request the recipe for a dish I "had a mouth for," as we said back in Colorado. Well, in the passing decades, I acquired quite a collection; all hand-inscribed on 3-by-5 cards. Some are now so dog-eared and smudged with use, I can barely read them. But I wasn't the only one of the Schulz's eight children who felt the need to recall past comforts from our dinner table. My sisters and brothers were always asking my mother for one or another of her recipes, too. A few years back, we were all happily surprised to find in our Christmas packages a hand-written, bound, soft-cover cookbook simply titled *Recipes from Home*. All our favorite childhood foods were there. A more comforting gift I can't imagine.

American food is free form. Unlike classic French and Chinese cuisines, our fare has no basic set of rules. American food scholars are hard put to present a recipe for a given dish as the *only* authentic rendering. Quite the contrary. Because our cooking is basically imprecise, and much improvised by the immigrant hands that stirred each pot, it's a cuisine of *echt* (true character). There are literally hundreds of variations of every American dish. Recipes that, in fact, change drastically with each locale and forebear. For this collection I have calculatedly limited the selection to the twelve "very best" of each that I know: from apple pies to waffles, a formidable display of originality at the stove.

This is a collection meant to be a celebration of America's best home fare. Wonderful dishes to be enjoyed casually and comfortably, which is true American style. A book that is at "home on everyone's range."

Apple Pies

JOHN CHAPMAN, alias "Johnny Appleseed," was not a pie baker and probably didn't give a piffle about pastry. But Chapman is indubitably the man responsible for America's love of apple pie, because he alone planted thousands of apple trees in this country in his venerable lifetime.

Artists tend to see Johnny Appleseed as a wild-eyed giant, scattering seeds from a bag slung across his narrow shoulders. He was eccentric without a doubt, but not the bumbling character depicted by legend and devised by lore. While it's true he had an obsession with apples, he was educated enough to know that apples grown from seed revert back to their wild state. Instead of seeds, Chapman planted *seedlings* in carefully planned orchard sites, beginning on the Atlantic coast and attempting to work his way across the U.S. Sad to say, he got only as far as Fort Wayne, Indiana by the time he died in 1845.

Apples were long established in New England by the time Chapman was born in Massachusetts in 1774. Apple pies, for that matter, had been part of British cuisine since Elizabethan times. The British prized that pie so dearly, Jane Austen once wrote, "Good apple pies are a considerable part of our domestic happiness." The Pilgrim women stashed their pie recipes along with rolling pins when they came to Plymouth Rock. They also brought apple cuttings from England and like the Colonists, the cuttings eventually flourished in the New World.

The apple was an important staple in eighteenth- and nineteenth-century New England. It could be served in one form or another at every meal. Apples were inevitably dished up for breakfast in pie form, a culinary notion that occasioned more than a few snickers in the rest of the country. When quizzed on this peculiarly Down East tradition, Ralph Waldo Emerson simply implored, "What (else) is pie for?"

By the end of the nineteenth century, eight thousand apple varieties were listed by the Department of Agriculture; today there are probably tens of thousands. Few, however, show up on supermarket shelves because of the unfortunate commercial demand for long keeping fruit. But, with the rising awareness of some consumers, and such innovations as inner-city green markets, locally grown apples of true bite and savor are once more becoming available.

Putting Your Pie in Apple-Pie Order My favorite apple for pie is the Rhode Island Greening. The next, and more available, choice would be the Granny Smith. Other fine regional pie apples include Empire, Gravenstein, MacCoun, Rome Beauty, Jonathan, and the York Imperial. Forget the ubiquitous Delicious. Like everything else that is over-mass-marketed these days (in crop size the Delicious is the number one apple in the world) it's long on shelf life, but virtually lifeless on tastebuds. Pick apples that are firm to the touch and "bruise free." Store them in the refrigerator unless you plan to use them in a day or two, in a loosely tied plastic bag with several holes poked in it. Apples need to breathe!

Whether one opts for flour, tapioca, ground crackers, or ground cornflakes as thickener depends not so much on the quirk of the cook, as the juiciness of the apple. I have often found even the best apples, because they were improperly stored or picked past their prime, exuding vast amounts of liquid after they are sliced. Some cooks add more thickening, others drain cut apples before they hit the pie shell. I use my eye, adding only enough liquid so the apples are well moistened, but *not* swimming in their own juice! When you slice apples in advance, keep them well covered in ice-cold water laced with lemon juice, to keep the fruit from turning brown. And always use a stainless steel knife to slice apples as carbon will turn an apple's crisp clean flesh to an ugly spotted mess. To test an apple for doneness when baked in a double-crusted pie, insert an ice pick or toothpick through one of the slashes to avoid damaging the crust.

When handling pastry dough, no matter how rich, the secret of success is *not* overworking the dough. I do not use a food processor for pastry dough. Like old-fashioned cooks, I believe pastry-making is a hands-on experience. Combine the shortening and flour with a pastry blender until it's of crumbly texture, then start adding water, about a tablespoon at a time, cutting the liquid into the dough with a knife or a fork. As the mixture starts to form a mass, use your fingertips to work in the remaining water. Touch will tell you when the dough is soft and pliable. Then, holding the dough in the outstretched palm of one hand, push it with the heel of the other, a bit at a time, until it stretches over your fingers. This ensures that the shortening is well incorporated. As the shortening will warm slightly during the kneading process, it is best to chill it before rolling, to make it easier to work with.

When rolling out pastry, use a well-balanced wooden rolling pin. A French pin, with its tapered ends, gives the pie maker the most control. In my opinion, marble rolling pins, while good in theory (marble stays cool), are much too unwieldy. Keep your board and pin *lightly* floured at all times. Use only enough flour to keep the dough from sticking to the board and avoid working extra flour into the dough as you roll it as extra flour turns a crust heavy. Always roll dough out away from you, lifting and turning it 90 degrees after every few rolls. This keeps the dough from sticking to the board. Remember, a light touch means a light crust later on. Practiced pastry makers can roll out even the "shortest" (richest) dough, which because of its high fat content is difficult to handle. Neophytes, however, may wish to place the dough between two sheets of floured wax paper before rolling. Once the dough is rolled out, gently peel away the top sheet. Flip the dough over the pie pan and carefully remove the remaining paper.

*I*N THE APPLE collection that follows, you will find the best regional pies I've tasted from Bangor, Maine, to Baja, California. At its best, apple pie should be served slightly warm with a pitcher of thick cream, a dipper of soft ice cream, or a boat of runny vanilla custard sauce. Name your own dietary downfall!

MY FIRST PIE

NOT THE FIRST by far that I ever ate, but certainly the one I cut my baking teeth on, was the apple pie made at The Store in Amagansett—America's first gourmet "take-out food" establishment—where I learned early in the 1970s all there was to know about making pie crust. I once figured I've made over a thousand so far. As Jonathan Swift wrote in "Polite Conversation" (1738), "Promises and pie crust are made to be broken." I, for one, take both promises and pie crusts alike with a grain of salt. Both should be "short" and sincerely made, as well.

For the pastry

2 cups all-purpose flour

1/4 teaspoon sugar

1/2 teaspoon salt

Pinch of ground cinnamon

1/2 cup (1 stick) unsalted butter, chilled

3 tablespoons vegetable shortening, chilled

5 tablespoons cold water (approximately)

For the filling

2 1/2 pounds green apples (about 5 large)

1 1/2 tablespoons all-purpose flour

1 cup sugar

Pinch of salt

1 tablespoon ground cinnamon

1/8 teaspoon freshly grated nutmeg

1 tablespoon lemon juice

Finely grated peel of 1 lemon

1/2 teaspoon vanilla

1 1/2 tablespoons unsalted butter

1 large egg, beaten

1. To make the pastry: Combine the flour with the sugar, salt, and cinnamon in a medium bowl. Cut in the butter and shortening with a knife. Blend with a pastry blender until the mixture has the texture of coarse crumbs. Add the water, about a tablespoon at a time, and mix gently with a fork or your fingertips to form a soft dough. Do not overwork. Refrigerate 1 hour.

2. Preheat the oven to 450° F.

3. To make the filling: Peel, core, and slice the apples into a large bowl. Sprinkle with the flour, and add the sugar, salt, cinnamon, nutmeg, lemon juice, lemon peel, and vanilla. Toss well.

4. Roll out slightly more than half the pastry on a lightly floured board. Line a 9-inch pie plate with the pastry. Pile the apple filling into the prepared pastry shell. Dot with the butter.

5. Roll out the remaining pastry and place over the pie. Seal, trim, and flute the edges. Cut several slashes in the top pastry to release steam. Brush with beaten egg. Place the pie on a foil-lined baking sheet and bake 15 minutes. Reduce the oven heat to 350° F. and bake until golden and the apples are tender, about 50 minutes longer.

Serves 8

AN AMERICAN CLASSIC

MY FATHER adores cheese with apple pie, preferably an aged cheddar from Wisconsin, his birth state. I've never really cottoned to the notion, but the coupling is so ingrained in our culture, it's known as a food marriage made in heaven. Eugene Field, the American poet, thought so too:

> But I, when I undress me
> Each night upon my knees
> Will ask the Lord to bless me
> With apple pie and cheese
> —*Apple Pie and Cheese, 1896*

For the pastry

2 1/2 cups all-purpose flour

1 teaspoon sugar

1/2 teaspoon salt

1/2 cup (1 stick) unsalted butter, chilled

1/2 cup vegetable shortening, chilled

1 teaspoon finely grated orange peel

4 tablespoons orange juice

For the filling

3 pounds green apples (about 6 large)

1/3 cup plus 1 1/2 tablespoons all-purpose flour

3/4 cup sugar

1 teaspoon ground cinnamon

1/8 teaspoon freshly grated nutmeg

1 teaspoon finely grated orange peel

1 teaspoon vanilla

1/2 cup honey

1/3 cup dark brown sugar (packed)

Pinch of ground ginger

3 1/2 tablespoons unsalted butter, chilled

1 large egg, beaten

Thinly sliced cheddar cheese

1. To make the pastry: Combine the flour with the sugar and salt in a medium bowl. Cut in the butter, shortening, and orange peel with a knife. Blend with a pastry blender until the mixture has the texture of coarse crumbs. Add the orange juice, about a tablespoon at a time, and mix gently with a fork or your fingertips to form a soft dough. Do not overwork. Refrigerate 1 hour.

2. To make the filling: Peel, core, and slice the apples into a large bowl. Sprinkle with 1 1/2 tablespoons flour, the sugar, 1/2 teaspoon cinnamon, nutmeg, orange peel, vanilla, and honey. Toss well. Let stand, tossing occasionally, 30 minutes.

3. Preheat the oven to 450° F.

4. Combine the remaining 1/3 cup flour with the remaining 1/2 teaspoon cinnamon, the brown sugar, and ginger in a small bowl. Mix well. Add 2 tablespoons butter and work the mixture with your fingers until it is mealy. Remove 1/4 cup and set aside.

5. Roll out slightly more than half the pastry on a lightly floured board. Line a 9-inch pie plate with pastry. Drain the apple slices, reserving the liquid. Layer the apples in the pastry shell, sprinkling with the flour mixture as you layer. Sprinkle the filling with 5 tablespoons of the reserved apple liquid. Dot the top with the remaining 1 1/2 tablespoons butter.

6. Roll out the remaining pastry and cut into 1/2-inch-wide strips. Weave the strips into a lattice pattern over the apples. Trim and flute the edges. Sprinkle the reserved 1/4 cup flour mixture in the open spaces. Brush the pastry with beaten egg. Place the pie on a foil-lined baking sheet and bake 15 minutes. Reduce the oven heat to 350° F. and bake, basting occasionally with any overflowing juices, until golden and the apples are tender, about 50 minutes longer. Serve with cheddar cheese slices.

Serves 8

APPLE AND CHEESE PIE

ANOTHER OLD American folk rhyme says it very succinctly. "Apple pie without cheese is like a kiss without a squeeze!" No puritan partnership, this version has the cheese *in,* not on, the pie. The recipe comes from the Dummerston Valley in Vermont where the crisp, toothsome "macs" provide a holy alliance with the champion local yellow cheddar. Surprisingly, native cooks serve up this pie with a *gob* of whipped cream.

For the pastry

2 cups plus 2 teaspoons all-purpose
    flour
2 teaspoons sugar
1/2 teaspoon salt
1/2 cup lard, chilled

1/4 cup vegetable shortening, chilled
1 large egg, lightly beaten
1 1/2 teaspoons red wine vinegar
2 tablespoons cold water

3/4 cup sugar

2 tablespoons all-purpose flour

Pinch of salt

1/2 teaspoon ground cinnamon

Pinch of freshly grated nutmeg

Finely slivered peel of 1 lemon

Juice of 1 lemon

2 1/2 pounds red or green apples (about 5 large)

1 cup grated sharp cheddar cheese

1 tablespoon unsalted butter

1 tablespoon heavy or whipping cream

1. To make the pastry: Combine 2 cups flour with the sugar and salt in a medium bowl. Cut in the lard and shortening with a knife. Blend with a pastry blender until the mixture has the texture of coarse crumbs. Add the beaten egg, vinegar, and water, about a tablespoon at a time, and mix gently with a fork or your fingertips to form a very soft dough. Do not overwork. Sprinkle with the 2 teaspoons flour. Refrigerate 1 hour.

2. Preheat the oven to 400° F.

3. To make the filling: Combine 1/2 cup sugar, the flour, salt, cinnamon, and nutmeg in a small bowl. Mix well.

4. Roll out slightly more than half the pastry on a lightly floured board. Line a 9-inch pie plate with pastry. Sprinkle the bottom with 2 teaspoons cinnamon mixture.

5. Combine the remaining 1/4 cup sugar with the lemon peel and lemon juice in a large bowl. Peel, core, and cut the apples into slices, adding them to the lemon mixture as you cut them.

6. Add the remaining cinnamon mixture to the apple mixture. Toss well and pile into the prepared pastry shell. Sprinkle the cheese over the top, tucking it into the spaces between the apples. Dot with butter.

7. Roll out the remaining pastry and place over the pie. Seal, trim, and flute the edges. Cut several slashes in the top pastry to release steam. Brush with cream. Place the pie on a foil-lined baking sheet and bake until golden and the apples are tender, about 50 minutes.

Serves 8

NUTTY SOUR CREAM APPLE PIE

FROM THE "red orchard" country of southeastern Pennsylvania comes an apple pie of a different stripe. Probably Amish in origin, it's a plain dessert neither too sweet nor too tart—but just right for a scoop of "cream" as the Plain Folk say.

For the pastry

2 1/2 cups all-purpose flour

1 teaspoon sugar

1/2 teaspoon salt

1/2 cup (1 stick) unsalted butter, chilled

1/2 cup vegetable shortening, chilled

1 teaspoon finely grated orange peel

4 tablespoons orange juice

For the filling

1/2 cup chopped pecans

3 tablespoons dark brown sugar

1 teaspoon ground cinnamon

3 tablespoons all-purpose flour

1/4 teaspoon salt

1/4 teaspoon freshly grated nutmeg

1/2 cup sour cream

1 large egg

1/3 cup honey

1/2 teaspoon vanilla

2 pounds green apples (about 4 large)

1 tablespoon heavy or whipping cream

1. To make the pastry: Combine the flour with the sugar and salt in a medium bowl. Cut in the butter, shortening, and orange peel with a knife. Blend with a pastry blender until the mixture has the texture of coarse crumbs. Add the orange juice, about a tablespoon at a time, and mix gently with a fork or your fingertips to form a soft dough. Do not overwork. Refrigerate 1 hour.

2. Preheat the oven to 425° F.

3. To make the filling: Combine the pecans, brown sugar, and cinnamon in a small bowl. Mix well. Set aside.

4. Roll out slightly more than half the pastry on a lightly floured board. Line a 9-inch pie plate with pastry.

5. Combine the flour, salt, and nutmeg in a large bowl. Whisk in the sour cream, egg, honey, and vanilla. Peel, core, and cut the apples into slices, adding them to the sour cream mixture as you cut them. Toss well and pile into the prepared pastry shell. Sprinkle the reserved pecan mixture over the top.

6. Roll out the remaining pastry and cut into strips. Place over the pie in a lattice pattern. Trim and flute the edges. Brush with cream. Place the pie on a foil-lined baking sheet and bake 25 minutes. Reduce the oven heat to 350° F. and bake until golden and the apples are tender, about 25 minutes longer.

Serves 8

INDIANA CRUMBED APPLE
AND PEAR PIE

A MATCHED PAIR of compatible local fruits is the basis of this Midwestern classic. The recipe was inspired by the ex-Governor of Indiana Robert D. Orr's prize-winning entry in *Ladies Home Journal*'s contest of state governor's apple pies—back in 1983.

For the filling

2/3 cup sugar

1/2 teaspoon ground cinnamon

1/8 teaspoon freshly grated nutmeg

2 pounds green apples (about 4 large)

1 pound pears (2 large)

2 tablespoons lemon juice

2 tablespoons unsalted butter

For the topping

1/2 cup light brown sugar (packed)

1/2 cup (1 stick) unsalted butter, softened

Finely grated peel of 1 lemon

1 cup all-purpose flour

1. Preheat the oven to 350° F.

2. To make the filling: Combine the sugar, cinnamon, and nutmeg in a large bowl. Peel, core, and cut the apples into thin slices, adding them to the sugar mixture as you cut them. Peel, core, and cut the pears into thin slices. Add to the apple mixture. Sprinkle with lemon juice. Toss well and layer the mixture into a 9-inch deep-dish glass pie plate. Do not add the excess juices. Dot the top with butter.

3. To make the topping: Using a wooden spoon, mix the sugar with the butter and lemon peel until smooth. Work in the flour with your fingers until the mixture is crumbly in texture. Place over the top of the pie. Place the pie on a foil-lined baking sheet and bake until golden brown and apples are tender, about 1 hour.

Serves 8

GERMANTOWN ICED APPLE AND RAISIN PIE

ANOTHER PEERLESS bit of pastry from Pennsylvania. The recipe is an old one, undoubtedly annexed from a middle-European dessert known as Dutch apple cake. But how or when it was altered to fit a pie shell is anyone in Germantown's guess.

For the pastry

2 cups all-purpose flour	1/2 cup vegetable shortening, chilled
1/2 teaspoon sugar	6 ounces cream cheese
Pinch of salt	2 to 3 tablespoons cold water

For the filling

1/4 cup all-purpose flour	1/2 cup sugar
1/2 cup dark brown sugar (packed)	1 teaspoon ground cinnamon
3 tablespoons unsalted butter, chilled	2 pounds green apples (about 4 large)
1/2 cup seedless raisins	1 tablespoon milk

For the icing

1/2 cup confectioners' sugar   1/4 teaspoon hot water
1 tablespoon lemon juice

1. To make the pastry: Combine the flour with the sugar and salt in a medium bowl. Cut in the shortening and cream cheese with a knife. Blend with a pastry blender until the mixture has the texture of coarse crumbs. Add the water, about a tablespoon at a time, and mix gently with a fork or your fingertips to form a soft dough. Do not overwork. Refrigerate 1 hour.

2. Preheat the oven to 400° F.

3. Roll out slightly more than half the pastry on a lightly floured board. Line a 9-inch deep-dish glass pie plate with pastry. Trim the edges.

4. To make the filling: Combine the flour with the brown sugar in a medium bowl. Cut in the butter with a knife. Blend with a pastry blender until well mixed. Stir in the raisins.

5. Combine the sugar with the cinnamon in a large bowl. Peel, core, and slice the apples, adding them to the sugar mixture as you slice them. Toss well.

6. Sprinkle a third of the raisin mixture over the bottom of the prepared pie shell. Add half the apples. Continue to layer with raisin mixture and remaining apples, ending with raisin mixture.

7. Roll out the remaining pastry on a lightly floured board. Place over the pie. Trim and flute the edges. Cut a slash in the center of the top crust to allow steam to escape. Brush with milk. Place the pie on a foil-lined baking sheet and bake until apples are tender, about 50 minutes. The top crust will get very dark. Reduce the oven heat to 300° F. if it begins to get too dark. Cool on a rack.

8. To make the icing: Whisk the confectioners' sugar with the lemon juice and water in a small bowl until smooth. Drizzle over the top of the pie in an attractive pattern.

Serves 8

HOW, AND WHEN, TO SERVE APPLE PIE

To some, the correct way to serve a slice of apple pie is just as important as what is in it. Henry Ward Beecher, as quoted by *The American Heritage Cookbook* (1964), summed it up most poetically:

> While it is yet florescent, white or creamy yellow, with the merest drip of candied juice along the edges, (as if the flavor were so good to itself that its own lips watered!) of a mild and modest warmth, the sugar suggesting jelly, yet not jellied, the morsels of apple neither dissolved nor yet in original substance, but hanging as it were in a trance between the spirit and the flesh of applehood . . . then, O blessed man, favored by all the divinities! eat, give thanks, and go forth, 'in apple-pie order!'

CLAREMONT DEEP-DISH
APPLE PIE

DEEP-DISH PIES originated in England. The custom of baking pies in round, shallow pans rather than deep squares or oblongs, the traditional British style, began with America's thrifty Colonists—confined circles helped stretch sparse comestibles! This deep-dish recipe hails from New Hampshire where thrift is considered a native inheritance, and a high virtue. This recipe apparently was developed at a time when butter was not always on hand in great supply. Lard was added to the crust along with the butter.

For the pastry

1 1/2 cups all-purpose flour

1/4 teaspoon salt

6 tablespoons (3/4 stick) unsalted
   butter, chilled

6 tablespoons lard, chilled

6 tablespoons ice water

For the filling

3 pounds green apples (about 6 large),
   plus 1 small green apple (about 1/3
   pound)

4 tablespoons (1/2 stick) unsalted butter

1/2 cup dark brown sugar (packed)

1/4 cup maple syrup

1/2 teaspoon ground cinnamon

Finely slivered peel of 1 orange

1 tablespoon milk

1. To make the pastry: Combine the flour with the salt in a large bowl.
Cut in the butter and lard with a knife. Blend with a pastry blender until the
mixture has the texture of coarse crumbs. Using the pastry blender, cut the
water into the flour to form a soft, sticky dough. Transfer to a well-floured
board.

2. Pat the dough with floured hands and turn over, using a long metal
spatula if necessary. Gently roll the dough, using a well-floured rolling pin,
to a rectangle about 15 inches long and 10 inches wide. The dough will still
be fairly sticky at this point. With the use of the spatula, fold the left third
of the dough over the middle. Then fold the right third over. Pick the dough
up with the spatula and reflour the board. Continue to roll the dough and
fold over in thirds nine more times, flouring the board, the pin, and your
hands as you work. After the last folding, fold the dough over on itself. Chill
4 hours or overnight.

3. Preheat the oven to 400° F.

4. To make the filling: Peel, core and cut the 6 large apples into 1/4-
inch-thick slices. Place in a medium saucepan with 2 tablespoons butter, the
sugar, maple syrup, cinnamon, and orange peel. Cook, stirring constantly,
over medium heat until the apples begin to release their juices, about 3 minutes. Reduce the heat. Cover and cook the apples over medium-low heat until

almost tender, about 12 minutes. Transfer the apples, using a slotted spoon, to a 9-inch deep-dish glass pie plate. (Reserve juices for use at another time, or discard.)

5. Peel, core, and cut the small green apple into very thin slices. Layer over the cooked apples. Melt the remaining 2 tablespoons butter. Drizzle over the apples.

6. Roll out the pastry on a lightly floured board and place over the pie. Seal, trim, and flute the edges. Cut several slashes in the pastry to release steam. Brush with milk. Place the pie on a foil-lined baking sheet and bake until golden, about 35 minutes.

Serves 8

TWISTED FRIED-APPLE PIE

A CAPACIOUS Californian contribution—one that no doubt made its way west in a Conestoga wagon. The apples are sautéed first, then layered over a caramel-coated crust later. The twist is in the braided lattice-work topping.

For the pastry

2 cups all-purpose flour

1/4 teaspoon sugar

1/2 teaspoon salt

1/8 teaspoon freshly grated nutmeg

1/2 cup (1 stick) unsalted butter, chilled

3 tablespoons vegetable shortening, chilled

5 tablespoons cold water (approximately)

For the filling

1 3/4 cups plus 1 tablespoon sugar

1 lemon, halved

3 pounds apples (about 6 large)

4 tablespoons (1/2 stick) unsalted butter

1 tablespoon all-purpose flour

1/2 teaspoon ground cinnamon

1/8 teaspoon freshly grated nutmeg

1 tablespoon milk

1. To make the pastry: Combine the flour with the sugar, salt, and nutmeg in a medium bowl. Cut in the butter and shortening with a knife. Blend with a pastry blender until the mixture has the texture of coarse crumbs. Add the water, about a tablespoon at a time, and mix gently with a fork or your fingertips to form a soft dough. Do not overwork. Refrigerate 1 hour.

2. Preheat the oven to 400° F.

3. Roll out slightly more than half the pastry on a lightly floured board. Line a 9-inch pie plate with pastry. Trim and flute the edges. Line the pastry with foil and weight down. Bake 10 minutes. Remove the foil; cool.

4. To make the filling: Place 1/4 cup of the sugar in a medium heavy saucepan over medium-high heat. Cook without stirring until the sugar begins to melt and turn golden. Stir until smooth and deep caramel in color. Drizzle over the sides and bottom of the pastry shell.

5. Squeeze the lemon halves into a large bowl of cold water, and add them to the water. Peel, core, and cut the apples across into 1/4-inch-thick slices. Add the slices to the lemon water as you cut them.

6. Place 1 1/2 cups sugar on a large plate. Dry the apple slices, about 5 at a time, and coat with sugar on both sides.

7. Melt 2 tablespoons butter in a large heavy skillet over medium heat. Add the coated apple slices and cook on both sides until the apples begin to soften, about 1 1/2 minutes per side. Do not allow the butter to brown. Transfer the slices with tongs to the prepared pie shell. Continue to sauté the apples, adding more butter as needed. When a third of the apple slices are done, sprinkle with a third of the flour, cinnamon, and nutmeg. Continue layering the apples, sprinkling with flour, cinnamon, and nutmeg. After the last apple slices are layered, raise the heat slightly under the skillet and cook the remaining mixture until it is thick and golden brown, 1 to 2 minutes. Pour over the apples.

8. Roll out the remaining pastry and cut into thin strips. Place the strips, twisting them like ribbon, over the pie. Gently press the ends into the edges of the bottom crust. Brush with milk and sprinkle with the remaining 1 tablespoon sugar. Bake until lightly browned, about 30 minutes.

Serves 8

APPLE CHIFFON PIE

IN UPPER New York State, they claim this is a local pie "to die over!" It may be true, for it's wickedly rich and insidiously creamy—as all desserts are meant to be. The baked gingersnap pie crust adds a nippy bite that offsets the smooth texture of the filling.

For the pastry

1 1/2 cups ground gingersnaps (about 60 of the commercial variety)

1/4 cup confectioners' sugar

6 tablespoons (3/4 stick) unsalted butter, melted

For the filling

4 egg yolks

1/4 cup sugar

1 1/2 tablespoons cornstarch

1/4 teaspoon vanilla

3/4 cup milk, scalded

2 teaspoons lemon juice

1/4 cup apricot preserves

1/2 cup light brown sugar (packed)

3 tablespoons golden rum

1 1/4 pounds green apples (about 3 medium)

1 envelope unflavored gelatin

1/4 cup apple juice

1/2 cup heavy or whipping cream

1 tablespoon confectioners' sugar

3 egg whites

1. Preheat the oven to 300° F.

2. To make the pastry: Combine the ground gingersnaps with the confectioners' sugar in a medium bowl. Stir in the butter with a wooden spoon until well mixed. Press mixture over the bottom and sides of a 9-inch deep-dish glass pie plate. Bake 12 minutes. Cool on a wire rack.

3. To make the filling: Whisk the egg yolks with the sugar, cornstarch, vanilla, and scalded milk in the top of a double boiler. Cook, stirring constantly, over boiling water until thick, about 8 minutes. Cool to room temperature. Cover and refrigerate until well chilled.

4. Combine the lemon juice with the apricot preserves, brown sugar, and rum in a medium saucepan. Peèl, core, and slice the apples, tossing them into the apricot mixture as you cut them. Heat, stirring constantly, to boiling; reduce the heat. Cook uncovered, stirring frequently, over medium heat until the mixture becomes syrupy, about 15 minutes. Transfer the apple mixture to the container of a food processor. Process until smooth. Force the pureed apple mixture through a sieve into a medium bowl.

5. Soften the gelatin in the apple juice in a small bowl. Place the bowl in a pan of hot water. Stir until the gelatin dissolves. Whisk into the apple mixture. Cool to room temperature. Refrigerate, stirring occasionally, until very thick, about 30 minutes. Do not allow gelatin to set.

6. Beat the cream with the confectioners' sugar in a large bowl until very stiff.

7. Fold the custard into the apple mixture. Fold in the whipped cream. Return to the refrigerator.

8. Beat the egg whites until stiff. Fold into the apple/custard mixture. Pour into the prepared crust. Refrigerate at least 4 hours before serving.

Serves 8 to 10

QUAD CITIES BAKED APPLE
AND PUMPKIN PIE

THE BEST of Iowa's fall offerings are herewith baked and pureed together into what just might become the next Thanksgiving Day tradition elsewhere in the country.

For the pastry

1 1/2 cups all-purpose flour

1 teaspoon sugar

1/2 teaspoon salt

6 tablespoons lard, chilled

1 large egg yolk, lightly beaten

1 teaspoon red wine vinegar

2 to 3 tablespoons cold water

For the filling

1 small pumpkin (about 4 pounds)	1/8 teaspoon freshly grated nutmeg
2 1/2 pounds red apples (about 5 large)	1/4 teaspoon ground cloves
3 tablespoons unsalted butter, melted	3 medium eggs, separated
1/2 cup sugar	1/2 cup milk
1/4 cup maple syrup	1/4 cup heavy or whipping cream
1 teaspoon ground cinnamon	Sweetened whipped cream

1. To make the pastry: Combine the flour with the sugar and salt in a medium bowl. Cut in the lard with a knife. Blend with a pastry blender until the mixture has the texture of coarse crumbs. Add the beaten egg, vinegar, and water, about a tablespoon at a time, and mix gently with a fork or your fingertips to form a very soft dough. Do not overwork. Refrigerate 1 hour or until needed.

2. Preheat the oven to 325° F.

3. To make the filling: Cut the pumpkin in half across and scrape out the seeds and strings. Place flesh-side down on a lightly buttered baking dish. Bake until tender, about 1 hour and 15 minutes. Cool.

4. Meanwhile, cut the apples in half lengthwise. Remove core areas and place cut-side down on a lightly buttered baking sheet. Bake until tender, about 1 hour. Cool.

5. Scrape out 1 1/2 cups pumpkin flesh into a bowl. Remove the skins from the apples and add to the pumpkin. Place the mixture, a third at a time, in the container of a food processor. Process, using the pulse switch, until smooth. Do not overprocess or the mixture will liquefy.

6. Transfer the pureed fruit mixture to a large bowl. Whisk in the butter, sugar, maple syrup, cinnamon, nutmeg, cloves, egg yolks, milk, and the 1/4 cup cream. Beat the egg whites until stiff; fold into the filling.

7. Roll out the pastry and line a 10-inch glass or ceramic quiche dish, building up the sides as much as possible. Trim and flute the edges. Gently pour in the filling. Place the pie on a foil-lined baking sheet and bake in the 325° F. oven until firm, about 1 hour. Serve at room temperature or slightly chilled with sweetened whipped cream.

Serves 8

CRANBERRY-APPLE-RAISIN PIE

THIS IS some late Colonist's contribution to the good life. A pie rich and dense as mincemeat, but a lot less work. The combination is a natural when you realize cranberries and apples are distant cousins in the garden.

For the pastry

2 1/2 cups all-purpose flour

1 teaspoon sugar

1/2 teaspoon salt

1/2 cup (1 stick) unsalted butter, chilled

1/2 cup vegetable shortening, chilled

4 tablespoons cold water

1 large egg beaten with 1 tablespoon water

For the filling

1 cup cranberries, picked over, washed

1/2 cup seedless raisins

1 cup plus 1 tablespoon sugar

1/2 cup dark brown sugar (packed)

Finely grated peel of 1 orange

2 tablespoons orange juice

1 tablespoon quick-cooking tapioca

1/2 teaspoon ground cinnamon

Pinch of ground cloves

1 pound green apples (about 2 large)

1/4 cup walnuts, chopped

1. To make the pastry: Combine the flour with the sugar and salt in a medium bowl. Cut in the butter and shortening with a knife. Blend with a pastry blender until the mixture has the texture of coarse crumbs. Add the water, about a tablespoon at a time, and mix gently with a fork or your fingertips to form a soft dough. Do not overwork. Refrigerate 1 hour.

2. Preheat the oven to 425° F.

3. Roll out slightly more than half the pastry and line a buttered 9-inch loose bottom tart pan. Build the edges up slightly higher than the pan. Trim. Brush with some of the egg and water mixture, set aside the rest.

4. To make the filling: Combine the cranberries with the raisins in a large bowl. Stir in the 1 cup sugar, the brown sugar, orange peel, orange juice, tapioca, cinnamon, and cloves.

5. Peel the apples and grate them directly into the cranberry mixture. Pour the mixture into the prepared pie shell.

6. Roll out the remaining pastry and cut into strips. Place over the pie in a lattice pattern. Trim and flute the edges. Brush the pastry with the remaining egg and water mixture. Insert the chopped walnuts in the spaces between the pastry. Sprinkle the top of the pie with the remaining 1 tablespoon granulated sugar. Place the pie on a foil-lined baking sheet and bake 15 minutes. Reduce the oven heat to 350° F. and bake until crust is golden and fruit is tender, about 35 minutes longer. Cool 5 minutes on a rack before carefully removing the sides of the pan.

Serves 8

MOM'S RHUBARB-APPLE PIE

EVERYONE THINKS their mother is the best pie maker in the world. But mine really is. Her pastry melts on the tongue and the fruit inside is always a perfectly baked amalgam that is tarter than sweet. For evidence, help yourself to a slice of Mildred Schulz's masterly rhubarb-apple pie.

For the pastry

2 cups all-purpose flour

1/4 teaspoon sugar

1/2 teaspoon salt

1/8 teaspoon ground ginger

1/2 cup (1 stick) unsalted butter, chilled

3 tablespoons vegetable shortening, chilled

4 to 5 tablespoons apple juice

For the filling

1 1/2 cups cubed fresh rhubarb (about 2 medium ribs)

3 tablespoons all-purpose flour

1/2 teaspoon ground cinnamon

1/8 teaspoon salt

1/4 teaspoon finely grated lemon peel

1/4 teaspoon finely grated orange peel

1 1/4 cups plus 1 tablespoon sugar

3 tablespoons unsalted butter, melted

1 medium red apple (about 1/3 pound)

3 large eggs, lightly beaten

1. To make the pastry: Combine the flour with the sugar, salt, and ginger in a medium bowl. Cut in the butter and shortening with a knife. Blend with a pastry blender until the mixture has the texture of coarse crumbs. Add the apple juice, about a tablespoon at a time, and mix gently with a fork or your fingertips to form a soft dough. Do not overwork. Refrigerate 1 hour.

2. Preheat the oven to 400° F.

3. Roll out slightly more than half the pastry on a lightly floured board. Line a deep 9-inch or regular 10-inch pie plate with pastry. Line the pastry with aluminum foil and weight with rice or beans. Bake 10 minutes. Remove the foil; cool.

4. To make the filling: Combine the rhubarb with the flour in a large bowl. Stir in the cinnamon, salt, lemon peel, orange peel, 1 1/4 cups sugar, and melted butter. Peel, core, and cut the apple into cubes the size of the rhubarb. Stir the cubed apples into the rhubarb mixture. Spoon into the prepared pie shell. Pour the beaten eggs evenly over the top.

5. Roll out the remaining pastry and cut into strips. Place over the pie in a lattice pattern. Trim and flute the edges. Sprinkle the top of the pie with the remaining 1 tablespoon sugar. Place the pie on a foil-lined baking sheet and bake 15 minutes. Reduce the oven heat to 350° F. and bake until crust is golden and rhubarb and apples are tender, about 45 minutes longer. Cool on a rack.

Serves 8

Baked Beans

DESPITE THEIR official nomenclature, "oven baked beans" began life as an outdoor food. That's probably why the dish still tastes at its best served al fresco. A genuine American original, baked beans were first cooked by Indians, who prepared them in covered clay pots in a hole in the ground—lined with hot stones. The technique was appropriated by early settlers who recognized a good thing when they tasted it! Three hundred years later, the "bean hole" is still common cooking currency at logging camps and trappers' lodges in the blue-jean country of the North and Northwest. However, nowadays, charcoal ash substitutes for fiery rocks to ensure the maximum heat for a tender and well-baked bean.

Volumes have been written about just what went into the first American pot of beans. Were they sweet or savory? Some food pundits insist Indian cooks used maple sugar along with chunks of juicy bear fat to sweeten the pot. Others claim there was no sweetening at all since early hand-scrawled receipts did not include that amenity. It was not until the middle of the nineteenth century, in fact, that the addition of molasses appeared in printed recipes; molasses, of course, was a heck of a lot easier to come by than sugar in those days. And it is no surprise that the earliest mention of baked beans was in a Boston cookbook.

Boston is justly famous for lots of good things to eat, but Saturday night bean suppers with brown bread is one of its oldest and best loved gastronomic traditions. Boston baked beans were of such culinary repute in the eighteenth century they earned the city its sobriquet, "Beantown." Saturday night bean suppers are not unique to Boston alone—the same menu can be found from Rockport to Provincetown, but true bean-o-philes claim the best are made in the small area of Boston south of Boylston Street and north of the Charles River.

Originally, bean suppers were served on Sunday. In early times, Pilgrims could not cook on the Sabbath because religious principles bid them only rest or pray. Of a consequence, beans were prepared in pots and hung over coals in an open hearth. There they simmered from sundown to sunup the following day. As the Colonists thrived and game dwindled, salt pork took the place of bear fat, and as religious scruples relaxed in time, bean suppers became an unrestricted weekend feast. And a cheap Saturday night event.

With the Industrial Revolution, life began to change in big cities like Boston. Working men found it cheaper and more convenient to eat around the corner at a "beanery" than travel home for lunch. *Harper's Weekly* (in 1877) reported that The Penny Restaurant had just opened on New York's Grand Street. Each item cost a penny. "A fair appetite could be appeased for five cents," said the reviewer. Business boomed and gave way to a whole era of "All-U-Kan-Eat-For-A-Nickel" counters, with baked beans on every menu.

For Those Who Don't Know Beans About . . . Beans There are countless regional variations on baked beans. But the basics of the dish remain pure and unsullied. First off, dry beans must be soaked before cooking. They can be *long soaked* overnight in cold water. Or they can be *quick soaked*. Here's how to do it. Cover the beans with cold water; heat to boiling and boil 2 minutes. Then let stand covered 1 hour. There are decided advantages to long soaking, particularly if you change the water several times. By soaking the beans, much of the complex sugars—oligosaccharides—which cause flatulence are released and washed down the drain. There are some nutrients lost with the water but this is minimal. I never use the soaking liquid to cook beans as so many purists still do. Those who insist might be wise to follow the old custom New Englanders had of stirring in healthy increments of freshly ground black pepper, supposedly the cure for what ails bean eaters.

While you may feel free with the pepper mill, hold off with the salt shaker. At least until the beans are tender. Salt affects the cell walls of the beans so they become less soluble resulting in beans "with a bite," even after hours and hours of cooking. It should also be noted that when using an acidic liquid, such as vinegar or tomato juice, to flavor beans, the cooking time will be extended considerably.

Dried beans of any color can be used interchangeably in a beanpot. Pea, navy, Great Northern are the white beans one usually finds on the supermarket shelf. Red beans include pink, pinto, kidney, and of course red. Cooking times may vary and you might notice a subtle difference in flavor, but do not panic if you can't find the bean called for in a specific recipe—merely substitute one at hand.

A last word on baked beans: The pot itself. The old-style clay pot is best because the amount of moisture lost in the baking is held to a minimum. Ceramic pots and cast-iron Dutch ovens with tight-fitting lids will do in a pinch but more liquid will be needed during the stint in the oven. In either case, when the beans are tender and if there appears to be too *much* liquid in the pot, simply remove the cover and continue to bake until just slightly wet. Baked beans should never be too dry.

The Nutritious Bean

Beans, beans, the musical fruit
The more you eat, the more you toot
The more you toot, the better you feel
So eat some beans at every meal!
—*The Brilliant Bean,* 1988

NO JOKE! Experts agree that the regular consumption of beans promotes a long and healthy life. Beans are good for the heart, help fight diabetes, and protect against colon cancer, constipation, and gallstones. Just by eating beans regularly (several times a week), you keep the body in tiptop shape. Beans are at their best if allowed to rest in the pot for a half an hour after cooking to allow the flavors to meld. Baked beans are compatible partners to ham, broiled chicken, and even grilled hot dogs. The recipes that follow represent a variety of baked bean dishes served up around the country.

BEACON HILL BAKED BEANS

And this is good old Boston
The home of the bean and the cod,
Where the Lowells talk to the Cabots,
And the Cabots talk only to God.
—John Collins Bossidy

AND THESE are definitely "upper crust" Boston baked beans. A touch of dark rum gives the dish true class.

1 pound dry white Great Northern
   beans
1 clove garlic, bruised

1 tablespoon English dry mustard
1 teaspoon curry powder
1/4 teaspoon Hungarian hot paprika

6 strips thick-cut bacon

1 large onion, finely chopped

2 tablespoons dark brown sugar

2 teaspoons Worcestershire sauce

1/4 cup molasses

5 tablespoons prepared chili sauce

1/4 teaspoon freshly ground black pepper

1/2 cup dark rum

1 1/2 cups V-8 juice (approximately)

1 teaspoon salt

1. Soak the beans according to one of the methods described on page 36. Drain.

2. Preheat the oven to 300° F.

3. Rub a buttered bean pot or heavy Dutch oven with garlic; mince the garlic.

4. Chop 3 strips bacon and sauté in a large pot over medium heat until crisp. Add the onion; cook 1 minute. Add the garlic; cook 2 minutes. Stir in the sugar, Worcestershire sauce, molasses, chili sauce, mustard, curry powder, paprika, pepper, rum, and 1/2 cup V-8 juice. Mix well. Stir in the drained beans.

5. Transfer the beans to the prepared pot. Place the remaining 3 strips bacon over the top. Cover and bake in oven 2 hours. Reduce the heat to 275° F. and continue to bake, adding additional V-8 juice as needed to keep the beans from drying out, until beans are tender, about 1 1/2 hours longer. Add salt to taste.

Serves 6 to 8

MARY SURINA'S SAN PEDRO BAKED BEANS

MARY SURINA is a dear, dear friend who also happens to be a remarkable cook. Her "traditional beans" have the added bite of the chili powder and the hot sauce that Southern Californians use to hot up a pot. Mary hails from Washington state, but has lived in San Pedro so long, she cooks like a native (albeit with slight Yugoslavian overtones).

1 pound dry pinto beans

5 strips bacon

1 large onion, chopped

1/4 teaspoon freshly ground black
pepper

1 teaspoon Worcestershire sauce

1/2 teaspoon Hungarian sweet paprika

1 teaspoon red wine vinegar

1/4 teaspoon ground allspice

Dash of hot pepper sauce

1 can (8 ounces) tomato sauce

1 can (6 ounces) tomato paste

3 1/2 cups chicken broth
(approximately)

1 clove garlic, crushed

1 tablespoon chili powder

1 tablespoon English dry mustard

3 tablespoons prepared chili sauce

2 tablespoons molasses

3 tablespoons dark brown sugar

Salt

1. Soak the beans according to one of the methods described on page 36. Drain.

2. Chop 3 strips of the bacon and cook in a medium saucepan over medium heat until light gold in color, 3 to 4 minutes. Add the onion; cook, stirring frequently, until golden brown, 8 to 10 minutes. Stir in the pepper, Worcestershire sauce, paprika, vinegar, allspice, hot pepper sauce, tomato sauce, tomato paste, and 2 cups chicken broth. Heat to boiling; reduce the heat. Simmer uncovered 30 minutes. Remove from heat.

3. Preheat the oven to 300° F.

4. Mix the garlic, chili powder, mustard, chili sauce, molasses, and brown sugar together in a small bowl. Stir into the cooked mixture. Stir in the drained beans.

5. Transfer the beans to a buttered bean pot or heavy Dutch oven. Cut the remaining 2 strips of bacon in half and place over the top of the beans. Cover and bake in oven 2 hours. Reduce heat to 275° F. and continue to bake, adding additional chicken broth as needed to keep the beans from drying out, until beans are very tender, about 5 hours longer. Add salt to taste.

Serves 6 to 8

SOUTH TEXAS'
CHUCK WAGON BEANS

WHETHER IN big "D" or out on the range, Texas is quintessential bean country. And down there they take their legumes seriously; refried or barbecued. The ingredient list for the following reads like the fixin's for an "honest-to-jaw" BBQ, LBJ-style. Leftovers? Unlikely, but a good ole country boy will spread any between two slices of white bread for tomorrow's lunch.

1 pound dry pink beans
2 tablespoons unsalted butter
1 medium onion, finely chopped
1 large clove garlic, minced
1 can (12 ounces) beer
1/4 cup Worcestershire sauce
1/4 cup brown sugar (packed)
1/2 lemon, sliced
1 tablespoon Hungarian sweet paprika
2 tablespoons Dijon mustard
2 tablespoons mild ground dried chiles (available in most gourmet grocers)

1 teaspoon crushed, dried hot red peppers
Pinch of dried marjoram
Pinch of dried thyme
1/4 teaspoon freshly ground black pepper
1 tablespoon tomato paste
3 cups tomato juice (approximately)
2 ounces salt pork, cut into strips
Salt

1. Soak the beans according to one of the methods described on page 36. Drain.

2. Preheat the oven to 300° F.

3. Melt the butter in a large heavy saucepan over medium-low heat. Add the onion; cook 1 minute. Add the garlic; cook 4 minutes. Stir in the beer, Worcestershire sauce, sugar, lemon slices, paprika, mustard, ground chilies, hot peppers, marjoram, thyme, ground pepper, tomato paste, and 1/2 cup of the tomato juice. Heat to boiling; reduce the heat. Simmer uncovered 15 minutes. Stir in the drained beans.

4. Transfer the beans to a buttered bean pot or heavy Dutch oven. Place the salt pork over the top of the beans. Cover and bake for 2 hours. Reduce the heat to 275° F. and continue to bake, adding additional tomato juice to keep the beans from drying out, until beans are tender, about 5 hours longer. Add salt to taste.

Serves 6 to 8

TOMATO BAKED BEANS
MULBERRY STREET-STYLE

"IF PALE BEANS bubble for you in a red earthenware pot / You can oft decline the dinners of sumptuous hosts." (*Martial—Epigrams*, Book XIII) Unless your host is making the beans herself and happens to be of Italian background. For example, the following beans are topped with a golden crust of crumbs and cheese that is broken into the pot as the dish is served.

1 pound dry white navy beans

3 tablespoons unsalted butter

3 tablespoons olive oil

1 large onion, chopped

2 large cloves garlic, minced

2 large fresh tomatoes, seeded, chopped (about 2 1/2 cups)

2 cups canned tomatoes, chopped

1 small rib celery, finely chopped

1 teaspoon chopped fresh basil, or 1/2 teaspoon dried

1 teaspoon chopped fresh oregano, or 1/2 teaspoon dried

Pinch of dried thyme

1 tablespoon sugar

1/4 teaspoon finely grated orange peel

1 cup tomato juice (approximately)

1/2 cup buttered bread crumbs

1/4 cup freshly grated Parmesan cheese

  1. Soak the beans according to one of the methods described on page 36. Drain.

  2. Preheat the oven to 300° F.

3. Heat the butter with the oil in a large pot or Dutch oven over medium-low heat. Add the onion; cook 1 minute. Add the garlic; cook 4 minutes. Add the tomatoes, celery, basil, oregano, thyme, sugar, and orange peel. Heat to boiling; reduce the heat. Simmer covered 45 minutes. Stir in the drained beans.

4. Transfer the beans to a buttered bean pot or heavy Dutch oven. Pour over 1/4 cup tomato juice. Cover and bake in oven 2 hours. Reduce the heat to 275° F. and continue to bake, adding additional tomato juice as needed to keep the beans from drying out, until beans are tender, about 1 1/2 hours longer.

5. Combine the bread crumbs and cheese. Spoon over the top of the beans and bake uncovered until nicely browned, about 25 minutes.

Serves 6 to 8

VERMONT
APPLE-BAKED BEANS

VERMONT MAY well be the northeastern corridor of baked bean country, for it is a rural state filled with exurbanites trying desperately to cultivate homely appetites. This update of a very old Newfane recipe is one of the best you will ever try. Maple syrup (only the Vermont kind will do) sweetens the pot; a chopped apple moistens the beans, and pork finishes the flavoring.

1 pound dry white navy beans

2 tablespoons vegetable oil

1 1/2 pounds country-style pork ribs, cut apart

1 medium onion, chopped

1 teaspoon English dry mustard

1/4 cup brown sugar (packed)

1/4 cup maple syrup

1/4 teaspoon freshly ground black pepper

1 cup water

1 red apple (about 1/2 pound), peeled, cored, diced

Salt

1. Soak the beans according to one of the methods described on page 36. Drain.

2. Preheat the oven to 300° F.

3. Heat the oil in a large heavy skillet over medium high heat. Sauté the pork ribs until well browned on all sides. Transfer to a plate.

4. Reduce the heat under the skillet to medium-low. Add the onion; cook 4 minutes. Do not brown. Sprinkle the onion with the mustard and stir in the brown sugar, maple syrup, pepper, and water. Combine with the drained beans in a large bowl. Stir in the diced apple.

5. Transfer the beans to a buttered bean pot or heavy Dutch oven. Place the pork ribs on top of the beans. Cover and bake in oven 2 hours. Reduce the heat to 275° F. and continue to bake until the beans are tender, about 1 1/2 hours longer. If the beans are still quite wet, remove the ribs and keep warm. Place the beans uncovered in the oven for about 20 minutes. Add salt to taste.

Serves 6

OHIO CRANBERRY BEAN BAKE

I FIRST TASTED this dish in Columbus. The small mottled pink beans are sweet and incredibly flavorsome. Unfortunately, they are not always easy to find. Make a phone call to your gourmet grocer or local healthfood store to find a pound. For this is one dish definitely worth a hill (make that mountain) of beans.

1 pound dry cranberry beans

1 pound sausage meat

1 large onion, finely chopped

2 large cloves garlic, minced

4 teaspoons Dijon mustard

3 tablespoons honey

1 1/2 cups chicken or vegetable stock (see page 378 or 379) (approximately)

1. Soak the beans according to one of the methods described on page 36.

2. Preheat the oven to 300° F.

3. Sauté the sausage meat, breaking the meat up into lumps, in a large heavy pot over medium-high heat until well browned. Pour off all but about 3 tablespoons grease. Reduce the heat under the pot to medium.

4. Add the onion to the sausage in the pot; cook 1 minute. Add the garlic; cook, stirring frequently, 4 minutes longer. Stir in the mustard and honey. Stir in 1 cup chicken or vegetable stock, scraping the sides and bottom of pot with a wooden spoon. Stir in the drained beans.

5. Transfer the beans to a buttered bean pot or heavy Dutch oven. Cover and bake in oven 2 hours. Reduce heat to 275° F. and continue to bake, adding additional stock as needed to keep the beans from drying out, until beans are tender, 1 1/2 to 2 hours longer.

Serves 6 to 8

Most dry beans (including kidney, navy, pea, pinto, pink, and black beans) belong to the common green bean family, *phaseolus vulgaris*, which was domesticated over 7,000 years ago in Mexico and Peru. One of the Indian triad (along with corn and squash), beans were considered to be an important staple in a tribe's diet. Beans tasted good, were adaptable, and energizing (beans being sky high in protein and carbohydrates). But equally important, colorful as well. The Hopis developed at least twelve kinds of beans, ranging from black to white. The most prized were the yellow, blue, red, white, multi-colored, and black varieties representing the six cardinal directions: east, west, north, south, up, and down.

BAKED BEANS CASSIE'S WAY

WHEN I was given this recipe in Maine, a dozen years ago, the donor did not specify who *Cassie* was. However, the dish seemed clearly European in character. Some while ago, while slicing and sautéing the lamb and pork sausages, it dawned on me that "Cassie's way" was probably a misheard version of provincial *cassoulet,* what one might call a bastard French Canadian invasion of Maine.

1 pound dry white navy or pea beans

4 tablespoons (1/2 stick) unsalted butter

1/4 cup diced, smoky country ham

3/4 pound sausage meat (preferably sweet Italian) formed into 8 patties

1 1/2 pounds shoulder lamb chops, bones and fat removed, cut into 1 1/2-inch pieces

1 teaspoon Dijon mustard

3 to 4 tablespoons goose fat (or additional unsalted butter)

1 large onion, chopped

1/2 teaspoon allspice berries, crushed

1 bunch scallions, bulbs and green tops, chopped

1 large clove garlic, minced

2 large carrots, coarsely chopped

1 can (17 ounces) plum tomatoes

1 1/2 cups beef broth (approximately)

1/2 cup dry white wine

Pinch of dried thyme

1 bay leaf

1/2 teaspoon freshly ground pepper

2 cups leftover cooked goose, cut into chunks, or substitute duck or game birds

1 cup fresh bread crumbs

Salt

Chopped fresh parsley

1. Soak the beans according to one of the methods described on page 36.

2. Drain. Return the beans to the pot and cover once more with cold water. Heat to boiling; boil 30 minutes. Drain.

3. Melt 1 tablespoon butter in a large heavy skillet over medium heat. Add the ham and cook, stirring constantly, until golden. Transfer with a slotted spoon to a bowl.

4. Add the sausage patties to the skillet and sauté until well browned on both sides. Drain on paper towels. Crumble and set aside.

5. Drain all but 1 tablespoon grease from the skillet. Add the lamb pieces and sauté until well browned on both sides. Stir in the mustard; cook 1 minute. Transfer to a plate.

6. Preheat the oven to 350° F.

7. Wipe out the skillet and add 2 tablespoons goose fat. Sauté the onion over medium-low heat 1 minute. Sprinkle the onion with the allspice and add the scallions and garlic. Cook, adding more goose fat if needed, until soft, about 15 minutes. Stir in the carrots, tomatoes, broth, wine, thyme, bay leaf, and pepper. Transfer to a heatproof bowl. Stir in the reserved ham. Stir in the drained beans.

8. Transfer a third of the beans to a buttered bean pot or heavy Dutch oven. Add half the goose meat, half the reserved lamb, and half the sausage. Repeat the layering. Top with the remaining beans. Bake uncovered 40 minutes.

9. Meanwhile, melt the remaining 3 tablespoons butter in a large skillet over medium heat. Add the bread crumbs and cook, stirring constantly, until the crumbs are golden, about 4 minutes.

10. After the beans have cooked for 40 minutes, spoon the crumbs over the top of the beans. Increase the oven heat to 400° F. Bake 25 minutes. Break the crumb topping and push it gently into the bean mixture and bake 15 minutes longer. (Add more broth to the beans if mixture becomes too dry.) Add salt to taste. Sprinkle with parsley before serving.

Serves 6 as a main course

GEORGIAN "GREENS AND BEANS"

SOUTHERN comfort food. From Atlanta to Augusta, the denizens agree there is nothing better for what ails you than a mess of greens cooked up with a ham bone—unless it's double dosed with healthy beans.

1 pound dry white Great Northern
   beans
2 tablespoons unsalted butter
1 large onion, chopped
2 cloves garlic, minced
1 tablespoon sugar
1 3/4 to 2 pounds mustard greens,
   washed, trimmed of stems, roughly
   chopped

1 1/2 cups chicken broth
1/8 teaspoon freshly grated nutmeg
1/2 teaspoon freshly ground black
   pepper
2 smoked pork knuckles (about 3/4
   pound each)
Red wine vinegar

1. Soak the beans according to one of the methods described on page 36. Drain.

2. Preheat the oven to 300° F.

3. Melt the butter in a large heavy pot or Dutch oven over medium heat. Add the onion; cook 1 minute. Add the garlic; cook 4 minutes longer. Sprinkle the mixture with sugar and add the mustard greens and chicken broth. Heat to boiling; reduce the heat. Simmer covered, stirring occasionally, until greens are wilted, about 20 minutes. Sprinkle the greens with the nutmeg and pepper. Remove from heat and stir in the drained beans.

4. Transfer the beans to a buttered bean pot or heavy Dutch oven. Tuck the pork knuckles into the beans. Cover and bake in the oven 2 hours. Reduce heat to 275° F. and continue to bake, stirring occasionally, until the beans are tender, about 1 1/2 hours longer.

5. Remove the pork knuckles from the beans. Cut off any meat and stir back into the beans. Pass the vinegar on the side.

Serves 6 to 8

BAKED HOPPIN' JOHN

ANOTHER Southern connection from the part of Low Country where half the denizens wear shoes, and the other half go shoeless—and the difference is not necessarily economics. Eaten on New Year's Day, Hoppin' John is said to bring good luck all year. To save time, I use frozen black-eyed peas instead of dried beans. Yes, black-eyed peas definitely are beans.

1/3 cup long grain rice

2 strips thick-cut bacon, chopped

1 cup cubed cooked ham

4 scallions, white bulbs and green tops, chopped

1 clove garlic, minced

1 package (10 ounces) frozen black-eyed peas

1 cup strong chicken (see page 378) or turkey stock

Pinch of dried thyme

1 tablespoon red wine vinegar

1/4 teaspoon freshly ground black pepper

Salt

2 tablespoons chopped fresh parsley

1. Add the rice to a large pot of boiling salted water. Stir until the water comes back to the boil. Boil 12 minutes. Drain in a colander. Place the colander over 1 inch of boiling water. Place a single layer of paper towels over the rice. Steam 15 minutes.

2. Preheat the oven to 300° F.

3. Sauté the bacon in a large heavy skillet over medium heat until limp, about 3 minutes. Add the ham and cook until bacon and ham turn golden brown, about 3 minutes longer. Reduce the heat slightly and stir in the scallions. Cook 1 minute. Add the garlic; cook 2 minutes. Stir in the black-eyed peas and 1/2 cup stock, breaking the peas apart with a wooden spoon. Stir in the rice and thyme. Raise the heat to medium high and cook, stirring constantly, until liquid is partially absorbed, about 3 minutes. Stir in the vinegar and pepper.

4. Transfer the beans to a buttered bean pot or heavy Dutch oven. Cover and bake in oven 1 hour. Stir in the remaining 1/2 cup stock. Continue to bake covered 30 minutes. Add salt to taste. Sprinkle with parsley before serving.

Serves 4

CUBANO BAKED BLACK BEANS

CONQUISTADORS are rumored to have brought the first black beans from the Caribbean to southern Florida where they flourished. Here's another Spanish gift; an expatriated version of Cuban baked beans, stirred up from Miami to Tampa Bay. *Con gusto!*

1 pound dry black turtle beans	1 large bay leaf
1/3 cup diced salt pork (about 3 ounces)	1/4 teaspoon dried oregano leaves, crushed
2 tablespoons olive oil	1/4 teaspoon cayenne pepper
1/2 cup diced cooked ham	Pinch of ground cloves
1 large onion, chopped	1 teaspoon red wine vinegar
2 large cloves garlic, minced	Salt and freshly ground pepper
2 1/2 cups beef broth (approximately)	Chopped fresh parsley

For garnish

1/3 cup finely diced cooked ham	2 hard-cooked eggs, finely chopped
1/3 cup sliced scallions	1/2 cup sour cream

1. Soak the beans according to one of the methods described on page 36.

2. Cook the salt pork in boiling water 5 minutes. Drain and pat dry with paper towels.

3. Preheat the oven to 300° F.

4. Heat the oil in a large heavy saucepan over medium heat. Add the salt pork and ham. Cook, stirring frequently, 5 minutes. Add the onion; cook 1 minute. Add the garlic; cook 4 minutes longer. Add 1 1/2 cups beef broth, scraping the sides and bottom of pan with a wooden spoon. Stir in the drained beans, the bay leaf, oregano, cayenne pepper, cloves, and vinegar.

5. Transfer the beans to a buttered bean pot or heavy Dutch oven. Cover and bake in oven 2 hours. Reduce the heat to 275° F. and continue to bake, adding additional beef broth as needed to keep the beans from drying out, until beans are tender, about 1 1/2 hours longer.

6. Remove 1 cup beans from the bean pot and place in the container of a food processor. Add 1/4 cup beef broth. Process until fairly smooth. Stir this mixture back into the bean mixture. Add salt and pepper to taste. Bake uncovered 20 minutes longer. Serve sprinkled with parsley and the suggested garnishes.

Serves 6 to 8

BAKED SWEET BILLY BEANS

ON THE coastline of Rhode Island, where I stumbled upon the next recipe some while ago, all pink beans sold at farm stands are dubbed "sweet billys." No one seems to know why. The cranberry bean, basis of the fruity smoky dish that follows, is the sweetest billy on record.

1 pound dry cranberry beans	1/4 cup Dijon mustard
3 tablespoons unsalted butter	1/2 teaspoon soy sauce
1 large onion, chopped	1 cup orange juice
2 cloves garlic, minced	1 1/2 cups water, approximately
3 cups cubed cooked smoky country ham	Salt and freshly ground pepper
1 cup apricot jam	

1. Soak the beans according to one of the methods described on page 36. Drain.

2. Preheat the oven to 300° F.

3. Melt the butter in a large heavy skillet over medium-low heat. Add the onion; cook 1 minute. Add the garlic; cook 4 minutes longer. Stir in the ham; cook 2 minutes. Stir in the jam, mustard, and soy sauce. Combine with the beans in a large bowl. Stir in the orange juice and 1/2 cup water.

4. Transfer the beans to a buttered bean pot or heavy Dutch oven. Cover and bake in oven 1 1/2 hours. Reduce the heat to 275° F. and continue to

bake, adding additional water as needed to keep the beans from drying out, until tender, about 4 1/2 hours longer. Add salt and pepper to taste.

Serves 6 to 8

BAKED ANASAZI BEANS

THE ANASAZI that grows in southwestern Colorado is a mottled, highly malleable dried bean that has been a mainstay of the Pueblo Indians' diet for centuries. These cliff dwellers claim that consumption of Anasazi beans is actually the secret of their long, active lives. And since many tribesmen live well past one hundred years, why argue the point? The following Pueblo-style baked bean dish, composed of Anasazis, beef, sausage, peppers, and corn, adds new life to old ingredients. This is served as a main dish. (Anasazi beans may be found at natural food stores or by mail order. Write: Adobe Milling Company, P.O. Box 596, Dove Creek, CO 81324 (303) 677-2620.)

1 pound Anasazi or pinto beans

2 tablespoons vegetable oil

2 pounds beef chuck neck bones

3 chorizos (Spanish sausages), (about 3/4 pound) chopped

2 medium onions, chopped

2 large cloves garlic, minced

1 small green bell pepper, seeded, chopped

2 small hot green peppers, seeded, deveined, chopped

1 teaspoon ground cumin

2 tablespoons chopped fresh basil, or 1 teaspoon dried

1 cup water

2 medium tomatoes, seeded, chopped

2 tablespoons chili powder

2 cups corn kernels (from 4 large ears)

1/4 cup chicken broth, if needed

Salt and freshly ground black pepper

1. Soak the beans according to one of the methods described on page 36.

2. Preheat the oven to 300° F.

3. Heat the oil in a large heavy skillet over medium-high heat. Add the neck bones and brown well on all sides. Transfer to a plate.

4. Add the chorizos to the skillet and sauté over medium heat until lightly browned. Stir in the onions; cook 1 minute. Add the garlic; cook, stirring constantly 2 minutes longer. Stir in bell pepper, hot peppers, cumin, basil, and water. Combine with the beans in a large bowl. Stir in the tomatoes.

5. Transfer the beans to a buttered bean pot or heavy Dutch oven. Place the neck bones over the top of the beans. Cover and bake in oven 1 1/2 hours.

6. Remove the bones from the pot and cut off any meat. Stir the meat into the beans along with the chili powder and corn. Reduce the heat to 275° F. and continue to bake, adding chicken broth if needed to keep the beans from drying out, until beans are tender, about 1 1/2 hours longer. Add salt and pepper to taste.

Serves 6 to 8

Barbecue Sauces

Barbecue is any four-footed animal—be it mouse or mastodon. . . . At its best it is a fat steer, and it must be eaten within an hour of when it is cooked. For if ever the sun rises upon Barbecue, its flavor vanishes like Cinderella's silks . . . staler in the chill dawn than illicit love.

SO WILLIAM ALLEN WHITE once wrote about Texans' favorite food. And it echoes *my* sentiments about outdoor grub exactly.

Long before Texas was a twinkle in the Southwest sky, barbecue socials played an all-important role in this country's well being, dating back to the days of Tidewater Jamestown. Wild boar was the staple meat in those days. What kind of sauce (if any) was slathered over the haunch as it spit-roasted is anyone's guess, but it definitely was neither sweet nor tomato-sticky. Those refinements came later. Nonetheless, barbecue was the attraction of many Southern political fund-raising events in eighteenth- and nineteenth-century America. Gentleman farmer and eventual President George Washington was even reported to have once profited politically from a three-day "pig out" at his plantation in Alexandria. So we know there were "cook-out" fans early on!

No one is absolutely sure where the notion of barbecue sauce comes from. Some credit its devise to the early Spanish settlers who were fond of splashing any chunk of roasted meat with sherry and roasted peppers. Others hold that a fermented tomato relish-type accompaniment, stirred up by native Americans, is the seasoning's forebear. But no matter, really. Barbecue sauce is strictly a regional affair that alters and amends itself from region to region.

Ages before sugary, ketchup-tinged formulas became synonymous with southern cook-outs, barbecue sauce was virtually nothing more than a spicy vinegar "moppin'" marinade, literally and liberally, applied with a clean mop, the residue of which was used for "soppin'" up the charred snippets of meat later. Vinegar marinades were particularly indigenous to the Carolinas, where to this very day, pit-purists decry any other embellishment. In parts of Texas, on the other hand, a "sass" is likely to be nothing more than slightly thickened Tabasco or a boiled mash of ripe jalapeños. But aside from such geographic palate eccentricities, the vast majority of barbecue sauces consumed today are tomato-based and most often mellowed with sweetening agents or syrups. Even so, it is precisely the blend and admixtures of varying ingredients in a barbecue sauce that establishes its territorial independence.

A Few Saucy Remarks While barbecue sauces are basically free form by nature (the proportion of ingredients need not be exact and can be increased or decreased to pamper individual tastes and tolerances), the correct use of a barbecue sauce is practically gospel. Sweet dressings, for instance, should never be used during the initial cooking process because they burn easily. A barbecue masterhand will generally marinate chicken or pork in a sweet sauce overnight to flavor the meat. The next day, however, he pours off and reboils the sauce till slightly thickened. Then, about 5 minutes before the food in question comes off the grill, he "mops" it with the mixture until it turns rosy-rust in color. Any remaining sauce is served warm, on the side. This technique, incidentally, works equally well when "barbecuing" under a broiler.

On quite the other hand, those aforementioned vinegar-based barbecue sauces are inevitably used as a marinade, *and* as a baste, during the cooking process as well. However, speaking generally of the country's tastebuds at large, it is the comingling of sweet and sour in a barbecue sauce that makes for the most conspicuous consumption.

*I*TALIANS have a saying: "Even an old boot tastes good if it is cooked over charcoal." And better by far, when sluiced with a good tangy sauce.

The following sauces represent a cross-section of America's best and unusual barbecue adjuncts. Some are more spirited than others, some sweeter; but all are meant to stimulate the tastebuds. Use them generously!

THE ALL-AMERICAN

IF ONE were forced to choose the most "emblematic" American barbecue sauce, this would undoubtedly be the top choice—right down to the obligatory ketchup, Worcestershire, and A-1 in the recipe's ingredient list. At the Settlement Inn, outside San Antonio, shrimp is first marinated in this sauce, then wrapped in bacon, and grilled to succulent perfection. A good all-purpose sauce.

1 tablespoon unsalted butter	1 tablespoon cider vinegar
1 onion, finely chopped	3 tablespoons dark brown sugar
3/4 cup ketchup	1/4 cup water
3 tablespoons Worcestershire sauce	Dash of hot pepper sauce
2 tablespoons A-1 steak sauce	

Melt the butter in a medium saucepan over medium-low heat. Add the onion; cook 5 minutes. Do not brown. Stir in the remaining ingredients. Heat to boiling; reduce the heat. Simmer, uncovered, 20 minutes.

Makes about 1 cup

OKIE HOTS

PULLIAM'S, long defunct, was a "barbecue joint" on the wrong side of the tracks in Oklahoma City—the side of the tracks, by the way, where most good barbecue can be found anywhere in the U.S.A. The original "hots" formula called for 1 tablespoon freshly ground black pepper, but I reduced it to suit my taste. Don't skimp on the cayenne, however. This sauce has a dark, rich taste with plenty of zip and is equally good on beef as well as pork or chicken.

1 tablespoon vegetable oil
1 small onion, finely chopped
1 small clove garlic, minced
1 bottle (14 ounces) ketchup
1/2 cup prepared chili sauce
3 tablespoons Dijon mustard
1 tablespoon English dry mustard
1 teaspoon freshly ground black pepper
1 1/2 teaspoons cayenne pepper

2 whole cloves
1/4 cup red wine vinegar
1/4 cup lemon juice
1/4 cup brown sugar (packed)
1/4 cup A-1 steak sauce
2 tablespoons Worcestershire sauce
1 1/2 teaspoons soy sauce
3/4 cup beer

Heat the oil in a medium saucepan over medium-low heat. Add the onion; cook 1 minute. Add the garlic; cook 4 minutes. Do not brown. Stir in the remaining ingredients. Heat to boiling; reduce the heat. Simmer, uncovered, 25 minutes. Remove the whole cloves.

Makes about 2 1/2 cups

SARA'S COUSIN JANE'S
ARIZONA BAR-B-CUE SAUCE

I MET Sara Eason Branscum at a barbecue cook-off. Where else? She is a food consultant, stylist, and darn good cook, transplanted to Oklahoma City from Arizona. Her cousin Jane Magavern's recipe has been in the family files for almost 30 years, and the sauce is traditionally slathered on chicken halves at family cook-outs. But, to turn a phrase of Alice B. Toklas, this is a sauce not only for the chicken, but for the goose, the gander, the duck, the turkey, and the Guinea hen, too!

4 tablespoons (1/2 stick) unsalted butter

1 small onion, minced

1 small clove garlic, minced

1 1/2 teaspoons English dry mustard

1/2 teaspoon salt

2 tablespoons chili powder

1 can (10 3/4 ounces) condensed tomato soup

3 tablespoons lemon juice

3 tablespoons red wine vinegar

1 cup water

Melt the butter in a medium saucepan over medium-low heat. Add the onion; cook 1 minute. Add the garlic; cook 4 minutes. Do not brown. Stir in the remaining ingredients. Heat to boiling; reduce the heat. Simmer, uncovered, 10 minutes.

Makes about 1 1/2 cups

SOUTH TEXAS' SOPPIN'

DEEP-DYED Lone Star denizens serve the following sauce "table-side" only. It's the perfect confederate for brisket and short ribs, and twice as tasty over smoky grilled chicken or spareribs. On the pungent side, the combination of cilantro, comino (or cumin), and anise give this topping a very tall-in-the-saddle flavor.

2 cloves garlic, roughly chopped

1 small dried, hot red pepper

2 teaspoons chopped fresh cilantro
(Chinese parsley)

1/4 teaspoon ground cumin

1/2 teaspoon anise seeds

1/2 teaspoon salt

2 tablespoons dark brown sugar

1 tablespoon Worcestershire sauce

1 cup cider vinegar

2 cups ketchup

Hot pepper sauce

Combine all ingredients except the ketchup and hot pepper sauce in the container of a food processor or blender. Process until smooth. Transfer the mixture to a medium saucepan and add the ketchup. Heat to boiling; reduce the heat. Simmer, uncovered, 30 minutes. Add hot pepper sauce to taste.

Makes about 3 cups

GEORGIA COKE

THE NEXT sauce has made more friends than any other I've ever served. I slather it over pork and chicken. Everyone goes home with the recipe, and it's not even mine! It was a gift of Atlanta's Nathalie Dupree, whose PBS series on cooking of the South, and her cookbook, *New Southern Cooking* (Knopf, 1986) has made her a real Southern comfort all over the country.

2 tablespoons unsalted butter

1 onion, finely chopped

2 cloves garlic, minced

1 bay leaf

2 cups ketchup

6 ounces Coca-Cola

1 tablespoon Worcestershire sauce

1 teaspoon Dijon mustard

2 teaspoons red wine vinegar

Salt and freshly ground pepper

Melt the butter in a medium saucepan over medium-low heat. Add the onion; cook 5 minutes. Do not brown. Stir in the remaining ingredients. Heat to boiling; reduce the heat. Simmer, uncovered, 20 minutes. Remove the bay leaf.

Makes about 1 1/2 cups

GEORGIAN MOPPIN' SAUCE

The other side of the deep South coin. A traditional, vinegar-based classic for pork, poultry, or game. This, too, is a pass-along recipe, from Pat Fusco, a Georgia native, and able barbecuer, now living in California.

1 teaspoon salt

1 tablespoon Hungarian sweet paprika

1/4 teaspoon cayenne pepper

1/4 teaspoon English dry mustard

1/2 teaspoon freshly ground black pepper

1/3 cup water

2 tablespoons Worcestershire sauce

1/3 cup red wine vinegar

4 tablespoons (1/2 stick) unsalted butter, cut into bits

Combine the dry ingredients in a medium saucepan. Stir in the water. Heat to boiling; remove from heat. Add the Worcestershire sauce and vinegar. Stir in the butter.

Makes about 1 1/4 cups

TULSA TOPPIN'

THIS SAUCE is the specialty of Skitch Henderson, maestro for all seasons—a man who can conduct a barbecue cook-out as brilliantly as he does the New York Pops Orchestra. Its zingy savor is a good match to beef, pork, poultry, and even grilled lamb.

2 tablespoons unsalted butter

1 large onion, finely chopped

1 clove garlic, minced

1 can (16 ounces) tomato sauce

1 cup cider vinegar

1 cup V-8 juice

1/2 cup prune juice

Finely slivered peel of 1/2 lemon

Juice of 1 lemon

1 bay leaf

6 juniper berries, crushed

1/2 teaspoon cayenne pepper

2 tablespoons light brown sugar

Melt the butter in a 4-quart saucepan over medium-low heat. Add the onion; cook 1 minute. Add the garlic; cook 2 minutes. Stir in the remaining ingredients. Heat to boiling; reduce the heat. Simmer, uncovered, until thickened, about 30 minutes. Remove the bay leaf.

Makes about 6 cups

Pages and pages have been written by food writers (myself included) about the origin of the word *barbecue*. The least authentic, but certainly most amusing, was offered by *Tar Heel* magazine. North Carolina's favorite monthly whimsically suggests the word developed from early nineteenth-century advertising. It is said that the owner of a Carolinian combination whiskey bar, beer parlor, pool hall, *and* cafe specializing in spit-roasted pork, wanted to let folks know just what to expect from his establishment. As the gent couldn't fit all that palaver on his storefront, he shortened it to "Bar-Beer-Cue-Pig!" Or, so the story goes.

OHIO VALLEY SOOTHING SYRUP

THEY SAY Ohio is the West of the East and the North of the South. Its cuisine, however, is pure Midwestern. At the myriad maple festivals during harvest time, barbecued chicken and ribs are smothered with this syrup-sweetened sauce that puts both the East and the South to shame.

2 tablespoons unsalted butter

1 tablespoon English dry mustard

1/2 cup maple syrup

1 cup prepared chili sauce

1/2 cup ketchup

1/2 cup cider vinegar

1 teaspoon celery seeds

1 teaspoon cayenne pepper

1/2 teaspoon salt

Combine all ingredients in a medium saucepan. Heat to boiling; reduce the heat. Simmer, uncovered, 20 minutes.

Makes about 2 cups

HAWAIIAN PORK SAUCE

GUAVAS, native to Brazil, have recently been cultivated in the Pacific as well, and are the basis of some recent tropical fruit drinks. Combined with apricots, the guava becomes the foundation for an intensely fragrant, sweeter-than-sour sauce. Use it on pork the Hawaiian way, but remember it is equally salutory to a chicken breast or turkey filet.

1/3 cup dried apricots

1 1/2 cups guava fruit drink (Ocean Spray's Mauna La'I Drink)

1 shallot, minced

3 tablespoons vegetable oil

1/2 cup tarragon wine vinegar

1/4 cup honey

1/2 teaspoon soy sauce

1/4 cup ketchup

1/2 teaspoon dried oregano

1/2 teaspoon salt

1/4 teaspoon freshly ground black pepper

1. Combine the apricots with the guava fruit drink in a small saucepan. Heat to boiling; reduce the heat. Cook, uncovered, over medium-low heat until apricots are tender, about 20 minutes. Cool slightly.

2. Place the apricot mixture into the container of a food processor. Process until smooth. Transfer to a medium saucepan and stir in the remaining ingredients. Heat to boiling; remove from heat.

Makes about 2 1/4 cups

DINAH'S BARBECUE SAUCE

THIS IS a sauce that elevates smoked brisket to a state of divinity. It is so called because the first burnishing of onion in the recipe got there by happenstance, or devilment; I have never determined which exactly. Dinah, my cat, distracted the cook! A chopped onion scorched, and a great sauce was born!

1 tablespoon unsalted butter
1 medium onion, sliced
1 clove garlic, chopped
1 cup prepared chili sauce

1 1/2 cups dark corn syrup
1/2 teaspoon bouillon powder
2 tablespoons soy sauce

1. Melt the butter in a heavy skillet over medium-high heat. Stir in the onion and garlic. Cook until the onion and garlic are well burnished (very dark, but not burned), about 10 minutes. Transfer to the container of a food processor or blender. Process until smooth.

2. Transfer the processed mixture to a medium saucepan. Stir in the remaining ingredients. Heat to boiling; reduce the heat. Simmer, uncovered, 30 minutes.

Makes about 2 cups

GINGERY BARBECUE SAUCE

GINGER IS the secret ingredient of the next semi-sweet barbecue adjunct. A happy alliance of fresh gingerroot and old-fashioned ginger ale makes a bracing compound that gives pork or poultry ultimate flavor.

2 tablespoons unsalted butter
1 medium onion, finely chopped
1 clove garlic, minced
1 teaspoon minced fresh gingerroot
1 cup prepared chili sauce

2 cans (8 ounces each) tomato sauce
1 bottle (10 ounces) ginger ale
1 tablespoon Worcestershire sauce
2 tablespoons cider vinegar

Melt the butter in a medium size, heavy saucepan over medium-low heat. Add the onion; cook 1 minute. Add the garlic and fresh gingerroot; cook 5 minutes longer. Stir in the remaining ingredients. Heat to boiling; reduce heat. Simmer, uncovered, until reduced by about a third, 35 to 40 minutes.

Makes about 1 3/4 cups

OREGON BERRY BRUSH

"IN COOKING, as in all the arts, simplicity is the sign of perfection." —Maurice Curnonsky. My favorite dapple for spareribs is simplicity itself. From the Portland area, home of the juiciest berries in the world, brush this fruity sauce on ribs as they twirl on a power-driven rotisserie, or smoke to crispness on a grill. The Oregon Berry Brush is, I might add, a noteworthy baste for chicken and turkey too.

1 jar (12 ounces) raspberry preserves
3 tablespoons red wine vinegar

1/2 cup prepared chili sauce
1 teaspoon Dijon mustard

Strain the preserves through a sieve into a medium saucepan. Pour the vinegar through the sieve to loosen the seeds. Discard the seeds. Add the chili sauce and mustard to the strained preserves. Heat to boiling; reduce the heat. Simmer 2 minutes.

Makes about 2 cups

Biscuits

*W*HETHER YOU *sit* on your "biscuit" to watch the world go by, or *use* your "biscuit" to get ahead in life is purely a personal matter. Don't, however, call someone "a son of a biscuit" unless you're looking for trouble! But then, *biscuit* has always been a slightly troublesome noun.

To set the matter straight: *Biscuit* is a French word (purportedly borrowed from the Italian, with Latin roots), literally meaning "twice cooked." It commonly came into English usage via the first Colonists who survived the rigors of trans-Atlantic crossings on a diet of "ship's biscuits." Hard, thin crackers meant to last forever. Apparently they did, for the first arrivals reported these wafers had to be boiled to a fare-thee-well before they could even be consumed. Unfortunately, mastication was not the only reason for boiling the biscuit. Old timers tell us that on long ocean voyages, even the hardiest sailors could not stomach consuming these wafers till after nightfall. After dark, we're told, they couldn't see the insect infestation that inevitably boiled with the biscuits!

The biscuit fared better on solid ground, but even after shortening was added to lighten the dough, early biscuits were still excessively chewy affairs. The South had one solution. Cooks' helpers—slaves—were pressed into service to literally beat the dough with mallets for hours on end until the mixture properly blistered in the oven. It is quite possible that the slaves taught this kitchen trick to their masters, for they were already adept at pounding grain and manioc into flour in their African homelands. But that, too, was a far cry from the biscuits we know and love today: delicate hot breads compounded of baking powder and shortening that are a miracle of American culinary ingenuity. Beaten biscuits nevertheless retain a place in Southern culinary culture.

How the biscuit came to *rise* is a story in itself. The first airy biscuits were levitated by yeast. And while yeast had been employed by professional bakers in the Old World since time immemorial, housewives on their own in the New World had to make this leavening from scratch; most often of fermented potatoes or hops, which smelled to high heaven! Cookbooks routinely included recipes for the home manufacture of yeast. And yeast in time became the basis of the most formidable biscuit of the nineteenth century: the *sourdough*.

While yeast was responsible for the biscuit's first inflation, baking soda was not far behind. At the end of the eighteenth century, pearlash, a derivative of the potassium carbonate in wood ashes, was found to produce carbon dioxide in heated dough—which made it rise as well. Pearlash, unfortunately, left a very bitter undertaste, and the first commercial baking soda marketed in 1840, though a refinement, wasn't much better. In time, however, chemists and kitchen savants discovered that by adding various acidic salts to baking soda, the astringency could be abated. The result of their labors, commercial baking powder, was introduced to the American public in 1856 and was judged an immediate success. And lightness became the biscuit's watchword ever since, along with a revolution in home baking. "Biscuit" to the British today usually refers to what Americans call crackers.

Using Your "Biscuit" About Biscuit Making Despite their universal appeal, biscuits have a special affinity to southern food and no meal below the Mason-Dixon Line is complete without a newly baked batch brought to the table. Much of the mystique behind the South's biscuit reputation is the flour used; southern flours are uniformly milled from soft winter wheat, low in gluten and high in starch, which produces the lightest, airiest biscuit imaginable. Southern flours are hard to come by in most of the country, but "cake flour," also made of soft wheat, can be substituted.

Nationally available "all-purpose" flour is a mixture of hard and soft wheats. All-purpose can be used freely in any biscuit recipe with a high butterfat content. High butterfat counteracts the tendency of baking powder to dry out all-purpose flour, which is not the case with soft wheat flours.

Making biscuits is similar to making pie crust, but it's a quicker and less awesome ritual, particularly for a kitchen novice. For the most part, shortening is merely blended into the flour mixture with a pastry blender, with just enough liquid added to form a soft dough. As with pie pastry, the more you handle the dough the tougher it gets, so remember to keep a light touch!

OLIVER WENDELL HOLMES said, "Life is a great bundle of little things." Well, a well baked, properly flaky biscuit qualifies as one of those "little things" in my book. Though not quite a bundle follows, the chosen dozen are worthy of a pat of butter or a slurp of gravy in anybody's book.

"OLD VIRGINNY" CREAM BISCUITS

THESE ARE the first biscuits I ever made that I literally could not resist. They are so good, I have sometimes consumed a half dozen at a single sitting. Having a less-than-perfect memory for culinary treats, I must confess to always carrying the recipe in my wallet. I've discovered that the greatest bread 'n' butter gift a weekend guest can give his host is a batch of cream biscuits whipped up for Sunday breakfast.

2 cups sifted all-purpose flour
2 1/2 teaspoons baking powder
1 teaspoon salt

3 tablespoons unsalted butter, chilled
2 tablespoons lard, chilled
3/4 cup heavy or whipping cream

1. Preheat the oven to 450° F.

2. Sift the flour with the baking powder and salt into a large bowl. Cut in the butter and lard with a knife. Blend with a pastry blender until the texture of coarse crumbs.

3. Slowly stir in the cream with a wooden spoon to form a soft dough. Roll the dough out on a lightly floured board 1/2-inch thick. Cut into 2 1/2-inch rounds. Place on an ungreased baking sheet. Bake until golden brown, 12 to 15 minutes.

Makes about 9 biscuits

SHARON TYLER HERBST'S EASY CREAMS

A DEAR FRIEND, and fellow ex-Coloradoan, Sharon is one of the best authorities on the art of baking I know. The following comes from her remarkable book, *Breads* (HP Books, 1983). She was taught this recipe by her Grandpa Buck when she was only eight years old. In her words:

> No cutting together of butter and flour is necessary. Instead, whipping cream is stirred into the dry ingredients. The heavier the cream, the richer the biscuit. In lieu of the traditional round shape, we used to cut the dough into squares— big, for grandpa-size appetites—and dip them in melted butter before baking.

2 cups all-purpose flour

4 teaspoons baking powder

2 teaspoons sugar

1 teaspoon salt

3/4 to 1 cup heavy or whipping cream, at room temperature (see note)

1/3 cup (2/3 stick) unsalted butter, melted

1. Preheat the oven to 450° F.

2. Place the flour with the baking powder, sugar, and salt in a large bowl. Slowly stir in enough cream with a wooden spoon to form a soft dough. Transfer the dough to a lightly floured board, knead briefly, and roll out 1/2-inch thick. Cut into 2-inch squares.

3. Dip the biscuits into butter and place on an ungreased baking sheet. Bake until golden brown, 12 to 15 minutes.

Makes about 12 biscuits

Note If your cream has less than 40 percent butter fat, add a tablespoon or two of melted butter.

KATE'S BISCUITS

KATE ALMAND is literally a southern institution. An Atlantan home cook, her biscuit recipe is so effortless there's no need to carry it in my wallet; the formula stays forever in my head. The batter is beaten to a soft pastelike consistency and coated with additional flour before baking. The only trick is to handle the dough as gently as possible during the coating process.

2 1/2 cups self-rising soft wheat or cake flour (see note)

1/2 cup Crisco shortening, chilled
1 cup milk

1. Preheat the oven to 500° F.
2. Place 1/2 cup flour in a medium bowl and set aside. Place the remaining 2 cups flour in a large bowl. Cut in the shortening with a knife. Blend with a pastry blender until the texture of coarse crumbs.
3. Add the milk and beat with a heavy wooden spoon until smooth, 1 to 2 minutes. With a spoon, scoop out some dough, about the size of a large egg. Roll in the flour to coat, tossing gently with your fingertips. Gently place on a lightly buttered baking sheet. Repeat procedure with the remaining dough. Bake in the top third of hot oven 10 minutes. Biscuits should be almost white, not golden brown.

Makes about 12 biscuits

Note To make self-rising flour, add 1 1/2 teaspoons baking powder plus 1/2 teaspoon salt to 1 cup soft wheat or cake flour.

HELEN'S BUTTERMILK SKYSCRAPERS

I CAME UPON these lofty biscuits in 1979 when I ate at Helen's tearoom in New Iberia, Louisiana, the heart of Cajun country. No Cajun cook, Helen is strictly old-time southern and an unbeatable baker. She serves her high-rise biscuits with a side of crisp bacon, sunny-side-eggs, and a mess of grits.

4 cups all-purpose flour

2 tablespoons baking powder

1 teaspoon baking soda

1 teaspoon salt

1 tablespoon plus 1 teaspoon sugar

2/3 cup (1 1/3 sticks) unsalted butter, chilled, plus 4 tablespoons (1/2 stick) unsalted butter, melted

1 1/2 cups buttermilk

1. Preheat the oven to 450° F.

2. Sift the flour with the baking powder, baking soda, salt, and sugar in a large bowl. Cut in the butter with a knife. Blend with a pastry blender until the texture of coarse crumbs.

3. Stir in the buttermilk with a wooden spoon to form a soft dough. Knead briefly on a lightly floured board. Roll dough out 1 1/4 inches thick. Cut into 3-inch rounds and arrange with sides touching in a buttered 9-inch square cake pan. Brush the tops with the melted butter. Bake until golden, about 25 minutes.

Makes 8 or 9 large biscuits

PAT'S CALIFORNIA TEA BISCUITS

PAT MCQUEARY of San Diego sent me this recipe a while back noting that the device first appeared in a 1930s Wesson Oil cookbook. Pat is a very good cook, and, as is usually the case with *good* cooks, could not resist adding her imprimatur to the recipe. Mayonnaise takes the place of the oil. With very tonic results, but see for yourself . . .

2 cups all-purpose flour

4 teaspoons baking powder

1/2 teaspoon salt

1 tablespoon sugar

1/4 cup mayonnaise

2/3 cup milk

1. Preheat the oven to 450° F.

2. Sift the flour with the baking powder, salt, and sugar in a large bowl.

3. Stir in the mayonnaise and the milk with a wooden spoon to form a soft dough. Roll out on a heavily floured board (dough will be slightly sticky) 1/2-inch thick. Cut into 2 1/2-inch rounds. Place on an ungreased baking sheet. Bake until golden, 12 to 15 minutes.

Makes about 9 biscuits

CAMPTON PLACE'S CARAWAY-RYES

CAMPTON PLACE is probably one of the most elegant hotels in the Western world. The Far West, that is, in downtown San Francisco. Campton Place is renowned for its food—and they serve wonderful breads, like this caraway-rye biscuit that goes well with all mild-flavored dishes.

1 1/2 cups all-purpose flour

1/2 cup rye flour

2 teaspoons baking powder

1/2 teaspoon baking soda

1/2 teaspoon salt

1 1/2 tablespoons caraway seeds

1/2 cup (1 stick) unsalted butter, chilled

1/2 cup buttermilk

1. Preheat the oven to 450° F.

2. Sift the flours with the baking powder, baking soda, and salt in a large bowl. Toss in the caraway seeds. Cut in the butter with a knife. Blend with a pastry blender until the texture of coarse crumbs.

3. Stir in the buttermilk with a wooden spoon to form a soft dough. Roll dough out on a lightly floured board 1/2-inch thick. Cut into 2 1/2-inch

rounds. Place on an ungreased baking sheet. Bake until golden, 10 to 12 minutes.

Makes about 9 biscuits

Speaking of the West, the Old West this time, legend tells of a lone couple who set off to meet a wagon train heading toward Oregon back in the 1880s. However, they became hopelessly lost and never did find the appointed rendezvous. So, they went West alone. One day after dusk near the Great Divide, a tribe of Indians surprised the family. The head of the house, not knowing how to react, offered the Indians glasses of milk fresh from their cow, while his wife prepared sourdough biscuits. The tribe, duly impressed with such unexpected hospitality, not only guarded them through the night, but actually escorted them westward the next day. The moral of this tale? Here are Louis Untermeyer's thoughts on the subject:

> What hymns are sung.
> What praises said.
> For homemade miracles of bread?
> —*Food and Drink*

RISEN SOURDOUGH BISCUITS

HERE'S THE breadstuff said to have won the West. Or, at the very least, kept the denizens of wagon trains hale and hearty enough to get there and win it! The old time recipe is only slightly updated in this rendering with a quick new method for making "sourdough" starter overnight. In the old days, maintaining starter on the westward trail was said to be a true art. And only an accomplished cook (pioneer wife or Conestoga wagon "cookie") was able to keep a batch replenished come rain, shine, heatwave, or blizzard.

For the sponge

1/2 cup warm water

1 teaspoon dry yeast

1/2 cup all-purpose flour

For the biscuits

The prepared sponge

6 tablespoons (3/4 stick) unsalted
    butter, melted, cooled

1/2 teaspoon salt

1/2 teaspoon sugar

1/2 teaspoon baking powder

1/4 teaspoon baking soda

1 3/4 to 2 cups all-purpose flour

1. To make the sponge: The day before serving the biscuits, place the water in a small bowl. Sprinkle with the yeast. Stir in the flour. Cover tightly and let stand at room temperature for at least 24 hours.

2. To make the biscuits: Scrape the sponge into a large bowl. Remove 1 tablespoon of the butter and set aside. Stir in the remaining butter, salt, sugar, baking powder, baking soda, and enough flour to make a soft dough. Roll the dough out on a lightly floured board, about 1/4-inch thick. Cut the dough into 9 2-inch rounds. Place the rounds snugly in a lightly buttered 8-inch square cake pan. Cover and let rise 1 hour.

3. Preheat the oven to 425° F.

4. Brush the biscuits with the remaining butter. Bake until golden and firm to the touch, 15 to 20 minutes.

Makes 9 biscuits

WHOLE WHEAT "ANGELS"

"BREAD, milk and butter are of venerable antiquity. The taste of the morning of the world."—Leigh Hunt, *The Seer*, 1840. More so when that bread is an honest-to-goodness early American yeast-risen biscuit. This biscuit was dubbed "angelic" to distinguish it from the "devilish" quality of the bespoke hard-to-chew biscuits that predated it. The recipe is highly authentic down to the addition of whole wheat, for the flour Colonists used was of much rougher mettle than the refined kind we use today.

1/2 cup warm water

1 1/2 teaspoons rapid rising granulated yeast

1/2 cup cake or soft wheat flour

7 tablespoons unsalted butter, melted, cooled to lukewarm

1/2 cup lukewarm milk

2 to 2 1/2 cups whole wheat flour

1/2 teaspoon sugar

1/2 teaspoon salt

1/2 teaspoon baking powder

1/2 teaspoon baking soda

1. Place the water in a large bowl. Sprinkle with the yeast. Stir in the cake flour. Cover and let stand in a warm place 20 minutes.

2. Remove 1 tablespoon of the butter and set aside. Stir the remaining butter and the milk into the yeast mixture. Stir in 1 cup whole wheat flour, the sugar, salt, baking powder, and baking soda. Stir in 1 more cup of flour and beat until smooth.

3. Transfer the mixture to a well-floured board (use whole wheat flour). Knead briefly and press dough down until 1/2-inch thick. Cut the dough into 9 2-inch rounds. Place the dough snugly in a lightly buttered 8-inch square cake pan. Cover and let rise 30 minutes. The dough should not be allowed to rise to more than half the depth of the pan or they will rise too much during baking.

4. Preheat the oven to 400° F.

5. Brush the biscuits with the remaining 1 tablespoon butter. Bake until firm to the touch, about 15 minutes.

Makes 9 biscuits

ALABAMA HAM AND CHEESE BISCUITS

SOUTHERN GENTRY invariably served "beaten biscuits" with snippets of country smoked ham tucked between the halves. This amended version, though definitely not a tried and true "beaten" biscuit, borrows the concept, incorporating not only ham, but cheese in the dough itself. A jot of spicy mustard ties "the bite" together. Serve with eggs for breakfast.

3 cups all-purpose flour

4 teaspoons baking powder

1/2 teaspoon salt

Pinch of freshly ground black pepper

6 tablespoons lard

3/4 cup ground cooked smoky country ham

1/4 cup finely grated cheddar cheese

1 teaspoon Dijon mustard

3/4 cup plus 1 tablespoon milk

1. Preheat the oven to 450° F.

2. Combine the flour, baking powder, salt, and pepper in a large bowl. Cut in the lard with a knife. Blend with a pastry blender until the mixture has the texture of coarse crumbs. Add the ham, cheese, and mustard. Continue to blend until well mixed.

3. Stir in 3/4 cup of the milk with a wooden spoon to form a soft dough. Knead briefly on a lightly floured board. Roll out the dough 1/2-inch thick. Cut into 2-inch rounds and arrange on an ungreased baking sheet. Brush the tops with milk. Bake until golden, about 15 minutes.

Makes 14 biscuits

SHAKER "SKILLET" BISCUITS

THE SHAKERS left a great kitchen legacy. They were not only frugal, but sensible cooks. During hot summer months, they rarely used stoves. Instead, they prepared their food on griddles or in stew pots over embers. Biscuits, a fixed part of every Shaker meal, were cooked over the same coals in heavy iron skillets set on gridirons. Shaker biscuits are still easy to make and so delectable, I predict you'll have a batch in the skillet all year long.

2 cups sifted all-purpose flour

1/2 teaspoon salt

2 teaspoons cream of tartar

1 teaspoon baking soda

4 tablespoons (1/2 stick) unsalted butter, chilled

2/3 cup heavy or whipping cream

1. Sift the flour with the salt, cream of tartar, and baking soda in a large bowl. Cut in the butter with a knife. Blend with a pastry blender until the mixture has the texture of coarse crumbs.

2. Slowly stir in the cream with a wooden spoon to form a soft dough. Roll the dough out on a lightly floured board 1/2-inch thick. Cut into 2 1/2-inch rounds.

3. Rub a cast-iron skillet with flour. Place over medium-low heat for 5 minutes. Add the biscuits, not touching, about 4 at a time. Cook until baked through, 8 to 9 minutes per side. Reduce heat if biscuits cook too quickly. They should be dark brown, but not burned.

Makes about 8 biscuits

NEW MEXICAN CHILE BISCUITS

THE NEXT BITE obviously hails from gringo country. In the Southwest, biscuits were once made entirely of cornmeal, which, to be dead honest, produced a dense, if somewhat leaden, quick bread. All-purpose flour brought to the Mexican kitchen at the turn of the century by newcomers from the East lightened the traditional biscuit immeasurably, but cornmeal is still present in the formula. Fresh Anaheim or Poblano chiles can be roasted and substituted for canned peppers. These mate well with grilled or broiled meats.

1 1/2 cups all-purpose flour

1/2 cup yellow cornmeal

1/2 teaspoon salt

2 teaspoons baking powder

1/2 teaspoon baking soda

7 tablespoons unsalted butter, melted

1/2 cup milk

1 can (4 ounces) chopped, mild green chiles

1. Preheat the oven to 450° F.

2. Combine the flour with the cornmeal, salt, baking powder, and baking soda in a large bowl. Remove 1 tablespoon of the butter and set aside. Stir in the milk, the remaining butter, and the chiles with a wooden spoon to form a soft dough.

3. Press the dough down on a floured board about 1/2-inch thick. Cut into 2-inch rounds and arrange on an unbuttered baking sheet. Brush the tops with the remaining 1 tablespoon melted butter. Bake until golden brown, about 15 minutes.

Makes 9 biscuits

OLD STYLE SHORTCAKE

WILLIAM BUTLER, seventeenth-century British writer, said of the strawberry: "Doubtless God could have made a better berry, but doubtless God never did." And doubtless, man could never have invented a more appropriate coupling for it than a crusty shortcake. This one is baked in the round, split asunder, topped with the juiciest berries one can find, lavished with mountains of whipped cream—and offered up with only two sublime words: "Dive in!"

2 1/2 cups all-purpose flour

1/2 cup sugar

4 teaspoons baking powder

1/2 teaspoon salt

3 ounces cream cheese

3 tablespoons unsalted butter, chilled; plus 2 tablespoons, melted

1 large egg, lightly beaten

2 tablespoons sour cream

1 3/4 cups heavy or whipping cream

1 quart fresh strawberries, cleaned and hulled

2 tablespoons Grand Marnier liqueur

1 tablespoon confectioners' sugar

1. Preheat the oven to 450° F.

2. Combine the flour with 1/4 cup sugar, the baking powder, and salt in a large bowl. Cut in the cream cheese and chilled butter with a knife. Blend with a pastry blender until the mixture has the texture of coarse crumbs.

3. Whisk the egg with the sour cream and 3/4 cup heavy cream in a bowl. Stir into the flour mixture to form a soft dough. Divide the dough in half. Press out dough on a lightly floured board into an 8-inch circle. Place in a greased 8-inch cake pan. Smooth with your fingertips. Repeat process with remaining dough. Place in the pan. Drizzle with melted butter. Bake 20 minutes. Turn off the heat and with the oven door ajar, cool the biscuit for 1 hour in the oven. Transfer to a rack. Split apart when cool. Transfer to a large round serving platter.

4. Halve any large berries. Lightly crush half the berries. Combine the berries with 1/4 cup sugar and the Grand Marnier. Refrigerate, covered, until serving.

5. Just before serving, beat the 1 cup cream with the confectioners' sugar until stiff. Spoon slightly more than half the berries over the bottom shortcake layer. Place the top on and spoon the remaining berries over the top. Cover the top with the whipped cream.

Serves 8

Bread Puddings

"PUDDING, like Topsy, seems to have 'just growed.'" So mused Irene Veal in *The Anthology of Puddings* (John Gifford, Ltd, 1942). According to Ms. Veal, puddings appeared under various spellings (*poding, poodying,* and even *pooddynge*) in England dating from the thirteenth century, but the earliest printed recipe didn't surface until three hundred years later. And, oddly enough, it called for bread.

> take crumbs of bread,
>
> yolks of egges and cowes milke,
>
> with saffron,
>
> seethe them together a lytle,
>
> as if to make a puddinge.

Etymologists seem to be confused about the word's actual origin. Some suggest it stems from the French *boudin* which is literally a meat pudding in a sausage casing. Moreover, they are quick to point out that the early English puddings were almost always wrapped (or encased, if you will) before they were boiled. Hence the link. However, according to Webster's International, the word *boudin* itself can be traced to *bood,* a Scottish word. For the record, Scottish haggis is one of the oldest meat puddings around.

Bread puddings, sometimes dubbed "hasty puddings" were popular in England long before the first settlers arrived on our shores. But, as wheat was not to be found in the New World, an American original was born out of necessity: Pilgrim-style hasty pudding made with cornmeal and sweetened with maple sugar or molasses.

As the Colonies flourished, so did wheat. And more pertinently, so did the number of bread pudding recipes logged by our forefathers. Some used slices; others, torn pieces or bread crumbs. Leftover biscuits, rolls, and even cakes wound up at the Colonist's table, whether the pudding was sweet or savory.

The first bread pudding was in fact a savory (tidbit consumed after a sweet dessert "to temper the palate"). Earliest French charlottes were un-sweetened as well, lined with butter-soaked bread, and not ladyfingers as we are accustomed to finding in our charlottes these days.

Bread pudding, in some form or other, is a standard sweet in every country of the world. The Chinese eat them stuffed with crushed nuts. In Russia, Poland, and the Balkans, crumbs (usually pumpernickel) are folded into whipped cream and sometimes jam to produce a dessert called *katchka*. But for most of us, bread pudding is a mixture of eggs, sugar, milk, and bread; baked to a fare-thee-well, till all the various ingredients fuse into one delicious confection no fork can resist.

Some Bread Pudding Pointers If ever there was a camp divided! Bread pudding mavens, that is. The battle lines are drawn over the simple question: crust or no crust? On one side are those who patiently "shave the bread of its covering," resulting in a smooth, velvety custard. On the other, the "real men don't eat quiche" types never trim their crusts. Texture with a bite, they argue, is what a great bread pudding is all about. I can be easily swayed one way or the other. But whether you prefer your bread sliced or torn, it should be at least a day old, preferably two, but not so stale you need to break it apart with a hammer. Oh yes, the white packaged stuff just won't do in a bread pudding; French- or Italian-style loaves are your best bet.

There are so many styles of bread puddings that no general rule of thumb covers all of them. When it comes to the basic, standard bread pudding, Fannie Farmer had the definitive word on the subject:

So many combinations make an excellent bread pudding that a recipe is only a general guide. If you prefer a sweeter pudding, add more sugar. Season discreetly with any spice. To make a firmer pudding, use less milk, even as little as 2 cups. To make a fluffier pudding, separate the eggs and add the whites last, beaten stiff. For a richer pudding, add 1 cup orange marmalade, chopped raisins, dates, or figs, or add 1/2 cup chopped nut meats.

Blessed be he that invented pudding, for it is a Manna that hits the Palates of all Sorts of People; a Manna better than that of the Wilderness, because the People are never weary of it . . .
    —Francoise Maximilien Mission (seventeenth-century France)

AND BLESSED be he that discovered that day-old bread need not be relegated to the birds. The recipes that follow prove that point admirably.

THE UNCLASSIC, CLASSIC BREAD PUDDING WITH HARD SAUCE

I DISCOVERED this recipe in Nora Ephron's tasty novel *Heartburn* (1983). It whetted my appetite uncontrollably at first reading and I have been making it ever since. Ephron got it from Chez Helene in New Orleans. It is unusual because it incorporates evaporated as well as fresh milk in the mixture—and enough butter to make it downright sinful.

1 loaf French- or Italian-style bread (8 to 10 ounces), torn into pieces
2 1/2 cups milk
1 cup (2 sticks) unsalted butter, softened
2 cups sugar
1 can (13 ounces) evaporated milk
2 tablespoons ground nutmeg
2 tablespoons vanilla
1 cup seedless raisins
Hard Sauce (recipe follows)

1. Preheat the oven to 350° F.
2. Combine the bread with the milk in a large bowl. Let stand 10 minutes.
3. Beat the butter with the sugar in a large bowl until light and fluffy. Beat in the evaporated milk, nutmeg, and vanilla. Stir in the bread mixture and raisins.
4. Pour mixture into a deep 3- to 4-quart baking dish. Place dish on a baking sheet. Bake 1 hour. Gently stir the mixture with a wooden spoon. Continue to bake until all liquid is absorbed, about 1 hour longer. Serve with Hard Sauce while still warm.

Serves 8 to 10

HARD SAUCE

1/2 cup (1 stick) unsalted butter, softened
1 cup confectioners' sugar
3 tablespoons dark rum

Beat the butter with the sugar in a large bowl until light and fluffy. Beat in the rum. Refrigerate, covered. Remove from refrigerator at least 30 minutes before serving. The sauce is best at room temperature.

Makes about 1 1/2 cups

OLD-FASHIONED APPLE
BREAD PUDDING

THIS RECIPE has been in Bert Greene's family for years and years. It was first printed in *Bert Greene's Kitchen Bouquets* (Contemporary Books, 1979), a dizzying collection of memories and memorable dishes, arranged by aroma and flavor. Apple brandy is the secret ingredient here; French Calvados is the best of all.

3 tablespoons unsalted butter
1 pound sweet apples (about 2 large),
    pared, cored, thinly sliced
1 1/3 cups sugar
1/3 cup seedless raisins
1/4 cup Calvados (apple brandy)
10 1/2-inch-thick slices French or
    Italian bread

6 large eggs
1 teaspoon vanilla
1 cup heavy or whipping cream
3 cups milk
Confectioners' sugar

1. Preheat the oven to 350° F.

2. Melt the butter in a large heavy skillet over medium-low heat. Add the apple slices and stir until well coated. Sprinkle with 1/3 cup sugar, the raisins, and Calvados; cook until heated. Set aflame; when flames subside, remove from heat.

3. Arrange the bread slices, slightly overlapping, in a buttered 9- by 13-inch baking dish. Spoon the apple mixture over the top.

4. Lightly beat the eggs in a large bowl. Beat in the remaining 1 cup granulated sugar, vanilla, cream, and milk. Spoon mixture over the apples. Let stand 10 minutes.

5. Place the baking dish in a large roasting pan. Pour hot water into the roasting pan to come halfway up the sides of the bread pudding pan. Bake until set, about 50 minutes. Cool for 20 minutes on a wire rack.

6. Generously dust the surface of the pudding with confectioners' sugar. Place under a preheated broiler until top is glazed, 2 to 3 minutes. Take care not to burn the sugar.

Serves 8

CHERRY BREAD PUDDING
WITH CHOCOLATE SAUCE

CHERRY was a favored fruit in America's dessert lexicon even before George Washington gave it "star" status. Martha Washington, coincidentally, was an excellent cook and often used cherry preserves in her bread pudding. Since most commercial cherry preserves are, frankly, "commercial" these days, I use whole cherries instead. Frozen, fresh, or even canned will do. The chocolate sauce, by the way, is a purely twentieth-century embellishment.

10-ounce loaf Italian bread, trimmed of crust, cut into 1/2-inch-thick slices

10 tablespoons unsalted butter, melted

2 cups milk

1 1/2 cups heavy or whipping cream

1 1/2 cups sugar

2 large egg yolks

1 teaspoon finely grated lemon peel

1/4 teaspoon freshly grated nutmeg

1 package (12 ounces) frozen, pitted dark sweet cherries, thawed (about 1 cup); 1/4 cup juice reserved

2 tablespoons Kirsch liqueur

1 teaspoon finely grated orange peel

1 tablespoon confectioners' sugar

Chocolate Sauce (recipe follows), warm

1. Cut the bread slices into triangles and brush both sides with melted butter. Set aside.

2. Combine the milk, 1/2 cup cream, and 1/2 cup sugar in a medium saucepan. Stir over medium heat until sugar dissolves. Remove from heat.

3. Beat the egg yolks in a large bowl until light. Slowly whisk in the warm milk mixture. Add the lemon peel and nutmeg.

4. Arrange half the bread triangles over the bottom of a 2 1/2- to 3-inch deep oval or rectangular baking dish. Spoon just enough of the custard over the bread to moisten.

5. Combine the cherries with the remaining 1 cup sugar, the Kirsch, and orange peel. Spoon over the bread in the dish. Place the remaining bread triangles over the cherries. Pour the remaining custard over the top. Let stand 20 minutes.

6. Preheat the oven to 350° F.

7. Bake the pudding until firm, about 40 minutes. Cool completely on a wire rack.

8. Beat the remaining 1 cup cream with the confectioners' sugar in a large bowl until stiff. Serve the pudding at room temperature with a dab of whipped cream on top. Spoon some of the warm Chocolate Sauce next to each piece on a plate.

Serves 6 to 8

CHOCOLATE SAUCE

4 ounces semi-sweet chocolate

2 1/2 tablespoons unsalted butter, cut into bits

2 tablespoons milk, at room temperature

2 tablespoons heavy or whipping cream, at room temperature

1 tablespoon dark rum

Melt the chocolate in the top of a double boiler over hot water. Stir in the butter, bit by bit, until smooth. Stir in the milk, cream, and rum. Let stand over warm water until ready to serve.

Makes about 1 cup

CHOCOLATE BREAD
AND BUTTER PUDDING

BRITISH POLITICIAN Clement Freud wrote in *Freud On Food* (1978):

In moments of considerable strain I tend to take to bread-and-butter pudding. There is something about the blandness of soggy bread, the crispness of the golden outer crust and the unadulterated pleasure of a lightly set custard that makes the world seem a better place to live.

Even more so when the bread and butter pudding is chocolate.

6 ounces sweet or semi-sweet imported chocolate (Lindt, Tobler, Maillard, etc.)

2 tablespoons unsalted butter, softened

6 to 8 1/4-inch-thick slices brioche or pound cake, trimmed (enough to line an 8-inch square pan)

3 large eggs

2 large egg yolks

1/2 cup light brown sugar (packed)

Pinch of salt

1 1/4 cups milk

1 1/2 cups heavy or whipping cream

1 1/2 teaspoons vanilla

1/8 teaspoon ground cinnamon

1/8 teaspoon ground nutmeg

Vanilla-flavored sweetened whipped cream

1. Preheat the oven to 325° F.

2. Roughly grate the chocolate over the bottom of an unbuttered 8-inch square cake pan. Butter the brioche or pound cake and place the slices over the grated chocolate. Do not crowd the slices.

3. Beat the eggs with the egg yolks in a large bowl. Beat in the sugar, salt, milk, 1 1/2 cups cream, the vanilla, cinnamon, and nutmeg. Pour over the brioche slices, pushing the slices down into the mixture until soaked.

4. Set the pan in a roasting pan. Pour hot water into the roasting pan to come halfway up the sides of the bread pudding pan. Bake until set, about 50 minutes. Do not allow the oven temperature to rise above 325° F. or the custard might separate. Cool pudding for at least 1 hour before serving with the vanilla-flavored whipped cream.

Serves 6

RICHMOND EGGNOG BREAD PUDDING

THE NEXT custardy-boozy bread pudding was invented out of necessity by a thrifty Virginia matron who had more eggnog than takers at a New Year's Day open house. Using her noggin', she sloshed half a loaf of bread with the residue in her punch bowl and baked it for a January 2 dessert. You don't have to wait for such dire party straits to whip up a batch, however. Any day can be New Year's if one has the necessary spirits!

Unsalted butter
5 to 6 1/2-inch-thick center-cut slices of challah bread
3 large eggs
3/4 cup sugar
1/4 cup cognac

1/4 cup dark rum
2 tablespoons bourbon
2 cups heavy or whipping cream
Pinch of ground cinnamon
1/8 teaspoon freshly grated nutmeg

1. Preheat the oven to 325° F.

2. Butter a 1-quart rectangular baking dish, about 2 inches deep. Butter the bread slices and arrange over the bottom of the dish. Do not crowd the pieces.

3. Beat the eggs with the sugar in a large bowl until light. Beat in the cognac, rum, bourbon, cream, cinnamon, and nutmeg. Pour over the bread slices. Let stand, pushing the bread down occasionally, 15 minutes.

4. Bake the bread pudding in the preheated oven until firm, about 30 minutes. Run under a preheated broiler to lightly brown the top. Cool on a rack.

Serves 6 to 8

SHAKER-STYLE COLD CHOCOLATE PUDDING

EVERY SHAKER village had its personal provincial bread pudding it seems. This one, adapted from a recipe that graced the supper tables at Hancock Village in Massachusetts over a century ago, is a hand's down winner. The chocolate caramel lurking beneath the velvety pudding should be spooned over the top of each slice as it is served. Take note: The meringue topping should be made no more than one hour before serving, even better at the last minute.

2 1/2 cups sugar

2 teaspoons unsweetened cocoa

3 ounces semi-sweet chocolate, chopped

2 cups milk

1 cup heavy or whipping cream

2 cups soft, day-old bread crumbs
   (from about 5 ounces bread)

4 large egg yolks

4 tablespoons (1/2 stick) unsalted
   butter, melted

1 teaspoon vanilla

5 large egg whites

1. Preheat the oven to 350° F.

2. Place a 3- to 4-inch deep 6- to 8-cup soufflé dish in the oven to warm.

3. Meanwhile, stir 1/2 cup sugar with the cocoa in a medium saucepan over high heat until sugar melts and turns caramel in color, about 4 minutes. Remove dish from oven and carefully pour caramel mixture over the bottom. Cool on a wire rack.

3. In a medium heavy saucepan, stir the chocolate with a wooden spoon over low heat until smooth. Slowly whisk in the milk until smooth. Whisk in the cream, 1 1/2 cups sugar, and the bread crumbs. Cook, stirring occasionally, 5 minutes.

4. Beat the egg yolks with the butter in a medium bowl until smooth. Stir this mixture into the bread crumb mixture and add the vanilla. Cook, stirring occasionally, 5 minutes. Do not allow to boil.

5. Pour the pudding mixture into the prepared dish. Bake until almost firm, about 20 minutes. Cool on a wire rack. Refrigerate, covered, overnight.

6. Just before serving, beat the egg whites in the large bowl of an electric mixer until soft peaks form. Slowly beat in the remaining 1/2 cup sugar until very stiff. Spread over the chilled chocolate pudding. Place the dish in a roasting pan and surround with ice. Place under a preheated broiler until the top is nicely browned, about 3 minutes. Serve immediately.

Serves 6 to 8

Remarkable, but true, not everybody loves bread pudding! Well, I can sight at least one example. Bert Leston Taylor even went so far as to pen the following stanza from his "Chant of Hate for Bread Pudding":

> Hate of the millions who've choked you down.
> In country kitchen or house in town,
> We love a thousand, we hate but one,
> With a hate more hot than the hate of the Gun
> —Bread Pudding!

What a pity Mr. Taylor never got to taste the recipes in this collection. For to paraphrase another oldie, "The proof of the pudding is in the eating."

CHOCOLATE MALTED
ICE BOX PUDDING

LOOSELY BASED on the bespoke Russian *katchka*, a dessert commonly served in expatriate Russian communities all over the U.S., the next recipe is a chocolate lover's downfall. But so simple, even a child can prepare it. All you need is a beater, a grater, and a sweet tooth.

3 cups heavy or whipping cream

3 tablespoons malted milk powder

1 tablespoon confectioners' sugar

1/2 teaspoon vanilla

4 ounces milk chocolate, finely grated

1 ounce semi-sweet chocolate, finely grated

4 ounces soft, day-old pumpernickel bread crumbs (from about 4 slices)

1. Beat 2 1/2 cups cream with the malted milk powder and confectioners' sugar in a large bowl until stiff. Beat in the vanilla. Fold in the grated chocolates. Fold in the bread crumbs.

2. Spoon the mixture into a 1 1/2- to 2-quart soufflé dish. Refrigerate, covered, overnight.

3. No more than 3 hours before serving, beat the remaining 1/2 cup cream in a medium bowl until stiff. Using a pastry bag fitted with a star tube, pipe the cream in concentric circles over the top. Keep chilled until ready to serve.

Serves 6 to 8

SANTA FE CUSTARD

THE FOLLOWING recipe is based on a classic Spanish recipe for baked custard, and takes on a remarkably new American dimension when coupled with bread cubes.

1 cup plus 2 tablespoons sugar

1/2 cup water

6 tablespoons Grand Marnier liqueur

1 1/2 cups 1/2-inch bread cubes (from about 4 ounces trimmed bread)

1 cup milk

3/4 cup heavy or whipping cream

1/2 teaspoon vanilla

2 large eggs

2 large egg yolks

1. Preheat the oven to 350° F.

2. Place a shallow 1-quart soufflé dish in the oven to warm.

3. Meanwhile, stir 1/2 cup sugar in a medium saucepan over high heat until the sugar melts and turns caramel in color, about 4 minutes. Remove the dish from oven and carefully pour the caramel mixture over the bottom,

tilting the dish to coat the sides as much as possible. Turn the dish upside down on a buttered piece of aluminum foil.

4. Place the saucepan in which the caramel was made over low heat and carefully add the water. Using a wooden spoon, scrape the sides and bottom of pan until all caramel residue has melted, about 4 minutes. Stir in 2 tablespoons sugar and 2 tablespoons Grand Marnier. Cool to room temperature and chill until ready to serve.

5. Place the bread cubes in a medium bowl. Sprinkle with the remaining 4 tablespoons Grand Marnier.

6. Combine the milk, cream, and vanilla in a medium saucepan. Stir over medium heat until hot. Do not allow to boil.

7. Beat the eggs with the egg yolks in a large bowl until light. Slowly beat in the remaining 1/2 cup sugar until light and fluffy. Beat in the warm milk mixture. Stir in the bread cubes. Let stand 15 minutes. Pour mixture into the prepared soufflé dish.

8. Set the dish in a roasting pan. Pour hot water into the roasting pan to come halfway up the sides of the bread pudding dish. Bake until set, about 45 minutes. Cool on a wire rack. Refrigerate, covered, overnight.

9. To unmold the pudding, heat 1/4-inch water in a heavy skillet to boiling. Turn off the heat. Dip a butter knife into the water and run around the edges of the pudding to loosen the sides. Place the dish in the water 30 seconds. Quickly invert dish onto a serving platter. Serve with the caramel sauce on the side.

Serves 6

FLORIDA KEYS BREAD PUDDING
WITH RUM SAUCE

AS PRIORLY NOTED, earlier Americans used whatever was leftover (bread or cake) to enrich their puddings. The following recipe depends on day-old sponge cake. Definitely tropical in nature, the device combines coconut milk, rum, and pineapple, but turns them all into a golden puff, rather than a piña colada. Top it with a cold custardy rum sauce.

1 package (7 ounces) flaked sweetened coconut

1 3/4 cup milk

1 cup heavy or whipping cream

3 large egg yolks

3/4 cup sugar

1 tablespoon dark rum

3 cups 1/2-inch cubes day-old sponge cake (about 5 ounces)

1 can (8 ounces) crushed pineapple, well drained

Rum Sauce (recipe follows)

1. Preheat the oven to 350° F.

2. Combine the coconut with the milk in the container of a food processor. Process until fairly smooth. Strain the milk into a bowl. Reserve the coconut for use at another time.

3. Combine 1 1/2 cups of the coconut milk with the cream in a medium saucepan. Heat over low heat until hot, about 5 minutes.

4. Beat the egg yolks with the sugar in a large bowl until light and fluffy. Slowly whisk in the hot coconut milk mixture. Transfer to the top of a double boiler. Cook over simmering water, stirring constantly, 5 minutes. Stir in the rum.

5. Place half the bread cubes over the bottom of a 1 1/2- to 2-quart soufflé dish. Spread the pineapple over the top. Cover the pineapple with the remaining bread cubes. Pour the hot egg mixture over the top; let stand 10 minutes.

6. Bake the pudding until set, about 40 minutes. Cool on a wire rack. Serve slightly warm or at room temperature with the Rum Sauce.

Serves 6 to 8

RUM SAUCE

2/3 cup heavy or whipping cream

1/4 cup milk

2 large egg yolks

1/3 cup sugar

2 tablespoons dark rum

1. Combine the cream and the milk in a medium saucepan. Heat over low heat until hot, about 5 minutes.

2. Beat the egg yolks with the sugar in a large bowl until light. Slowly whisk in the hot liquid. Whisk in the rum. Transfer to the top of a double boiler. Cook over simmering water, stirring constantly, until thick enough to coat a spoon, about 10 minutes. Cool to room temperature. Serve at room temperature or slightly chilled.

Makes about 1 1/2 cups

JERSEY PUDDING
WITH AMARETTO SAUCE

THIS NEXT recipe is a true original. It is the handiwork of Suzan Gross who lives, and eloquently cooks up a storm, in New Jersey. Her pudding was the winner of the *Hour Magazine* television cooking contest a few years back. It is still one of the most winning desserts around.

1 challah bread (1 pound), torn into
    1-inch pieces
3 cups milk
1 cup heavy or whipping cream
3 large eggs
1 1/2 cups sugar

2 tablespoons almond extract
3/4 cup sliced almonds
3/4 cup golden raisins
3/4 cup chopped dried apricots
Amaretto Sauce (recipe follows)

1. Preheat the oven to 325° F.

2. Combine the bread with the milk and cream in a large bowl. Let stand 10 minutes.

3. Whisk the eggs with the sugar in a medium bowl until well mixed. Whisk in the almond extract. Pour over the challah bread. Stir with a wooden spoon until the bread is well coated. Stir in the almonds, raisins, and apricots.

4. Spoon the mixture into a greased 9- by 13- by 2-inch glass baking dish. Bake until set, about 50 minutes. Cool on a rack. Serve slightly warm or well chilled with Amaretto Sauce.

Serves 10 to 12

AMARETTO SAUCE

1/2 cup (1 stick) unsalted butter   1 large egg, lightly beaten
1 cup confectioners' sugar   1/4 cup Amaretto liqueur

Melt the butter in the top of a double boiler over boiling water. Whisk in the sugar until smooth and the sugar dissolves. Remove from heat and whisk in the beaten egg. Cool slightly and whisk in the Amaretto liqueur. Serve warm.

Makes about 1 2/3 cups

CAPE COD CRANBERRY
BREAD BAKE

FROM THE Massachusetts' Cape, where the cranberry is always the fall fruit of choice, comes this rosy recipe. Homemade cranberry sauce is drizzled betwixt bread and custard to make a refreshingly different "Down East" dessert; a notable change for the-day-after-Thanksgiving dinner menu.

1 large seedless orange
2 cups cranberries, picked over
2 1/4 cups sugar
1/3 cup water
2 large eggs
Pinch of ground cinnamon
1 1/2 cups milk

1/2 cup heavy or whipping cream
3 tablespoons Grand Marnier liqueur
1 teaspoon vanilla
8 ounce loaf, French- or Italian-style bread, trimmed of crust, cut into thin slices
Heavy or whipping cream

1. Finely grate the peel from the orange. Remove the skin and membranes from the orange. Section the orange and cut each section across into thin slices. Combine the orange peel, the orange slices, the cranberries, 1 1/2 cups sugar, and the water in a medium saucepan. Heat to boiling; reduce the heat.

Simmer covered 10 minutes. Remove cover and continue to cook until slightly thickened, about 5 minutes. Remove from heat.

2. Preheat the oven to 325° F.

3. Beat the eggs with the cinnamon in a large bowl until light. Beat in the remaining 3/4 cup sugar, the milk, 1/2 cup cream, Grand Marnier liqueur, and vanilla.

4. Place a layer of bread over the bottom of a buttered 2-quart soufflé dish. Using a ladle, add enough egg mixture to cover the bread. Spoon one third of the cranberry mixture over the top. Repeat the layers two more times, adding all the egg mixture to the dish before spooning on the last third of the cranberries. Bake until firm, about 1 hour. Serve slightly warm or at room temperature with heavy cream.

Serves 8

SISTER CORA'S BREAD PUDDING

SISTER CORA HAMPTON of New Orleans was a chef who worked as a taxi driver when away from the range. She was a talker. The talk was all food. One tip she passed on was how to perk up a boring gravy—stir a jot of mustard into it. But, more to the point, the following recipe was given off the cuff—scribbled on a stolen writing pad from the previous city's hotel.

8-ounce loaf crusty French bread, torn into pieces
2 cups milk
1 cup heavy or whipping cream

1/4 cup plus 1 tablespoon bourbon
6 large eggs, separated
2 cups sugar
Pinch of salt

1. Preheat the oven to 350° F.

2. Place the bread in a large bowl. Stir in the milk, cream, and 1/4 cup bourbon. Mix well; let stand 15 minutes.

3. Beat the egg yolks in a large bowl until light. Slowly whisk in 1 cup sugar. Beat until light and fluffy.

4. Spoon the bread mixture into a buttered 8-inch square or 9-inch round glass dish about 2 inches deep. Pour the egg yolk mixture over the top. Bake until firm, about 30 minutes. Cool on a rack.

5. Before serving, beat the egg whites with a pinch of salt in the large bowl of an electric mixer until soft peaks form. Slowly beat in the remaining 1 cup sugar and the remaining 1 tablespoon bourbon to make a meringue. Beat until stiff and shiny. Spoon meringue over the top of the pudding and run under a preheated broiler until the top is nicely browned, about 2 to 3 minutes.

Serves 6 to 8

Brownies

*I*T'S NO SECRET that all the world loves brownies, but to set a plateful, unadorned, before the leaders of the world takes guts, or perhaps, just supreme chocolate confidence. That's exactly what Maida Heatter, "America's undisputed queen of desserts," served the distinguished guests who attended President Reagan's 1983 Economic Summit in Williamsburg. The reaction? Maida recalls, "The message came back that the dignitaries wanted more!" The American brownie became an international star overnight.

Who actually invented the brownie is a matter of conjecture. One persistent legend is that of a newly hired chef at the long vanished Hotel Touraine in Boston. As the story goes, back in the 1920s a small fire broke out in the kitchen while this fellow was simultaneously melting chocolate for pudding and stirring a batch of butter cookies. As wreaths of smoke filled the room, he shut his eyes and, snatching up the about-to-scorch chocolate, poured it into the nearest bowl at hand, which, of course, contained cookie batter. Being a thrifty New Englander and new at his job, he was loath to throw out the expensive mess. Instead, he poured the mixture into a pan and baked it. The result: A rich, moist, and rather chewy confection—a cross between cake, candy, and pudding, too. Slicing it into squares, he listed it on the day's menu as "Boston Brown Bars," which in time became happily abbreviated to "Boston Brownies."

Maida Heatter, on the other hand, offers a different genesis. She credits a former librarian in Maine with the happy invention.

Brownie Schrumpf is her name and years ago, when she was baking a chocolate cake, she forgot to add the baking powder. Undaunted by the flatness of the cake, she simply cut it into squares and served it anyway.

These little brown cakes were an instant hit with her friends, who affectionately dubbed the new dessert "Brownies" in her honor.

No matter which story you choose to nibble, everyone agrees this chocolate treat came into being sometime after World War I. However, brownies did not really come into their own until the mid-1930s. Since more women joined the work force during The Depression than ever before, a quick, easy, and comforting dessert was exactly what overworked mothers needed. All the major chocolate purveyors came up with versions of brownie recipes, printing them on the backs of chocolate wrappers, cocoa tins, and cellophane packets. The brownie became such a part of American life that it was voted the most popular snack in America during the days of World War II rationing—when most chocolate lovers could only dream about them longingly. The brownie seems to have come full circle once again. In today's current era of two household incomes, the majority of consumer requests from Nestlè's, Baker's, Hershey's, et al., are all for brownie recipes.

Some Brownie Pointers Brownies are kid food. No matter what age we are, they always remind us of mother, home, and happier times. Perhaps that's why we talk on about them so passionately. Wars could be fought over the "correct" texture of a brownie. Fudgy and indecently rich, or cakey and not so calorically moist? That is the question. (I take mine somewhere between undersize and overkill!)

Other than precisely measuring out the amount of butter and chocolate, there is one simple way to control a brownie's texture. If, for instance, you have a recipe in your collection whose taste absolutely slays you, but the texture leaves something to be desired, try making it in a different sized pan. The smaller the container, the cakier the brownie. A slightly larger pan, on the other hand, will produce a decidedly fudgier bar.

When melting chocolate, always use the top of a double boiler placed over not-quite-simmering water (or in a microwave). Chocolate burns easily, so unless you have a very heavy pot and an equally sure hand, do *not* attempt to melt it over direct heat. Also, unless you are melting chocolate in a large amount of butter, take great care not to let any moisture drip into the pan. A scant drop of water will make chocolate "seize." Or, in other words, turn into a cohesive and immovable lump. Should this ever happen when you are making brownies, or anything else for that matter, there *is* a solution. Add just enough shortening, in very small increments, until the mixture can be beaten smooth again.

If, by some trick of fate, you find that you're fresh out of chocolate when the brownie urge strikes, don't panic. Just remember that 3 level tablespoons of cocoa mixed with 1 level tablespoon of shortening (liquid or solid) equals 1 ounce of unsweetened chocolate.

ASIDE FROM the fact that brownies are easy to whip up, they are popular with home cooks for a few other pertinent reasons. They are durable for one thing—they have been known to travel great distances to homesick progeny, parents, and paramours, *intact*. They are also highly versatile. Any brownie recipe can be altered slightly to satisfy the maker's tastes. And they are always welcome meal endings—whether packed in a lunch box or placed before kings and presidents. Brownies can be consumed unadorned, or lavished with whipped sweet cream or a scoop of vanilla ice cream for overkill.

"Bring on the dessert. I think I am about to die," were the reputed last words of Pierette Brillat-Savarin in 1911. Better yet, bring on the brownies! Some "to-die-for" recipes follow.

OMAHA
GRANDMOTHERLY BROWNIES

BROWNIE RECIPES are highly prized, often closely guarded, and sometimes hotly contested family secrets. The best, in my opinion, are those passed down from grandmother to mother to daughter. There was once a notable court case (in Nebraska) of a brownie recipe left to a favorite child in a will. The other deprived heirs contested the legacy, however, and the bequest declared invalid. No one knows for sure what grandmother was the author of the following fudgy formula, but it sure is a welcome inheritance.

2 ounces unsweetened chocolate

1/2 cup (1 stick) unsalted butter, cut into pieces

2 large eggs

1 cup sugar

1 teaspoon vanilla

1/2 cup all-purpose flour

Pinch of salt

1/4 cup sour cream

2/3 cup chopped walnuts (about 2 2/3 ounces)

1. Preheat the oven to 325° F.

2. Melt the chocolate with the butter in the top of a double boiler over hot water until smooth. Cool slightly.

3. Beat the eggs with the sugar in a large bowl until light. Slowly beat in the chocolate mixture. Stir in the vanilla. Sift in the flour, 2 tablespoons at a time, mixing well after each addition. Stir in the salt, sour cream, and walnuts.

4. Pour the batter into a greased 8-inch square cake pan. Bake until a toothpick inserted in the center comes out fairly clean, about 25 to 30 minutes. The center should be slightly cakey. Cool completely on a wire rack before cutting into bars.

Makes about 20 brownies

GREENWICH VILLAGE
"BROWNSTONE" BROWNIES

BROWNIES KNOW no geographic boundaries. One of the richest and nut-tiest versions was logged by an eminent food authority and long time Green-wich Village resident, Cecily Brownstone. As the story goes, Brownstone patterned her recipe after the offerings of a long-vanished bakery near the Village's Patchin Place. An indomitable old lady with a terrible temper owned the shop, but her brownies rivalled chocolate caramels as a chewy addiction.

3 ounces unsweetened chocolate

4 tablespoons (1/2 stick) unsalted
    butter, softened

1/2 teaspoon vanilla

1 cup sugar

1/2 cup light brown sugar (packed)

1/3 cup light corn syrup

3 large eggs

1 cup all-purpose flour

1/8 teaspoon salt

1 1/2 cups pecan halves or large pieces
    (about 6 ounces)

1. Preheat the oven to 350° F.

2. Butter an 8-inch square cake pan. Line the pan with wax paper. Butter the paper; flour the pan.

3. Melt the chocolate in the top of a double boiler over hot water until smooth. Remove from heat.

4. Beat the butter in a large bowl until light. Beat in the vanilla, both sugars, and the corn syrup. Add the eggs, one at a time, beating thoroughly after each addition. Slowly beat in the melted chocolate, the flour, the salt, and 1 cup pecans.

5. Spoon the batter into the prepared pan. Sprinkle the remaining 1/2 cup pecans over the top. Bake until a toothpick inserted in the center comes out fairly clean, about 1 hour. Cool in the pan on a wire rack 30 minutes.

6. Cover the pan with another rack and invert. Remove the pan and peel off the paper. Invert back onto a wire rack and let stand until completely cool.

7. Chill the brownie cake for about 30 minutes before cutting into bars.

Makes about 24 brownies

AUNT MARY'S CALIFORNIA CONGO BARS

HAVE A bicoastal bestowal. The following, golden-pecan-plus-chocolate-chip confection is the sweet handiwork of (Aunt) Mary Guidry, who lives and bakes in San Bernardino, California. Aunt Mary's niece, who donated the treasure to this collection, does not know *how* the recipe got its name, but clearly remembers how fast a batch was "cannibalized" at every family picnic.

2/3 cup vegetable shortening

2 3/4 cups sifted all-purpose flour

2 1/2 teaspoons baking powder

1/2 teaspoon salt

2 1/4 cups light brown sugar (packed)

3 large eggs

1 cup chopped pecans (about 4 ounces)

6 ounces semi-sweet chocolate chips

1. Preheat the oven to 350° F.

2. Melt the shortening in a large heavy saucepan over medium-low heat. Cool slightly.

3. Sift the flour with the baking powder and salt.

4. Beat the sugar into the shortening. Add the eggs, one at a time, beating thoroughly after each addition. Stir in the flour mixture, pecans, and chocolate chips.

5. Pour the batter into a greased 8-inch square cake pan. Bake until a toothpick inserted in the center comes out fairly clean, about 40 minutes. Cool completely on a wire rack before cutting into bars.

Makes about 20 brownies

BROTHERLY LOVE BARS

BEING A malleable feast, the brownie has a way of acquiring extra dividend flavorings prior to the oven. One of the most spectacular of those confederations comes from Philadelphia. A while back, some uninhibited Pennsylvanian had the happy notion of adding chopped chocolate to nutty brownie batter, then layering the mixture with whipped marshmallows. The result? Baked heavenly hash.

2 ounces unsweetened chocolate

1/2 cup (1 stick) unsalted butter

2 large eggs

1 cup sugar

1 teaspoon vanilla

1/2 cup all-purpose flour, sifted

Pinch of salt

1/4 cup heavy or whipping cream

1/2 cup chopped walnuts (about 2 ounces)

2 ounces semi-sweet chocolate, chopped

1/2 to 2/3 cup whipped marshmallow topping

1. Preheat the oven to 325° F.

2. Melt the chocolate with the butter in the top of a double boiler over hot water until smooth. Cool slightly.

3. Beat the eggs with the sugar in a large bowl until light. Slowly beat in the chocolate mixture. Stir in the vanilla. Add the flour, 2 tablespoons at a time, the salt, cream, walnuts, and chopped semi-sweet chocolate.

4. Pour one third of the batter into a greased 8-inch square cake pan. Drop 1/2 teaspoonfuls of marshmallow topping evenly over the surface, using about half of the total amount. Pour another third of batter over the top and dot with the remaining marshmallow topping. Pour in the remaining batter. Bake until a toothpick inserted in the center comes out fairly clean, about 40 minutes. Cool completely on a wire rack before cutting into bars.

Makes about 20 brownies

BLACK AND WHITE BROWNIES

THERE ARE countless formulas for fudge extant but very few instructions for the ultimate fudgy brownie. The next recipe is a contender for that honor. A dark, rich bar of estimable density, it also harbors a textural surprise: nubbins of velvety white chocolate in every bite.

3 ounces unsweetened chocolate

6 tablespoons (3/4 stick) unsalted butter

1 cup sugar

1/4 teaspoon baking powder

1/4 teaspoon salt

2 large eggs, lightly beaten

1 teaspoon vanilla

1/2 cup all-purpose flour

4 ounces white chocolate, chopped
(about 1/2 cup)

1. Preheat the oven to 325° F.

2. Melt the chocolate with the butter in the top of a double boiler over hot water until smooth.

3. Transfer the chocolate mixture to a medium bowl. Stir in the sugar, baking powder, salt, eggs, and vanilla. Beat well and stir in the flour, 2 tablespoons at a time. Stir in the white chocolate.

4. Pour the batter into a greased 8-inch square cake pan. Bake until a toothpick inserted in the center comes out fairly clean, about 20 to 25 minutes. Cool completely on a wire rack before cutting into bars.

Makes about 20 brownies

THE UNBEATABLE MS. HEATTER'S
PALM BEACH BROWNIES

THERE ARE brownies and there are brownie makers in the world. When one thinks of the ultimate pairing of the art and artist, the bespoke Maida Heatter comes to mind. Although Ms. Heatter estimates she has probably created half a hundred brownie recipes over the years, the Palm Beach Brownie, with its complex flavorings of chocolate, coffee, and almond is indubitably her finest hour. This recipe, from *Maida Heatter's Book of Great Desserts* (Knopf, 1980), is a little tricky because the brownies are a bit difficult to handle, but worth the extra care.

8 ounces unsweetened chocolate

1 cup (2 sticks) unsalted butter

2 1/2 tablespoons instant coffee powder

3 3/4 cups sugar

5 large eggs

1 tablespoon vanilla

1 teaspoon almond extract

1/4 teaspoon salt

1 2/3 cups sifted all-purpose flour

8 ounces (2 generous cups) walnut halves

1. Preheat the oven to 400° F.

2. Line a 9- by 13-inch baking pan as follows: Invert the pan, cover it with a long piece of aluminum foil, and press the foil around the sides and corners to shape it like the pan. Turn the pan over and gently press the foil inside the pan. Brush the foil with very soft, or melted, butter.

3. Melt the chocolate with the butter in the top of a large double boiler over hot water until smooth. Set aside.

4. Combine the eggs, vanilla and almond extracts, the salt, coffee powder, and sugar in the large bowl of an electric mixer. Beat on high speed for 10 minutes. On low speed, beat in the chocolate and then the flour, just until well mixed. Stir in the nuts.

5. Pour the batter into the prepared pan. Bake 30 minutes. Brownies will look slightly underdone. Cool completely on a wire rack.

6. When the pan is cool to the touch, invert onto a cookie sheet. Carefully, remove the foil. Invert onto another cookie sheet. Let stand 6 hours. Cut into squares with a sharp knife, wiping the blade each time you cut. The brownies will be very moist in the center. Store in an air-tight container.

Makes about 32 brownies

CHICAGO CHOCOLATE MALTIES

TWO OF THE most indelible flavors of a Midwest childhood, *chocolate* and *malt,* are happily fused in the following rich, candylike squares. Each piece has the virtue of being crisp, chewy, and comforting as a corner malt shop in Oak Park—all at the same time.

2 ounces semi-sweet chocolate

1/2 cup (1 stick) unsalted butter

1 teaspoon vanilla

3 large eggs

1 cup sugar

1/2 cup all-purpose flour

1/4 cup malted milk powder

3 tablespoons heavy or whipping cream

1/2 cup chopped pecans (about 2 ounces)

1. Preheat the oven to 350° F.

2. Melt the chocolate with the butter in the top of a double boiler over hot water until smooth. Stir in the vanilla. Cool slightly.

3. Beat the eggs with the sugar in the large bowl of an electric mixer until light and fluffy. Slowly beat in the chocolate mixture.

4. Sift the flour with the malted milk powder and add to the batter, 2 tablespoons at a time. Stir in the cream and pecans.

5. Pour batter into a greased 8-inch square cake pan. Bake until a toothpick inserted in the center comes out fairly clean, about 25 minutes. Cool completely on a wire rack before cutting into bars.

Makes about 20 brownies

Scoring brownie points with an employer has, it seems, not always been such a wise course to follow. When George R. Brown became general superintendent of the Fall Brook Railway (New York Central) in 1885, he was dismayed with the railroad's habit of suspending workers for practically no reason whatsoever. Instead of suspensions, Brown instituted a system of demerits. Which, needless to say, became known as "Brownies." A fractious employee was allotted a set amount of "Brownie Points." And only after he exceeded the limit was he "rail-roaded" off the job.

MARBLED WONDER BROWNIES

OLD-FASHIONED recipes have a way of becoming lost-and-found legends in the American dessert lexicon. Take the following heirloom devise for example. It dates back to the late nineteenth century when it was known as Streaky Tea Cake. The name never caught the home baker's fancy and tea cakes (like afternoon tea itself) vanished forever after World War I. Or almost forever. In the "brownie revival" of the late 1960s, the Streaky Tea Cake recipe surfaced once more. Still the same moist coffee bar striped with chocolate of the past, it was given a new name: Marbled Wonders, and a new life, too.

1 cup (2 sticks) unsalted butter, softened

4 extra-large eggs

1 tablespoon orange liqueur

1/4 teaspoon salt

2 tablespoons instant espresso powder

2 cups sugar

1 1/4 cups all-purpose flour

8 ounces roughly chopped pecans (about 2 cups)

3 ounces unsweetened chocolate, melted

1. Preheat the oven to 325° F.

2. Beat the butter in the large bowl of an electric mixer until light. Beat in the eggs, one at a time, beating thoroughly after each addition. Beat in the orange liqueur, salt, espresso, and sugar. Beat on medium-low speed 5 minutes. Stir in the flour and pecans.

3. Divide the batter into two equal portions. Combine one portion with the chocolate and pour into a greased 9- by 13-inch baking pan. Swirl the other portion through the chocolate mixture to create a marbled effect. Bake until a toothpick inserted in the center comes out fairly clean, about 40 minutes. Cool completely on a wire rack before cutting into bars.

Makes about 36 brownies

OLD-TIME MINNESOTA COCOA BARS

IN MINNESOTA, where the winters are cold, long, and lingering, this is the high-rated brownie of the younger set. As easy to make, it seems, as a cup of hot cocoa, these rich chocolate bars have school children across the state buttering cookie pans from early November to late April.

1/2 cup (1 stick) unsalted butter, softened

1 cup sugar

1 teaspoon vanilla

2 large eggs

1/2 cup all-purpose flour

1/2 cup unsweetened cocoa powder

1/4 teaspoon baking powder

1/4 teaspoon salt

1/2 cup pecan or walnut halves, chopped (about 2 ounces)

1. Preheat the oven to 350° F.

2. Beat the butter in the large bowl of an electric mixer until light. Slowly beat in the sugar. Beat in the vanilla and then the eggs, one at a time, beating thoroughly after each addition.

3. Combine the flour, cocoa, baking powder, and salt. Slowly add to the butter mixture. Stir in the walnuts.

4. Spoon the batter into a buttered 8-inch square cake pan. Bake until a toothpick inserted in the center comes out fairly clean, about 20 to 25 minutes. Cool completely on a wire rack before cutting into bars.

Makes about 20 brownies

FROSTED BALTIMORE BRUNETTES

COCOA BEAN addicts have been known to travel halfway across the globe for a fudgy fix. The next chocolate-on-chocolate brownie is worthy of just such an extravagant excursion. Reputedly the invention of a pastry chef at Baltimore's Moscone Restaurant, this confection never made it to the dessert trolley. Why? It was too good! The kitchen help "et 'em up" before they ever got to the customers!

3 large eggs

1 cup light brown sugar (packed)

3 ounces semi-sweet chocolate, grated

1 1/2 cups all-purpose flour

1 teaspoon ground cinnamon

1/2 teaspoon baking soda

1/2 teaspoon salt

1/4 cup honey

1 cup chopped almonds (about 3 ounces)

1 1/2 ounces unsweetened chocolate

1/2 can (7 ounces) condensed milk

4 tablespoons (1/2 stick) unsalted butter, cut into pieces

1 small egg yolk, beaten

1/2 teaspoon vanilla

1. Preheat the oven to 325° F.

2. Beat the eggs in a large bowl until light. Slowly beat in the sugar, grated semi-sweet chocolate, flour, cinnamon, baking soda, and salt until smooth. Beat in the honey. Stir in the almonds.

3. Pour the batter into a 9- by 13-inch baking pan. Bake until a toothpick inserted in the center comes out fairly clean, about 25 minutes. Cool completely on a wire rack.

4. Melt the unsweetened chocolate in the top of a double boiler over hot water. Stir in the condensed milk, butter, egg yolk, and vanilla. Beat until smooth and thick. Spread over brownies. Let stand until set. Cut into bars.

Makes about 36 brownies

JEANETTE'S BARS

THE FOLLOWING chocolate and butterscotch bars were sent to me one year for Christmas by my sister Jeanette Deschamps, who lives in Naperville, Illinois. Jeanette's pale brownies were so admired by friends, they literally disappeared at a sitting. The original recipe (it turns out), was once printed on a Land O'Lakes butter carton, but had since undergone major alteration in my sister's kitchen and I can't think of a happier collaboration.

2 cups all-purpose flour
1 1/2 cups light brown sugar (packed)
1/2 cup (1 stick) unsalted butter, softened; plus 2/3 cup butter

1 cup pecan halves (about 4 ounces)
1 bar (5 ounces) milk chocolate, cut into bits (about 1 cup)

1. Preheat the oven to 350° F.

2. Combine the flour, 1 cup sugar, and the 1/2 cup softened butter in the medium bowl of an electric mixer. On low speed, beat the mixture until mixed. On medium speed, beat the mixture until smooth, 3 to 4 minutes.

3. Pat the mixture evenly over the bottom of an ungreased 9- by 13- by 2-inch baking dish. Spread the pecans evenly over the mixture.

4. Combine the 2/3 cup butter with the remaining 1/2 cup sugar in a medium saucepan. Heat to boiling, stirring constantly, over medium heat. Boil 1 minute. Spread evenly over crust in pan. Bake until golden and bubbly, about 18 minutes.

5. Remove the bars from the oven and immediately sprinkle the chocolate bits over the top. Allow to melt slightly and then, using the sharp point of a knife, cut through the chocolate, making swirls. Do not spread the chocolate. Cool completely on a wire rack before cutting into bars.

Makes about 36 brownies

VERMONT CHOCOLATE-CARAMEL CHEWIES

THE FINAL recipe in this collection is the all-time favorite at cake and bake sales in the Green Mountain country of Vermont. Oatmeal gives this brownie its bounce, while caramel adds the quintessential crumble. The original formula comes from a yellowed mimeographed sheet entitled, "The Townshend Vermont Mother's Club Bulletin," circa 1938.

1/2 cup (1 stick) plus 1 1/2 tablespoons
    unsalted butter, softened
1 cup dark brown sugar (packed)
2 ounces unsweetened chocolate, melted
1 large egg
2 teaspoons vanilla
1 1/4 cups all-purpose flour

1/2 teaspoon baking soda
1/2 teaspoon salt
1 1/2 cups rolled oats
1 cup chopped pecans (about 4 ounces)
7 ounces caramels
1/2 can (7 ounces) condensed milk

1. Preheat the oven to 350° F.

2. Beat 1/2 cup butter in the large bowl of an electric mixer until light. Beat in the brown sugar. Beat on medium speed 3 minutes. Slowly beat in the melted chocolate, egg, and 1 1/2 teaspoons vanilla.

3. Sift the flour with the baking soda and salt. On low speed, slowly add to the chocolate mixture. Stir in the rolled oats, and 1/2 cup pecans. Press two-thirds of this mixture into a greased 8-inch square cake pan.

4. Melt the caramels with the condensed milk and 1 1/2 tablespoons butter in the top of a double boiler over hot water. Stir in 1/2 cup pecans and 1/2 teaspoon vanilla. Pour over the mixture in the pan. Carefully sprinkle the remaining rolled oat mixture over the top. Bake until golden brown, about 30 minutes. Cool completely on a wire rack before cutting into bars.

Makes about 20 brownies

Chilis

Wish I had time for just one more bowl of chili.
—(Alleged) dying words of Kit Carson

CARSON wasn't the only cowpoke in Texas who felt that impassioned about chili. The James brothers, Frank and Jesse, reputedly spared the banks of Fort Worth from hold-ups and shootouts because a favorite chili parlor was in the immediate vicinity. In their matter-of-fact opinion, "anyplace with a chili joint this good just ought'a be treated better!"

Ask any denizen of the Lone Star State about the genesis of chili and, ten to one, he will tell you it was invented in San Antonio. But that's not so. And while it is true that *chili con carne* gained its first celebrity in the sluggish Texas river town, the dish's reputation stemmed more from its saucy purveyors than any ingredient in its sauce.

Around the middle of the eighteenth century, according to Texas chroniclers, the first band of "Chili Queens" gathered along the dark side of San Antonio's Military Plaza to ply their wares. By lantern light, these Mexican ladies stirred up pots of highly seasoned stew that they sold the voracious militia. Or at least that's how the legend goes. And while it is well documented that the "Queens" were a San Antonio institution for almost two hundred years, chili may *not* have been the only commodity they offered. How chili came to San Antonio is another story.

Centuries, or perhaps millenniums, before the first Spanish explorers touched down in the Americas and sampled native fare, the Inca, Aztec, and

Mayan Indians were stirring up compounds of meat, beans, and peppers for their subsistence. Hot peppers, they found, preserved the meat they hunted—so it was only natural that the fiery capsicums that grew wild in their land would keep their stews from spoiling as well. The Spanish obviously liked what they tasted of South American Indian cooking, for when they returned home they were loaded down with many New World ingredients (including peppers and beans) that would add zest to traditional Hispanic dishes forever after.

Several hundred years later, around 1723, a handful of colonists from the Canary Islands came to America. Missionaries, by and large, they settled in the Southwest Texas territory to build churches and cathedrals, with the formidable task of converting the already pious Indians to Christianity. As part of their daily rituals, the priests shared meals with the Indian tribes, doling out a "Spanish" stew of (you guessed it) meat, beans, and peppers. Chili, it seems, (then and now) makes converts after the first spoonful reaches the tongue. But back to the Chili Queens.

These stirring ladies of the evening did play a major role in popularizing chili in Texas and may have even refined it, but it was the roving cowboys and the roguish cattle drovers passing through town who spread the dish's fame from the Rio Grande to the Great Salt Lake—and even beyond.

Checking Out Chili There are no hidden secrets or tricks to making a "good bowl of red," as they say west of the Pecos. But few agree on what really goes into the pot. Beef? Cubed, chopped, or ground? Pork? (Not in Texas!) Tomatoes? Beans? And on and on and on. The subject gets even hotter when it comes to serving chili. Au naturel? With only the amendment of oyster crackers? Or the whole shootin' match: minced onion, sour cream, and grated cheddar cheese? In the end, whatever suits your taste is the answer!

Chili makers are advised, however, to use only prime seasonings. Spices lose potency after a long stay in the kitchen cupboard, so when in doubt, throw the offending tins away. Traditionalists frown on commercial "chili powder." The main reason being that supermarket varieties contain more filler than ground chile peppers, most often dried garlic, powdered onion, cumin, oregano, cloves, and coriander. Seasoned chili makers stick to only pure ground dried Colorado (mild) or New Mexico (hot) peppers, but these are not easy to come by on supermarket shelves. Fortunately, specialty grocers and even gourmet departments of major food chains are getting wise to cognoscenti chili makers' demands for the "right" ingredients. Pecos River brand is one of the more widely found "pure" chile powders. If you must use a commercial spice off the rack, test its bite by mashing a spoonful in a speck of oil. If its flavor leans heavily toward cumin or is just too mild-mannered for your palate, adjust the other seasonings in the recipe accordingly. After all, it is the essential flavor of chile pepper that ultimately gives a bowl of well-made chili its glower or glow! When dealing with the hot varieties, wash your hands thoroughly when through mincing the peppers. Do not touch your eyes or any other vital parts until you do.

Many old-fashioned chili recipes call for a measure of cornmeal to be stirred into the pot just before it goes to the table. Although cornmeal will certainly thicken a pot of runny chili, there is a more serious premise to the notion. Oldtimers, you see, never drained the fat from a pan of sautéed meat. The grease, they believed, gave chili its vital character. A tablespoon or so of cornmeal added after the dish is cooked absorbs any floating fat, distributing it evenly throughout the stew, leaving nary a trace of grease. Clever!

MARTINA and William Neely spent years and years researching the subject of chili and ended up writing a book called *The International Chili Society Official Chili Cookbook* (St. Martin's Press, 1981). The earliest recipe for chili that this adventurous pair came up with reads something like this:

Cut up as much meat as you think you will need in pieces about the size of a pecan. Put it in a pot, along with some suet, and cook it with about the same amount of wild onions, garlic, oregano, and chiles as you have got meat. Put in some salt. Stir it from time to time and cook it until the meat is as tender as you think it's going to get.

A very basic recipe. Some "not so basic" renditions follow.

BERT GREENE'S BOWL OF RED

TRADITIONAL in theory, this recipe is exceptional in practice. Thin strips of pork are combined with beef to add a flavorsome contrast to the stew, while in true Mexican style, a smidgen of grated bitter chocolate is stirred in—to add bite to Greene's bounty. Serve with the works.

2 strips bacon

1/4 pound salt pork, diced

1 pound lean pork, cut into 2-inch long strips, about 1/2-inch thick

1 pound chuck steak, cut into 2-inch long strips, about 1/2-inch thick

2 medium onions, chopped

3 cloves garlic, minced

1 medium jalapeño pepper, seeded, deveined, minced

1 ounce unsweetened chocolate, grated

1/2 teaspoon dried oregano

1/4 teaspoon ground cumin

3 tablespoons chili powder

1 teaspoon salt

1/4 teaspoon freshly ground black pepper

1 can (28 ounces) imported plum tomatoes with juice, crushed

1/2 cup tomato juice

1. Sauté the bacon strips in a large heavy pot or Dutch oven until crisp. Drain on paper towels; crumble and set aside.

2. Add the salt pork to the pot and sauté until golden, about 4 minutes. Transfer to a plate with a slotted spoon.

3. Sauté the strips of pork and beef, about 10 at a time, until well browned on both sides. Transfer to the plate with the salt pork.

4. Preheat the oven to 350° F.

5. Add the onions to the Dutch oven and cook over medium heat 1 minute. Add the garlic and jalapeño pepper; cook 4 minutes longer. Return the salt pork and meat to the pot. Toss well and stir in the chocolate, oregano, cumin, chili powder, salt, and pepper. Mix well and stir in the tomatoes and tomato juice.

6. Heat the chili to boiling on top of the stove. Cover and transfer to the oven. Cook until meat is tender, about 1 hour and 15 minutes. Remove cover and sprinkle with the reserved crumbled bacon. Cook, uncovered, 10 minutes longer.

Serves 6

"WILD ABOUT CHILI" CHILI

THIS IS *my* basic "red neck" bowl of chili. What makes it special is two different cuts of beef. Ground meat gives body to the stew, while the strips of chuck steak add chewy texture. Cumin is absent in this dish as it undercuts the delicate balance of the other flavorings.

1 pound dry pinto beans

6 tablespooons (3/4 stick) unsalted butter

1 tablespoon vegetable oil

1 1/2 pounds beef steak (chuck), cut into strips 2 inches long, about 1/2 inch wide

1 1/2 pounds lean ground beef

2 large onions, chopped

2 cloves garlic, minced

4 tablespoons chili powder

2 large tomatoes, seeded, chopped

1 can (10 ounces) mixed tomatoes and green chiles

1 teaspoon brown sugar

1 bay leaf

Pinch of dried thyme

1 teaspoon cayenne pepper

1/2 teaspoon ground allspice

1/2 teaspoon crushed dried hot red peppers

1 teaspoon soy sauce

Dash of hot pepper sauce

1 1/4 cups beef broth (approximately)

1 teaspoon salt

1/2 teaspoon freshly ground black pepper

1. Soak the beans overnight in cold water.

2. Preheat the oven to 300° F.

3. Heat 3 tablespoons butter with the oil in a large heavy skillet over medium heat. Pat the beef strips dry with paper towels and sauté about 10 pieces at a time, until well browned on both sides. Transfer to a large heavy pot or Dutch oven.

4. Add the ground beef to the skillet. Cook over medium-high heat, breaking up the lumps with a wooden spoon, until lightly browned. Transfer with a slotted spoon to the pot with the beef strips.

5. Discard all grease from the skillet. Add the remaining 3 tablespoons butter and melt over medium heat. Add the onions, scraping the bottom and sides of the pan with a wooden spoon. Cook 3 minutes. Add the garlic; cook 2 minutes longer. Transfer to the Dutch oven.

6. Stir the chili powder into the meat mixture. Add the fresh tomatoes and the mixed tomatoes and chiles. Stir in the remaining ingredients (except the beans) and heat to boiling. Cover and transfer to the preheated oven. Bake until the meat is tender, about 2 hours.

7. Meanwhile, drain the beans and place in a heavy pot. Cover with cold water. Heat to boiling; reduce the heat. Simmer, stirring occasionally, until tender, about 1 hour. Drain.

8. When the meat is tender, stir the beans into the chili and return to the oven. Bake, uncovered, 30 minutes. (Add more beef broth if mixture seems dry.)

Serves 6 to 8

CALIFORNIA "PURIST'S" CHILI

AN INCREDIBLE (and extraordinarily simple) recipe. It comes from John Knuehman, a chili lover who lives in southern California. The touch of ripe orange is the California equivalent of a South American tamarind. Orange peel is sautéed with onion and garlic to tinge the beef in a browned marmalade sauce. Note that this chili is *hot!* Reduce the jalapeños if you're weak-tongued.

4 strips of bacon, chopped

1 medium onion, chopped

1 large clove garlic, minced

Finely slivered peel of 1 orange

1 1/2 pounds boneless beef chuck, finely chopped

2 tablespoons chili powder

2 teaspoons ground cumin

1/4 teaspoon freshly ground black pepper

1/3 cup water

2/3 cup beef broth

2 teaspoons Hungarian hot paprika

3 canned jalapeño peppers, finely chopped

1. Sauté the bacon in a large heavy saucepan over medium heat until almost crisp. Stir in the onion; cook 1 minute. Add the garlic and orange peel; cook 4 minutes longer.

2. Raise the heat to medium-high and stir in the chopped beef. Cook, stirring constantly, until the beef is light brown in color, about 4 minutes. Stir in the remaining ingredients. Heat to boiling; reduce the heat. Cook, covered, stirring occasionally, until the beef is tender and the chili has thickened, about 1 hour and 15 minutes.

Serves 4

LUSHINGTON CHILI

HAVE A MIX of beef and ham simmered to velvety smoothness in beer, and for overkill, slaked with red wine; hence the boozy cognomen. No beans mar this dish's texture. Monterey Jack cheese is stirred directly into the chili at the last minute, rather than reserved for a topping. Serve this with sour cream on the side.

6 tablespoons vegetable oil

2 pounds beef chuck, cut into 1/4-inch cubes

1/4 teaspoon cayenne pepper

1/2 teaspoon dried oregano

2 cans (8 ounces each) tomato sauce

(ingredients continued)

2 medium onions, finely chopped

2 large cloves garlic, minced

6 tablespoons dry red wine

4 tablespoons chili powder

1 teaspoon ground cumin

1/2 teaspoon Hungarian sweet paprika

2 cups cubed (1/4 inch) cooked ham

1 cup beer

1 teaspoon salt

1/4 pound Monterey Jack cheese, cut into 1/4-inch cubes

1. Heat the oil in a large saucepan over high heat until hot but not smoking. Stir in the meat all at once and cook, stirring, until the meat loses its color, about 3 minutes. Stir in the onions; cook 1 minute. Add the garlic; cook, stirring constantly, 4 minutes longer. Sprinkle with the wine and reduce the heat to medium. Cover and cook 5 minutes.

2. Stir the chili powder into the meat mixture along with the cumin, paprika, cayenne pepper, and oregano. Cook 1 minute. Stir in the tomato sauce, ham, beer, and salt. Heat to boiling; reduce the heat. Cook, covered, stirring occasionally, over medium-low heat 1 1/2 hours. Remove from heat and let stand, uncovered, 5 minutes.

3. Stir in the cheese and serve immediately.

Serves 6

KANSAS CITY WHITE CHILI

KANSAS CITY brings to mind barbecue, chicken fried steak, and some of the best beef found east of the Rockies. This brilliant "chicken chili" is another K.C. culinary original. It is adapted from an outstanding recipe in the excellent local Junior League's 1984 cookbook, *Beyond Parsley*. White chili makes a great party dish served over rice. Pass a bowl of grated Monterey Jack on the side.

1 pound dry white beans

6 cups chicken broth (approximately)

2 cloves garlic, minced

2 medium onions, chopped (divided)

2 teaspoons ground cumin

1 1/2 teaspoons dried oregano

1/4 teaspoon ground cloves

1/4 teaspoon cayenne pepper

1 tablespoon olive oil

2 cans (4 ounces each) chopped green chiles

1 1/2 pounds skinned boneless chicken breasts, cut into 1-inch strips

1. Place the beans in a medium pot and cover with cold water. Heat to boiling; boil 2 minutes. Let stand 1 hour. Drain.

2. Combine the beans, chicken broth, garlic, and 1 onion in a large heavy pot or Dutch oven. Heat to boiling; reduce the heat. Simmer, covered, until beans are almost tender, about 1 1/2 hours.

3. Heat the oil in a medium skillet over medium-low heat. Add the onion; cook 5 minutes. Do not brown. Stir in the chiles, cumin, oregano, cloves, and cayenne pepper. Cook, stirring constantly, 1 minute.

4. Stir the onion/chile mixture into the bean mixture. Add the chicken pieces. Heat to boiling; reduce the heat. Simmer partially covered 1 hour (adding more chicken broth if chili becomes too dry).

Serves 6 to 8

Chili is a shorthand version of the name *chile con carne* (peppers with meat). It received its moniker in somewhat reverse order, however, which is often the Texas way. In the eighteenth century, a wise and beautiful woman (who happened to be a nun), Sister Mary of Agreda, was sent from a priory in Spain to help the missionary fathers introduce the Indian natives to a Christian God. As she was a good cook, Mary of Agreda invited all potential parishioners to a Sunday family dinner that she called *carne con chile* (meat with peppers). Unfortunately, she cooked so well, she often had more converts than meat for them at her table—so she added more peppers, and then some more; until the dish became *chile con carne,* once and for all!

TUCSON-TO-TOMBSTONE
TURKEY CHILI

NEXT COMES an old Arizona hand-me-down recipe. Originally made with Thanksgiving leftovers chopped and chilied to a fare-thee-well, it has moved from one part of the sunshine state to another over the years, but the formula remains resolutely the same. My only update is the uncooked ground turkey in the ingredient list, which makes for a juicier dish.

1/4 cup finely chopped salt pork

2 1/2 pounds ground fresh turkey

2 tablespoons vegetable oil

2 large onions, finely chopped

2 large cloves garlic, minced

2 teaspoons ground cumin

1 teaspoon Hungarian hot paprika

4 tablespoons chili powder

1/4 teaspoon dried oregano

1 teaspoon salt

4 jalapeño peppers, seeded, deveined, finely chopped

2 large red bell peppers, seeded, chopped

1 quart chicken broth

2 tablespoons chopped fresh cilantro (Chinese parsley)

1. Sauté the salt pork in a large heavy saucepan over medium heat until golden, about 5 minutes. Transfer with a slotted spoon to a bowl.

2. Pour off all but 2 tablespoons grease from the pan. Add the meat and sauté over high heat, breaking up the lumps with a wooden spoon until the meat loses its color. Transfer, along with the pan juices, to the bowl.

3. Heat the oil in the same saucepan over medium heat. Add the onions; cook 1 minute. Add the garlic; cook, stirring frequently, 4 minutes longer. Return the meat with its juices to the pan, scraping the bottom and sides of pan with a wooden spoon. Stir in the cumin, paprika, chili powder, oregano, and salt. Cook 4 minutes. Add both peppers and the chicken broth. Heat to boiling; reduce the heat. Cook, uncovered, stirring occasionally, over medium-low heat 1 hour. Raise the heat slightly if the chili is too thin.

4. Stir 1 tablespoon cilantro into the chili. Sprinkle the remainder over the top.

Serves 6 to 8

ANTIC ANCHO CHILI

ANCHO CHILES are dried (mild) poblanos that rise a bit more in temperature as they dehydrate. Here, the dried peppers are cooked and then processed till they become a garnet-hued sauce for the tender chunks of beef. The recipe comes from a young and enormously talented food writer, Jill Gardner of San Francisco, who flouts tradition in everything she does. Here, notably, passing white goat cheese as a garnish for her chili in lieu of cheddar.

3 dried ancho chiles

1 tablespoon unsalted butter

1 tablespoon olive oil

2 1/2 pounds boneless beef chuck, cut into 1-inch pieces

1 large onion, chopped

2 cloves garlic, minced

1 tablespoon tomato paste

1/2 teaspoon chopped fresh oregano, or 1/4 teaspoon dried

1 teaspoon ground cumin

1/2 teaspoon salt

1/4 teaspoon freshly ground black pepper

1 1/4 cups beef stock (see page 377)

1/2 cup dry white wine

1 1/2 teaspoons chopped fresh cilantro (Chinese parsley)

4 ounces goat cheese, crumbled

1. Remove the stems from the dried chiles. Slit the chiles lengthwise and scrape out the seeds. Transfer the chiles to a small saucepan. Add just enough water to cover. Heat to boiling; reduce the heat. Simmer over medium-low heat until tender, about 15 minutes. Set aside.

2. Heat the butter with the oil in a large pot or Dutch oven over medium heat. Sauté the beef cubes, a few at a time, until golden on all sides. Transfer to a plate. Add the onion to the pot; cook 1 minute. Add the garlic; cook 2 minutes. Reduce the heat to medium-low and cook 4 minutes longer.

3. Drain the chiles, reserving 1/2 cup liquid. Transfer to the container of a food processor or blender. Process until smooth. Stir the pureed chiles into the onion mixture. Return the meat and add the tomato paste, oregano, cumin, salt, pepper, beef stock, and wine. Heat to boiling; reduce the heat. Cook,

covered, over medium-low heat until the meat is tender, 1 1/2 to 2 hours. Remove the cover and raise the heat slightly. Cook, stirring frequently, until thickened. Sprinkle with cilantro. Serve the goat cheese on the side.

Serves 4 to 6

GREEN CHILIED PORK WITH POLENTA

THE SAME talented Jill Gardner inspired this dish when she wrote me a long letter about the marriage of pork and polenta. It's a combination made in heaven—but in this instance, highly dependent upon the smoky flavor of a third party, roasted green pepper.

For the green chilied pork

3 large or 4 medium green bell peppers

4 tablespoons bacon drippings

2 1/2 pounds boneless pork shoulder, cut into 1/2-inch cubes

2 large onions, chopped

2 large cloves garlic, minced

2 tablespoons all-purpose flour

4 cans (4 ounces each), mild green chiles, drained, chopped

4 cups chicken broth

Salt and freshly ground black pepper

For the polenta

2 cups milk

2 cups water

1/2 teaspoon salt

1 cup coarse yellow cornmeal

1. To make the green chilied pork: Roast the peppers over a gas flame or under a broiler until charred all over. Carefully wrap the peppers in paper towels. Place them in a plastic bag and set aside until cool. Rub off the skins with the paper towels, seed, and chop. Set aside.

2. Heat the bacon drippings in a large pot or Dutch oven over medium heat. Sauté the pork pieces, a few at a time, until lightly browned. Transfer to a plate.

3. Add the onions to the bacon drippings; cook 1 minute. Add the garlic; cook 2 minutes longer. Return the meat to the pot and reduce the heat to medium-low.

4. Sprinkle the pork mixture with the flour. Cook, stirring constantly, 1 minute. Stir in the roasted peppers, the canned peppers, and the chicken broth. Heat to boiling; reduce the heat. Simmer, partially covered, until the pork is tender, about 1 hour and 15 minutes. Raise the heat slightly if the chili is too thin. Add salt and pepper to taste.

5. Meanwhile, to make the polenta: Combine the milk, water, and salt in a medium saucepan. Heat slowly to boiling; reduce the heat to low. Slowly whisk in the cornmeal and cook, whisking constantly, until thick, about 5 minutes.

6. To serve, spoon the polenta into shallow bowls and ladle the chili over the top.

Serves 6

TATTOOED CHILI

JOE DEFRATES, the only man ever to win both the National and the World Chili Championships, said: "Chili powder makes you crazy!" To prove his point, try the next formula. It comes from the federal penitentiary at Gainesville, Texas—and was reputedly found inscribed on the forearm of an inmate who had it tattooed there for safekeeping.

1 pound dry pigeon peas (grandules)

5 tablespoons olive oil

1 pound Spanish sausages (chorizos), cut into 1/2-inch thick slices

3 pounds beef chuck, cut into 1-inch cubes

1 large onion, chopped

3 cloves garlic, minced

2 tablespoons masa harina (corn flour available at Spanish grocers)

3 tablespoons chili powder

1 teaspoon ground cumin

1 1/2 cups chopped, peeled, and seeded fresh tomatoes

1 can (17 ounces) plum tomatoes, crushed

(ingredients continued)

2 poblano peppers, roasted, peeled, seeded, chopped

2 jalapeño peppers, seeded, deveined, minced

1 teaspoon salt

1/2 teaspoon freshly ground black pepper

1 cup beef broth (approximately)

1. Soak the pigeon peas overnight in cold water. Drain. Place in a large pot. Cover with water. Heat to boiling; reduce the heat. Simmer uncovered, stirring occasionally, until tender, about 1 hour. Drain.

2. Preheat the oven to 350° F.

3. Heat 2 tablespoons of the oil in a large pot or Dutch oven. Sauté the sliced chorizos until well browned on both sides, about 10 minutes. Transfer with a slotted spoon to a plate.

4. Discard all grease from the skillet and add the remaining 3 tablespoons oil. Pat the beef cubes dry with paper towels. Sauté the cubes, a few at a time, over medium-high heat. Transfer to the plate with the sausage slices.

5. Add the onions to the pot; cook over medium-low heat 1 minute. Add the garlic, poblano peppers, and jalapeño peppers. Cook, scraping the sides and bottom of pan with a wooden spoon, 5 minutes. Return the sausage and beef to the pot. Stir in the masa harina. Add the chili powder, cumin, tomatoes, salt, pepper, and beef broth. Heat to boiling. Cover and transfer to oven. Bake until meat is tender, about 2 hours.

6. Remove the cover and stir the beans into chili mixture. Add more beef broth if too dry. Bake uncovered in oven 25 minutes longer.

Serves 6 to 8

GULFPORT SEAFOOD CHILI

IN THE coastal town of Gulfport, Mississippi (pronounced "Guff-Port" by every native), the ethnic mix is inherent in this next dish. It's a chili with Italian, Creole, and Black antecedents.

2 pounds sweet Italian sausage, removed from casings

1 large red bell pepper, seeded, chopped

1 large rib celery, finely chopped

2 large onions, finely chopped

2 large cloves garlic, minced

1 teaspoon dried oregano

2 teaspoons ground cumin

4 tablespoons chili powder

2 teaspoons Hungarian sweet paprika

1 teaspoon cayenne pepper

1/2 teaspoon ground coriander

1 large green bell pepper, seeded, chopped

1 large red bell pepper, seeded, chopped

1 large rib celery, finely chopped

1 can (28 ounces) plum tomatoes with juice, chopped

2 cups clam juice

3 to 4 teaspoons cornmeal

1/2 pound small shrimp, shelled, deveined

1 pound thick-cut white fish (cod, haddock, etc.), cubed

1/2 pound bay scallops or sea scallops, quartered

Salt and freshly ground black pepper

Chopped fresh parsley

1. Sauté the sausage meat in a large heavy saucepan over medium-high heat until it loses its color. (Unless the sausage is excessively greasy, do not drain.) Stir in the onions; cook 1 minute. Add the garlic; cook, stirring frequently, until the meat and onions are well browned, about 10 minutes. Stir in the oregano, cumin, chili powder, paprika, cayenne pepper, and coriander. Mix well and add the bell peppers, the celery, tomatoes, and clam juice. Heat to boiling; reduce the heat. Cook, uncovered, stirring occasionally, over medium-low heat 30 minutes. Cook, covered, stirring occasionally, 45 minutes longer.

2. Stir just enough cornmeal—about 3 to 4 teaspoons—into the chili to absorb the grease. Stir in the shrimp; cook 2 minutes. Stir in the fish and scallops; cook 3 to 4 minutes longer. Add salt and pepper to taste. Sprinkle with parsley.

Serves 6 to 8

BLEECKER STREET VEGGIE CHILI

A VEGETABLE chili, served by Michael McLaughlin at his Manhattan Chili Company restaurant in New York City, inspired the next formula. In his book *The Manhattan Chili Co. Southwest American Cookbook,* (Crown, 1968), Michael credits Southwest doyenne Jane Butel with the original notion of substituting bulgur as a textural stand-in for ground meat. Nonvegetarians are guaranteed to love it, too! Serve with grated cheddar cheese and sour cream on the side.

1/2 cup bulgur wheat

2 cups V-8 or tomato juice

3 tablespoons olive oil

1 large onion, chopped

2 large cloves garlic, minced

3 tablespoons chili powder

4 teaspoons ground cumin

1/2 teaspoon ground coriander

1/2 teaspoon dried oregano

1/2 teaspoon dried thyme

1/2 teaspoon cayenne pepper

Pinch of ground cinnamon

1 teaspoon salt

1/2 teaspoon freshly ground black pepper

1 can (28 ounces) tomatoes

2 cups vegetable stock (See page 379)

1 red bell pepper, seeded, chopped

1 package (10 ounces) frozen black-eyed peas, thawed

1 package (10 ounces) frozen baby lima beans, thawed

1 1/2 cups fresh corn kernels (from 3 medium ears)

2 teaspoons chopped fresh cilantro (Chinese parsley)

1. Place the bulgur in a medium bowl and cover with 1 cup V-8 juice. Let stand 1 1/2 hours.

2. Meanwhile, heat the oil in a large heavy pot or Dutch oven over medium-low heat. Add the onion; cook 1 minute. Add the garlic; cook 10 minutes longer.

3. Combine the chili powder in a small bowl with the cumin, coriander, oregano, thyme, cayenne pepper, cinnamon, salt, and freshly ground pepper. Stir into the onions; cook 5 minutes. Add the tomatoes with juice. Mash the tomatoes with a vegetable masher until fairly smooth. Add the remaining 1 cup V-8 juice and the vegetable stock. Heat to boiling; reduce the heat. Cook, covered, over medium-low heat 20 minutes.

4. Add the bell pepper to the chili. Continue to cook, partially covered, 20 minutes.

5. Add the bulgur and black-eyed peas. Cook, stirring often, partially covered, 25 minutes. Remove cover and raise the heat slightly if the chili is too thin.

6. Add the lima beans and corn to the chili. Cook, uncovered, 10 minutes. Sprinkle with cilantro before serving.

Serves 6 to 8

SMOKED BOAR AND BLACK BEAN CHILI

A CHILI GOURMET'S delight. Boar, not truly wild in this country any longer, is available at many specialty butcher shops around the country and is indubitably the perfect mate for a pot of smoky black chilied beans. The preparation takes a while, but it is definitely well worth the effort. The dish is best made in a home water smoker, but will still rate a Lone Star salute if you follow the pointers for making it a more conventional way.

1/4 cup bacon drippings

2 large cloves garlic, crushed; plus 3 medium cloves garlic, minced

3 tablespoons chili powder

1/8 teaspoon ground cumin seeds

1/4 teaspoon freshly ground black pepper

3 1/2 pounds saddle of wild boar

1 pound dry black turtle beans

1/2 cup diced salt pork

2 tablespoons olive oil

2 medium onions, chopped

1 large red jalapeño pepper, seeded, deveined, minced

1 cup diced cooked, smoky ham (about 5 ounces)

3 1/2 cups beef broth (approximately)

1 bay leaf

1 teaspoon chopped fresh oregano, or 1/2 teaspoon dried

2 teaspoons red wine vinegar

2 tablespoons dark rum

4 scallions, sliced

2 hard-cooked eggs, finely chopped

1. Combine the bacon drippings with the crushed garlic, 2 tablespoons chili powder, the cumin, and freshly ground pepper in a small bowl. Spread over the boar. Let stand while preparing the beans.

2. Place the beans in a large pot. Cover with cold water and heat to boiling; boil 2 minutes. Remove from heat and let stand, covered, 1 hour. Drain.

3. Wipe out and return the beans to the pot. Cover with cold water and heat to boiling; reduce the heat. Simmer, uncovered, 30 minutes. Drain.

4. Meanwhile, cook the salt pork in boiling water 5 minutes. Drain and pat dry with paper towels.

5. Preheat a two-tiered water smoker. (Charcoal smokers will require a full pan of briquets.)

6. Heat the oil in a large saucepan over medium heat. Add the salt pork; cook 3 minutes. Stir in the onion; cook 1 minute. Add the minced garlic and jalapeño pepper; cook 3 minutes. Stir in the ham; cook 2 minutes longer.

7. Stir the remaining 1 tablespoon chili powder into the onion mixture. Add the beans, 3 cups of the broth, the bay leaf, oregano, vinegar, and rum. Mix well. Transfer to an enamel-coated pan that will fit in the smoker. (I use the water pan.)

8. Add presoaked wood chips or chunks to the smoker's heat source. Place the beans on the lower food rack of the smoker. Place the wild boar on the upper food rack directly over the beans. Cover and smoker-cook, keeping the temperature between 200° and 225° F. for 2 hours. Stir the beans and add another 1/2 cup broth. (Add more briquets if using a charcoal grill.) Continue to smoker-cook until the beans are tender (add more broth if too thick), and the boar juices run yellow when the meat is pricked with a fork (internal temperature on a meat thermometer should register 170° F.), about 2 hours longer.

9. To serve: Slice the meat and press lightly into the beans. Garnish with scallions and hard-cooked eggs.

Serves 6 to 8

Note To make this chili in a conventional oven, place the bean mixture, using only 2 cups broth (step 7), in a large heavy Dutch oven. Place the boar over the beans and bake, covered, in a 325° F. oven, stirring the beans once or twice, until the beans and meat are tender, about 2 hours. If the bean mixture is too wet, place uncovered over medium-high heat on top of the stove and cook, stirring frequently, until thickened.

Chocolate Cakes

Oh, cakes and friends we should choose with care,
Not always the fanciest cake that's there
Is the best to eat! And the plainest friend
Is sometimes the finest in the end!
—"On a Rainy Day," by Margaret E. Sangster

CERTAINLY, no one considers an American chocolate cake "fancy." Unlike a French dacquoise or Viennese Sacher torte, it takes no special skill to turn out a layer cake, even when it's enriched with chocolate. But, this was not always the case.

In Colonial America, all baking was done in fireplaces. If one was lucky enough to live in a large settlement, unbaked cakes could be taken to a community oven, but for most pioneer housewives, improvisation was the key kitchen word. Earliest cakes were baked in large iron pots known as Dutch ovens which were placed on trivets, away from the direct heat of the fire. Later, baking cavities were built directly into side walls of fireplaces. These brick ovens were preheated by placing live coals inside the well until the "oven" became hot enough for baking bread, or more pertinently, cake. It was, however, a very primitive business. To judge an oven's readiness, a conscientious home baker could throw a handful of flour onto the bricks to see if it scorched, or worse yet, place her hand directly in the hot oven and count off the seconds she could "take the heat."

The first cakes were single layers, most often pound cakes, embellished with fruit for special occasions. But the lack of reliable leavening left much to be desired texturally. Although some yeast was employed in Colonial cake making, it was a more common practice to force a cake's rise by beating eggs till they were so stiff the batter virtually levitated before it hit the oven. In the eighteenth century, it was not uncommon for a housewife to use as many as twenty eggs in one cake! On top of that, she had to beat the eggs *by hand* anywhere from 3 to 5 hours to ensure feathery lightness. The next hundred years was a boon for American bakers in general and for those who favored chocolate cake in particular. For one thing, baking powder was introduced and for another, chocolate became highly refined thanks to the cocoa press. Even more important, the first practical freestanding wood stove was invented and changed the course of home baking forever after.

A Boston cooking teacher named Maria Parloa was the undisputed pioneer who developed chocolate cake in America. Although Parloa penned three "cookery" books by 1880, the general populace regarded her chocolate cake recipes with distinct suspicion. Parloa relied on baking powder for leavening and baking powder was still a new and highly mistrusted ingredient for many housewives. Miss Parloa was a determined missionary, however, and eventually sold her ideas to Baker's, a chocolate company that had been thriving with moderate success in Massachusetts since 1765. Once a major chocolate purveyor joined the fray, it didn't take long for chocolate cake to find willing hands at the oven. In time it became America's favorite dessert.

Having Your Cake . . . And Eating It Too When making a chocolate layer cake, use only sturdy pans made of aluminum. Stainless steel, contrary to most opinions, is *not* a good heat conductor. To prepare a cake pan for baking, grease it well with shortening and then lightly sprinkle the inner surface with flour, shaking out the excess flour afterward. Lining the bottoms of cake pans with parchment paper is an advisable precaution when making dense extra-chocolately cakes, as these rich batters sometimes have a tendency to irremediably stick. If you opt for a lining, grease the pan as well as the parchment paper before dusting its surface with flour.

Soft wheat, or cake flour, is the most common flour used for cake baking as it produces a light, airy texture. However, there are times when all-purpose flour (a mixture of hard and soft wheats) is best-suited for a moist, dense finish. For the recipes in this collection, sift the flour before it is measured. This helps aerate the flour which makes it easier to absorb liquids. Also, as many Americans have not yet adapted to the practice of measuring by weight, it helps to achieve the most accurate calibration. To measure flour, fill a dry measure cup with sifted flour and scrape it level with the back of a knife.

Always bake cakes in the middle of the oven for best air circulation. To test a cake for doneness, insert a toothpick or cake tester in the center. It should come out clean. A well-baked cake will also bounce back when pressed lightly with your hand.

One good thing about all cakes, and most particularly the chocolate layer, is that they are at their best made a day before they are to be served. Once cooled, freshly baked cakes can be placed in airtight bags and kept at room temperature overnight. Never refrigerate a buttery chocolate cake. Cakes that must be made in advance should be frozen, rather than refrigerated, but the texture of the cake will, sad to say, alter after a stint in the freezer.

*J*OSEPH AMENDOLA and Donald E. Lundberg, authors of *Understanding Baking* (CBI publishing, 1979) added this grace note to their book about layer cakes in general:

> Few pleasures are greater than turning out a perfect cake . . . Such creations can bring happiness to both our childhood and mature years, for few, if any, people are immune to their charm, and memories of them . . . lighten the dark corners of life.

Amen.

I am a deep-dyed chocolate cake fan and find that chocolate cake is the one dessert I serve to dinner guests that always elicits a sigh of pleasure first and a second helping afterward.

OLD-FASHIONED LAYER CAKE WITH FUDGE FROSTING

HERE IS the very best cake that ever came out of South Pekin, Illinois. It may, in passing, be the best cake to ever come out of the state for that matter. The frosting is Bert Greene's. Old-fashioned? You bet. Melting? Like a dipper of fresh fudge. Hard to make? It's a piece of cake.

For the cake

4 ounces semi-sweet chocolate, chopped
1 cup milk
1 cup light brown sugar (packed)
3 large egg yolks
2 cups sifted cake flour
1 teaspoon baking soda

1/2 teaspoon salt
1/2 cup (1 stick) unsalted butter, softened
1 cup sugar
1/4 cup water
1 teaspoon vanilla
2 large egg whites

For the frosting

3 ounces unsweetened chocolate
1 can (14 ounces) sweetened condensed milk

8 tablespoons (1 stick) unsalted butter, cut into bits
1 egg yolk, lightly beaten
1 1/2 teaspoons vanilla

1. Preheat the oven to 375° F. Grease and flour two 9-inch round cake pans.

2. To make the cake: Combine the chocolate, 1/2 cup milk, the brown sugar, and 1 egg yolk in the top of a double boiler. Cook, stirring constantly, over hot water until smooth. Remove from heat.

3. Sift the flour with the baking soda and salt into a small bowl.

4. Beat the butter in the large bowl of an electric mixer until light. Slowly beat in the sugar. Beat until light and fluffy. Beat in the remaining 2 egg yolks, one at a time, beating thoroughly after each addition. Beat in the chocolate mixture.

5. Combine the water with the remaining 1/2 cup milk and the vanilla. Add to the batter in thirds, alternating with thirds of the flour mixture.

6. Beat the egg whites until stiff; fold into the batter.

7. Pour the batter into the prepared pans. Bake until a toothpick inserted in the center comes out fairly clean, about 25 minutes. Cool on a wire rack before unmolding.

8. To make the frosting: Melt the chocolate in the top of a double boiler over hot water. Stir in the condensed milk until smooth. Stir in the butter, bit by bit, until smooth. Stir in the egg yolk and vanilla and cook until slightly thickened. Cool slightly and then frost the bottom layer, the sides, and top of the cake.

Serves 8 to 10

NOTHING BEATS CHOCOLATE BEET CAKE

IN ITS LONG confectionery past, chocolate has gotten mixed up with a lot of odd flavorings. One of its more felicitous connections is the following Midwest farm wife's legacy. Here, a rich fudgy cake depends, surprisingly, on pureed beets to keep it moist. The recipe was brought to California by covered wagon over a hundred years ago. And it is still a trail blazer today. Serve this dusted with confectioners' sugar or sweet cocoa, and let your waistline be your guide regarding whipped cream.

3 ounces semi-sweet chocolate

1 cup vegetable oil

1 3/4 cups sugar

2 cups sifted all-purpose flour

2 teaspoons baking soda

1/4 teaspoon salt

(ingredients continued)

3 large eggs	Confectioners' sugar
2 cups puréed, drained, cooked or canned beets	2 cups heavy or whipping cream, whipped (optional)
1 teaspoon vanilla	

1. Preheat the oven to 375° F. Grease and flour a 10-cup bundt pan.

2. Melt the chocolate with 1/4 cup oil in the top of a double boiler over hot water. Cool slightly.

3. Beat the sugar with the eggs in the large bowl of an electric mixer until light and fluffy. Slowly beat in the remaining 3/4 cup oil, the beet puree, the chocolate mixture, and the vanilla.

4. Sift the flour with the baking soda and salt in a medium bowl. Slowly stir into the batter. Pour the mixture into the prepared pan. Bake in the preheated oven until a toothpick inserted in the center comes out clean, about 1 hour. Cool on a wire rack for 15 minutes before unmolding. Dust with confectioners' sugar before serving, and top with the cream if you choose.

Serves 8

ROSE LEVY BERANBAUM'S
CHOCOLATE FUDGE CAKE WITH
MILK CHOCOLATE BUTTERCREAM

IN *Your Horoscope and Dreams* by Ned Ballantyne and Stella Coeli (Books, Inc. 1940), the authors tell us:

> To dream of cake fortells advancement for the laborer and enhancement for the industrious . . . Those in love will be especially gratified. Layer cake denotes satisfaction . . . A fluffy rich icing on a cake predicts gaiety.

Rose Levy Beranbaum is not only one of the dream bakers of America, but a "dessert scientist" in the bargain. She knows everything there is to know about cake and has written one of the most important baking books of the century, *The Cake Bible* (William Morrow & Co., 1988). Her chocolate fudge cake is so extravagant, it is indeed the stuff that dreams are made of.

For the cake

3/4 cup plus 3 tablespoons unsweetened cocoa

1 1/2 cups boiling water

3 large eggs

1 1/2 teaspoons vanilla

3 cups sifted cake flour

2 cups light brown sugar (packed)

2 1/4 teaspoons baking powder

3/4 teaspoon baking soda

3/4 teaspoon salt

1 cup (2 sticks) unsalted butter, softened

For the frosting

1 pound milk chocolate, chopped

8 ounces semi-sweet chocolate, chopped

1 1/2 cups (3 sticks) unsalted butter, softened

1. Preheat the oven to 350° F. Line the bottoms of two greased 9-inch cake pans with parchment paper. Grease and flour the pans.

2. Whisk the cocoa with the boiling water in a medium bowl until smooth. Cool.

3. Beat the eggs with 1/4 cup of the cocoa mixture and the vanilla. Set aside.

4. Combine the flour, sugar, baking powder, baking soda, and salt in the large bowl of an electric mixer. Beat on low speed 30 seconds. Add the butter and the remaining cocoa mixture. Beat on low speed until just mixed. Beat on medium speed 1 1/2 minutes. Scrape down the sides and add the reserved egg mixture in three batches, beating the batter for 20 seconds after each addition.

5. Pour the batter into the prepared pans. Bake until a toothpick inserted in the center comes out clean, about 25 minutes. Cool on a wire rack. Unmold and remove parchment paper.

6. To make the frosting: Melt the chocolates in the top of a double boiler over hot water. Cool.

7. Beat the butter in a large bowl until light. Slowly beat in the cooled chocolate until light and fluffy. Spread over the bottom layer, the sides, and top of cake.

Serves 10

BROWNSTONE STOOP

THE NEXT cake is called brownstone for an obvious reason. Made in a 9- by 13-inch pan, it looks a bit like the cornerstone its cognomen implies. How the cake actually got the name is a matter of conjecture, but there are actually two brownstone cakes of record. One is a dark caramelized spice cake. The other, the rich chocolatey devise that follows. "Would yee both eat your cake and have your cake?" asked poet John Heywood back in the fifteenth century. If it's Brownstone Stoop, the answer is clearly, yes.

2 ounces unsweetened chocolate, chopped	1/2 cup (1 stick) unsalted butter, softened
1 cup water	2 cups dark brown sugar (packed)
1 teaspoon baking soda	2 large eggs, separated
2 1/2 cups sifted cake flour	1 teaspoon vanilla
1 teaspoon baking powder	1/2 cup sour cream
1/4 teaspoon salt	Confectioners' sugar

1. Preheat the oven to 325° F. Grease and flour a 9- by 13-inch glass cake pan. If using other than glass, preheat the oven to 350° F.

2. Combine the chocolate, water, and baking soda in the top of a double boiler. Cook, stirring occasionally, over simmering water until smooth. Cool slightly.

3. Sift the flour with the baking powder and salt into a medium bowl.

4. Beat the butter with the brown sugar in the large bowl of an electric mixer until smooth. Beat in the egg yolks, one at a time, beating thoroughly after each addition. Beat in the vanilla.

5. On low speed, beat in the cooled chocolate mixture in thirds, alternating with thirds of the flour mixture. Beat in the sour cream.

6. Beat the egg whites until stiff. Fold into cake batter. Pour mixture into the prepared pan. Bake until a toothpick inserted in the center comes out clean, about 40 to 45 minutes. Cool on a wire rack. Dust with confectioners' sugar.

Serves 12

COLORADO CELEBRATION CAKE

IN MY home state, actually in my home as well, this is the chocolate cake for all seasons and reasons—it has been made to celebrate everything from a B+ report card to the acquisition of a new Ford, and even a fiftieth anniversary party. What's so celebratory about this dessert is the fudge and marshmallow topping, swirled into a frosting while the cake is still warm.

3 tablespoons unsalted butter or shortening, softened

3/4 cup plus 2 tablespoons sugar

1 large egg

1/2 teaspoon vanilla

1/3 cup unsweetened cocoa

1/3 cup plus 2 tablespoons boiling water

1/2 teaspoon baking soda

1 1/4 cups sifted cake flour

Pinch of salt

1/2 cup sour milk or buttermilk (see note)

1 ounce unsweetened chocolate, chopped

1 tablespoon unsalted butter

1 cup confectioners' sugar

10 marshmallows, cut in half across

1. Preheat the oven to 350° F. Grease and flour a 9-inch springform pan.

2. Beat the softened butter or the shortening with the sugar, egg, and vanilla in the large bowl of an electric mixer until light and fluffy.

3. Combine the cocoa with 1/3 cup boiling water in a heatproof bowl. Whisk until smooth. Beat in the soda. Let stand until the mixture is mahogany in color and bubbles slightly.

4. Beat the cocoa mixture into the butter mixture until smooth. Slowly add the flour, salt, and sour milk or buttermilk.

5. Pour the batter into the prepared pan. Bake until a toothpick inserted in the center comes out fairly clean, about 25 minutes (because of its fudginess, the toothpick won't be completely dry).

6. Meanwhile, in the top of a double boiler, melt the chocolate with the butter over hot water until smooth. Stir in the confectioners' sugar. Add the 2 tablespoons boiling water, a bit at a time, to make a slightly thin icing.

7. When the cake is baked, place the marshmallows over the top. Return the cake to the oven until the marshmallows soften, 2 to 3 minutes. Then spoon the icing over and around the marshmallows, slightly swirling the marshmallows. Cool on a wire rack 20 minutes. Remove the sides of the pan; cool completely before serving.

Serves 8

Note To make sour milk, add 1 teaspoon lemon juice or vinegar to 1/2 cup milk.

INDIANA'S FAMOUS
"COKE" CAKE WITH CHOCOLATE-COKE
BUTTERCREAM

ECCENTRIC soft drink fans have been sloshing down chocolate Cokes for years, so it's not surprising to discover that some inspired Indianapolis homemaker decided to flavor a chocolate cake with a healthy splash of "Classic Coke" a while back. A knockout confection, it's dense, dark, and utterly "refreshing."

For the cake

1 cup (2 sticks) unsalted butter

1/2 cup chopped marshmallows

1/4 cup unsweetened cocoa

1 cup Coca-Cola

1 cup sugar

1 cup light brown sugar (packed)

2 cups all-purpose flour

1 teaspoon baking soda

2 large eggs, lightly beaten

1/2 cup buttermilk

For the icing

6 ounces semi-sweet chocolate

1/3 cup Coca-Cola

1 cup (2 sticks) plus 2 tablespoons
    unsalted butter, softened

3 large egg yolks

2/3 cup confectioners' sugar

1. Preheat the oven to 350° F. Grease and flour two 9-inch round cake pans.

2. To make the cake: Combine the butter with the marshmallows in a medium saucepan. Cook, stirring occasionally, over low heat until marshmallows melt, about 8 minutes. Stir in the cocoa and Coca-Cola until smooth. Remove from heat.

3. Combine the sugars with the flour and baking soda in the large bowl of an electric mixer. Beat in the chocolate mixture on low speed. Add the eggs and buttermilk and continue to beat on low speed just until mixed. Pour the batter into the prepared pans. Bake in the preheated oven until a toothpick inserted in the center comes out clean, about 35 to 40 minutes. Cool on a wire rack before unmolding.

4. To make the icing: Combine the chocolate with the Coca-Cola in the top of a double boiler. Cook, stirring occasionally, over boiling water until smooth. Cool and chill.

5. Beat the butter in the large bowl of an electric mixer until light and fluffy. Beat in the egg yolks, one at a time, beating well after each addition. Slowly beat in the chocolate mixture and confectioners' sugar. Frost the bottom layer, the sides, and top of the cake.

Serves 8 to 10

Chocolate cake left its muddy print on American history long before Miss Parloa ever baked a layer. In Salem, Massachusetts a witchcraft trial was based on evidence of—you guessed it—devil's food cake. Tituba was the baker's name. A half-Caribe Indian, half-black woman from Jamaica, she came to America as a household slave in the employ of a Reverend Parris in Salem, years before any tales of witches hit town. Old and motherly, her only duty was to watch over Parris's daughter and niece. And, on occasion, to bake a cake. What a cake it was! A wondrous deep chocolate cake, virtually untasted in New England at the time.

Tituba, who told fortunes and read tea leaves, entertained the children at night with stories of island voodoo rituals, while doling out slices of her chocolate cake to sweeten their sleep. But on one occasion, the children grew ill, and all of Tituba's home remedies failed to make them well again. A local physician could find no cause for their indisposition—so he declared the girls bewitched. Others in Salem had recently been accused of witchcraft and Tituba was added to the list.

To prove her innocence, she was ordered by the town elders to make a cake that would cure the children. But the family dog must eat a slice first. Tituba scorched the cake out of agitation, and the dog would not touch a crumb—actually howled when she tried to force the issue. Tituba was sentenced to life imprisonment (though truly she might have been hanged), but in time, her famous cake recipe surfaced again, with a dark name she bestowed upon it from her prison cell: "Devil's Food."

BANGOR TOMATO
DEVIL'S FOOD CAKE WITH
CLASSIC BOILED ICING

A FALLEN angel among chocolate desserts is obviously devil's food cake. What makes this one so irresistible is a can (yes, a whole 8 ounces) of tomato sauce in its devising. Does tomato make chocolate more satanic? Well, according to the natives of Bangor, where the recipe came to hand, it adds an unexpectedly fudgy depth of flavor. And that's good enough for most chocoholics.

For the cake

4 ounces sweet chocolate

1/2 cup milk

1 cup dark brown sugar (packed)

3 large egg yolks

2 cups sifted cake flour

1 teaspoon baking soda

1/2 teaspoon salt

1/2 cup (1 stick) unsalted butter

1 cup sugar

1 can (8 ounces) tomato sauce

1 tablespoon heavy or whipping cream

1 teaspoon vanilla

2 large egg whites

For the frosting

1/2 cup water

1/3 cup light corn syrup

2 1/2 cups sugar

2 large egg whites

Pinch of salt

1 teaspoon orange juice

1 1/2 teaspoons vanilla

1. Preheat the oven to 350° F. Grease and flour two 9-inch round cake pans.

2. To make the cake: Combine the chocolate, milk, brown sugar, and 1 egg yolk in the top of a double boiler. Cook, stirring constantly, over hot water until smooth. Remove from heat.

3. Sift the flour with the baking soda and salt into a medium bowl.

4. Beat the butter in the large bowl of an electric mixer until light. Slowly beat in the sugar until light and fluffy. Add the two remaining egg yolks, one

at a time, beating thoroughly after each addition. Slowly add the chocolate mixture.

5. Combine the tomato sauce, cream, and vanilla in a small bowl. Add to the batter in thirds, alternating with thirds of the flour mixture.

6. Beat the egg whites until stiff; fold into the batter.

7. Pour the batter into the prepared pans. Bake until a toothpick inserted in the center comes out clean, about 25 minutes. Cool on a wire rack before unmolding.

8. To make the frosting: Combine the water, corn syrup, and sugar in a medium saucepan. Heat to boiling; boil until the mixture thickens and forms a ball when a small spoonful is dropped into cold water (about 240° F. on a candy thermometer).

9. Beat the egg whites in the large bowl of an electric mixer until stiff. Slowly beat in the hot syrup. Continue to beat until spreading consistency. Beat in the orange juice and vanilla. Spread over the bottom layer, the sides, and top of cake.

Serves 8 to 10

KANSAS COCOA GOODIE CAKE
WITH CARAMEL NUT FROSTING

A CAKE with lineage, my Grandmother Moehlenbrink, who was born in Bremen (pronounced Brie-man), Kansas, practically on the Nebraska border, always called this her "goodie cake." As kids we called it her "soap cake" because it seemed to have a slightly foamy flavor. Grandma made hers with sour milk. I use buttermilk instead—and the suds are only a memory now. I realize what I haven't said about "cocoa goodie cake" is how good it was, and still is. My grandmother never frosted hers, but having a sweet tooth, I do.

For the cake

2 large eggs

Pinch of salt

1 cup light vegetable oil

1 cup buttermilk

2 cups sugar

1/4 cup unsweetened cocoa (preferably Lindt or Droste's)

3 cups sifted all-purpose flour

1 tablespoon baking soda

1 cup very hot water

For the frosting

3/4 cup light brown sugar (packed)

6 tablespoons (3/4 stick) unsalted butter

3 tablespoons heavy or whipping cream (approximately)

1 teaspoon vanilla

1 1/2 cups confectioners' sugar

2/3 cup chopped pecans (about 2 2/3 ounces)

1. Preheat the oven to 325° F. Grease and flour a 9- by 13-inch glass cake pan. If using other than glass, preheat oven to 350° F.

2. To make the cake: Beat the eggs with the salt in the large bowl of an electric mixer until light. Slowly add the oil and buttermilk. Beat well. Beat in the sugar.

3. On low speed, slowly add the cocoa, flour, baking soda, and water (in that order) to the buttermilk mixture. Beat only until mixed. Pour the mixture into the prepared pan. Bake until a toothpick inserted in the center comes out clean, about 50 minutes. Cool on a wire rack.

4. To make the frosting: Combine the brown sugar and butter in a medium saucepan. Cook over low heat until smooth. Stir in the cream and raise the heat slightly. Gently simmer the mixture, stirring occasionally, 5 minutes. Cool. Stir in the vanilla and confectioners' sugar until smooth. Add a splash more cream if needed to make the frosting a spreadable consistency. Stir in the nuts. Carefully spread over the cake with the aid of two knives so that the top of the cake does not pull.

Serves 12

SWEET GEORGIA BROWN CAKE

Pat-a-cake, pat-a-cake, baker's man
Bake me a cake as fast as you can
Pat it and prick it and mark it with a B
Put it in the oven for baby and me.
                              —Old nursery rhyme

IN THIS CASE the *B* in the verse above stands for brown, not baby, for here is a rich and upright chocolate pound cake of remarkable russet-to-umber hue. This is the kind of cake a prideful Atlanta baker of fifty years ago would dub, "Sweet Georgia Brown."

3 1/2 cups sifted cake flour

3 cups sugar

1 cup unsweetened cocoa (preferably Lindt or Droste's)

3 teaspoons baking powder

1 teaspoon salt

1 cup (2 sticks) unsalted butter, softened

1 1/2 cups milk

1 tablespoon vanilla

3 large eggs

1/4 cup light cream or half-and-half

Confectioners' sugar

1. Preheat the oven to 325° F. Rub a 10-inch tube pan with oil. Do not flour.

2. Sift the flour with the sugar, cocoa, baking powder, and salt into the large bowl of an electric mixer. Make a well in the center and add the butter, milk, and vanilla. Beat on low speed 1 minute. Beat on medium speed 4 minutes.

3. Add the eggs to the batter, one at a time, beating thoroughly after each addition. Beat in the light cream.

4. Pour the batter into the prepared pan and bake until firm to the touch and a toothpick inserted in the center comes out clean, about 1 hour and 30

to 40 minutes. Cool on a wire rack before unmolding. Dust with confectioners' sugar before serving.

Serves 8 to 10

COCOA MAYO CAKE
WITH BURNT SUGAR FROSTING

THIS IS an all-American state and country fair winner that was invented when bottled mayonnaise replaced homemade and a woman's urge to be creative was most often executed in the kitchen. Cocoa and mayonnaise are responsible for a moist dense layer cake that still holds up as a "just dessert" fifty years later when women are creative all over the place.

For the cake

3 large eggs

1 2/3 cup sugar

1 teaspoon vanilla

1 cup store-bought mayonnaise

2 cups sifted all-purpose flour

1 1/4 teaspoons baking soda

1/4 teaspoon baking powder

2/3 cup unsweetened cocoa (preferably Lindt or Droste's)

1 1/3 cups water

For the frosting

1 1/2 cups light brown sugar (packed)

1/3 cup water

1 tablespoon light corn syrup

2 large egg whites

3 tablespoons white crème de cacao

    1. Preheat oven to 350° F. Grease and flour two 9-inch round cake pans.

    2. To make the cake: Beat the eggs with the sugar in the large bowl of an electric mixer until light and lemon in color. Beat in the vanilla and mayonnaise.

3. Sift the flour with the baking soda, baking powder, and cocoa in a medium bowl. Add to the batter in thirds, alternating with thirds of the water.

4. Pour the batter into the prepared pans. Bake until a toothpick inserted in the center comes out clean, about 25 minutes. Cool on a wire rack before unmolding.

5. To make the frosting: Combine the sugar with the water, corn syrup, and egg whites in the top of a double boiler. Beat with an electric hand-held mixer over simmering water until of spreading consistency, about 7 minutes. Beat in the crème de cacao. Spread over the bottom layer, the sides, and top of the cake.

Serves 8 to 10

MISSISSIPPI MUD

ARE THERE some chocolate cakes that are fudgy to a fault? It's a rhetorical question because the answer is a resounding "*no*" from chocolate lovers everywhere. The following prodigious device was first stirred up by a housewife in Natchez—but like little Eva, its fame soon outgrew its local purlieus. Now it's a world-famous confection. Serve it with unsweetened whipped cream to ameliorate the richness.

Unsweetened cocoa

1 1/4 cups strong coffee

1/4 cup bourbon

5 ounces unsweetened chocolate

1 cup (2 sticks) unsalted butter, cut into pieces

2 cups sugar

2 1/4 cups sifted all-purpose flour

1 teaspoon baking soda

Pinch of salt

2 large eggs, lightly beaten

1 teaspoon vanilla

Confectioners' sugar

Unsweetened whipped cream (optional)

1. Preheat the oven to 275° F. Grease a 9-inch tube pan (3 1/2 inches deep) and sprinkle with cocoa.

2. Heat the coffee with the bourbon in a medium saucepan over medium-low heat. Add the chocolate and butter. Cook, stirring frequently, until smooth. Remove from the heat and stir in the sugar. Let stand 5 minutes. Transfer to the large bowl of an electric mixer.

3. Sift the flour with the baking soda and salt into a medium bowl. Add to the batter on low speed in four batches. Beat in the eggs, one at a time, beating thoroughly after each addition. Beat in the vanilla.

4. Pour the batter into the prepared pan. Bake until a toothpick inserted in the center comes out clean, about 1 1/2 hours. Cool completely on a wire rack before unmolding. Serve dusted with confectioners' sugar or topped with whipped cream.

Serves 10

RED-FACED BIRTHDAY CAKE
WITH COLORADO SNOW TOPPING

THE NEXT blushing entry is very dear to my heart for it has commemorated my birthday for as long as I can remember. When I left home, it even followed me, first to the Army and then across the entire continent. Four rosy layers, wrapped in plastic, were mailed along with a recipe for the *snow* frosting. My mother, Mildred Schulz, a heck of a baker, once heard that the formula originated at the old Waldorf Astoria Hotel at the turn of the century and migrated west with some silver-rich Coloradoan who paid $1,000 for it. It's a good story, but the cake is even better. Why is it red-faced? Don't tell the secret, but there is 1/4 cup red food coloring in the batter. But it's not red dye #2—so breathe easier and enjoy.

For the cake

1/2 cup (1 stick) unsalted butter,
   softened
1 1/2 cups sugar
2 large eggs
2 ounces red food coloring
1 teaspoon vanilla
2 tablespoons unsweetened cocoa

1 teaspoon salt
1 cup buttermilk
2 1/4 cups sifted cake flour
1 teaspoon baking soda
1 teaspoon cider vinegar

For the frosting

3 tablespoons all-purpose flour
1 cup milk
1 cup (2 sticks) unsalted butter,
   softened

1 cup sugar
1 teaspoon vanilla

1. Preheat the oven to 350° F. Grease and flour two 9-inch round cake pans.

2. To make the cake: Beat the butter with the sugar in the large bowl of an electric mixer until light and fluffy. Beat in the eggs, one at a time, beating thoroughly after each addition.

3. Stir the food coloring with the vanilla and cocoa in a small bowl to form a paste. Beat into the batter.

4. Combine the salt and buttermilk. Add to the batter in thirds, alternating with thirds of the flour.

5. Combine the baking soda and vinegar. Stir into batter.

6. Pour the batter into the prepared pans. Bake until a toothpick inserted in the center comes out clean, about 30 minutes. Cool on a wire rack before unmolding.

7. When the cake is completely cool, cut each layer in half to form four layers.

8. To make the frosting: Slowly whisk the flour with the milk in a medium saucepan until smooth. Cook, stirring frequently, over medium heat until thick, about 5 minutes. Cool.

9. Beat the butter with the sugar in the large bowl of an electric mixer until light and fluffy. Beat in the vanilla. Slowly beat in the cooled milk mixture. Spread the frosting over each cake layer. Place one on top of the other and ice the sides and top of cake.

Serves 8 to 10

Chocolate Chip Cookies

THE VERY FIRST cookie is said to have been invented by the sugar-loving Persians back in the seventh century. But it took a quantum leap to the twentieth century for the cookie to achieve real immortality. Enter the "chocolate chip," invented by happy accident in 1930.

Jennifer Harvey Lang, in her book *Tastings* (Crown, 1986), tells the tale of what was destined to become America's favorite kitchen mishap. Almost sixty years ago, Ruth Wakefield, the owner of the Toll House Inn in Whitman, Massachusetts, set about making her weekly batch of chocolate cookies. But instead of melting the chocolate, as she customarily did, Mrs. Wakefield gave into an impulse. She chopped the chocolate into small pieces and stirred it into a butter cookie batter, fully expecting the chocolate to melt in the oven. Well, it didn't. And another legend was born: Toll House Cookies.

Mrs. Wakefield's chocolate-dotted creations made the Toll House Inn famous, it glorified the state of baking in New England in general, and set cookie makers all over America on a kitchen collision course: chopping chocolate into bite-size morsels.

In 1939, the Nestlé Company began packaging chocolate chips with the Toll House recipe printed on the package. Under the terms of an agreement with Mrs. Wakefield, Nestlé was required to run the recipe without change for forty years. Forty years later to the day, they altered the recipe, no longer sifting the flour, eliminating the water, and dictating ungreased baking sheets in lieu of buttered. The difference is subtle, but highly noticeable to anyone who truly drooled over the original formula. You will find the original one here.

Some Tips on Chocolate Chips Whether one likes them soft and chewy, or hard and crisp, I've yet to meet anyone who doesn't opt for seconds of a well-made chocolate chip cookie. Most likely our preferences were stamped by our mothers' individual methods for making them. But make a mental note here: Any chocolate chip cookie can be changed from the hard, crisp variety to the soft, chewy type merely by substituting vegetable shortening for butter, and by reducing the baking time by about 2 minutes.

It is best to bake chocolate chip cookies on a middle rack of an oven for optimum air circulation. If you are baking two sheets of cookies at one time, be sure to rotate the pans halfway through the baking time for even results. If you are reusing baking sheets, allow them to cool and then wipe them thoroughly before adding fresh cookie dough. If you don't cool and clean the pan, the dough will start baking before you get it into the oven and the texture of the cookies will change irremediably. And do watch your oven heat as chocolate chips have a tendency to scorch. Remember what Sir James Barrie wrote in his foreword to Peter Pan. "Whenever cookies burn in the kitchen, an unhappy child makes a plan to run away from home!"

Always allow freshly baked chocolate chip cookies to rest for about 1 minute before removing them from the baking sheets. Then place them individually on a wire rack to prevent the bottoms from becoming damp. Store the cooled cookies in airtight containers, preferably with wax paper dividing the layers.

"**WHAT IS** patriotism but the love of the good things we ate in our childhood." (Lin Yutang) And so, even though rising entrepreneurs like Wally Amos (Famous Amos cookies) and Debra Field (Mrs. Field's cookies) have made personal fortunes packaging chocolate chip cookies, most patriotic Americans still prefer to make their own. From scratch. In fact, more than half of all cookies made in the home are chocolate chips. The best from my enormous collection follow.

MRS. WAKEFIELD'S ORIGINAL
TOLL HOUSE COOKIE

INCREDULOUS as it may seem, chocolate chip cookies did not bear a stamp of authority back in the 1930s, '40s, even '50s, unless they came to table with "Toll House" prefixed to the name. There was a reason. Unscrupulous bakers often offered up compromise versions that had neither the butteriness, nor the chocolate bit, of Mrs. Wakefield's original. If it said "Toll House," however, one knew it was the real thing. Here's the genuine article.

1 cup plus 2 tablespoons sifted all-purpose flour
1/2 teaspoon baking soda
1/2 teaspoon salt
1/2 cup (1 stick) unsalted butter, softened
6 tablespoons sugar
6 tablespoons light brown sugar (packed)

1/2 teaspoon vanilla
1/4 teaspoon water
1 large egg
6 ounces (1 cup) semi-sweet chocolate chips
1/2 cup chopped nuts (about 2 ounces)

1. Preheat the oven to 375° F.
2. Sift the flour with the baking soda and salt into a bowl.
3. Beat the butter with the sugars, vanilla, water, and egg until creamy. Stir in the flour mixture; mix thoroughly. Stir in the chocolate chips and nuts.

4. Drop the cookie batter by tablespoonfuls onto greased cookie sheets. Bake until edges are golden, 10 to 12 minutes. Cool on the baking sheet for a few minutes before transferring to a wire rack to cool completely.

Makes about 24 cookies

SOFT CHOCOLATE CHIPS

THE ORIGINAL "chocolate chip" cookie was crisp and crumbly—and always left an unmistakable trail from the cookie jar. That fact has gotten many a kid into all sorts of trouble. Taking note of a Bible passage, "A soft answer turneth away wrath," a soft cookie likewise leaves no telltale evidence for retribution.

1 1/2 cups plus 2 tablespoons sifted
    all-purpose flour
1/2 teaspoon baking soda
1/4 teaspoon salt
1/2 cup vegetable shortening
6 tablespoons sugar
6 tablespoons light brown sugar

1/2 teaspoon vanilla
1/4 cup milk
1 large egg
6 ounces (1 cup) semi-sweet chocolate
    chips
1/4 cup chopped nuts (about 1 ounce)

1. Preheat the oven to 350° F.
2. Sift the flour with the baking soda and salt into a bowl.
3. Beat the shortening with both sugars until creamy. Beat in the vanilla, milk, and egg. Stir in the flour mixture; mix thoroughly. Stir in the chocolate chips and nuts.
4. Drop the cookie batter by tablespoonfuls onto greased cookie sheets. Bake 10 minutes. Cool on the baking sheet for a few minutes before transferring to a wire rack to cool completely.

Makes about 24 cookies

ALABAMA-BOUND
DOUBLE-CHOCOLATE SNAPS

IN BIRMINGHAM a while back I made a rash statement that I was a chocolate-chipaholic. (Probably because as a child, *my* toothfairy left little packages of chocolate chips instead of nickels or dimes under my pillow.) Southern bakers being generous to a fault, I left town with a dozen recipes. The best of the lot is the following deep fudgy cookie spliced with melting chocolate chips to compound the caloric downfall.

2 ounces unsweetened chocolate	1 teaspoon baking powder
3 tablespoons unsalted butter	1/4 teaspoon salt
2 large eggs	6 ounces (1 cup) milk chocolate chips or coarsely chopped white chocolate
1 cup sugar	
1 1/4 cups all-purpose flour	3 to 4 tablespoons sifted confectioners' sugar

1. Melt the chocolate with the butter in the top of a double boiler over hot water until smooth. Remove from heat.

2. Beat the eggs with the sugar in a medium bowl until light. Beat in the chocolate mixture. Beat in the flour, baking powder, salt, and chocolate chips. Refrigerate, covered, 1 hour.

3. Preheat the oven to 300° F.

4. Spread the confectioners' sugar over a shallow dish. Scoop up the batter, using about 1 1/2 teaspoons for each cookie, and roll in your hands to form a ball. Roll each ball in the confectioners' sugar and place on lightly buttered baking sheets. Press lightly with your fingers to flatten each ball of cookie batter to about 1/4-inch thickness.

5. Bake 18 minutes. Cool on the baking sheet for a few minutes before transferring to a wire rack to cool completely.

Makes about 50 cookies

CHOCOLATE GINGER CHIPS

"SUGAR AND SPICE and everything nice (including chocolate chips). That's what little cookies are made of." A highly spiced, super soft gingersnap, this one is enriched with just the right amount of chocolate chips to enhance, yet not detract from, its original sassy flavoring.

1/2 cup vegetable shortening

1/2 cup sugar

1/4 cup molasses

2 large egg yolks

1 1/2 teaspoons ground ginger

1 teaspoon ground cinnamon

1/2 teaspoon ground cloves

1/2 teaspoon baking soda

1/8 teaspoon salt

1 cup all-purpose flour

6 ounces (1 cup) semi-sweet chocolate chips

1. Preheat the oven to 350° F.

2. Beat the shortening with the sugar in a large bowl until light. Beat in the molasses, egg yolks, ginger, cinnamon, cloves, baking soda, and salt. Stir in the flour; mix thoroughly. Stir in the chocolate chips.

3. Drop the cookie batter by rounded teaspoonfuls onto lightly greased baking sheets. Press flat. Bake 10 to 12 minutes. Cool on the baking sheets for a few minutes before transferring to a wire rack to cool completely.

Makes about 34 cookies

MARIN COUNTY CHOCOLATE CHIPPERS

HAVE A Wild West (Coast) version of the chocolate chip that's like no other. Concocted by Sharon Tyler Herbst of Greenbrae, California, for her tasty tome, *The Joy of Cookies* (Barron's, 1987), it is both moist and crunchy at the same time and crammed with every conceivable sweetmeat besides chocolate chips.

2 cups all-purpose flour

1 teaspoon baking soda

1/2 teaspoon salt

1 cup flaked coconut

1 cup rolled oats

1 tablespoon unsweetened cocoa

1 cup (2 sticks) unsalted butter, softened

1 1/2 cups light brown sugar (packed)

2 teaspoons vanilla

2 large eggs

12 ounces (2 cups) semi-sweet chocolate chips

1 1/2 cups chopped nuts

1. Preheat the oven to 375° F.

2. Sift the flour with the baking soda and salt into a bowl.

3. Combine the coconut, rolled oats, and cocoa in the container of a food processor. Process until finely ground. Stir into the flour mixture.

4. Beat the butter with the sugar and vanilla in the large bowl of an electric mixer until light. Beat in the eggs, one at a time, beating thoroughly after each addition.

5. Stir the processed coconut/flour mixture into the batter; mix thoroughly. Stir in the chocolate chips and nuts.

6. Scoop up the batter, using 2 tablespoons for each cookie, and place it on lightly buttered baking sheets about 2 inches apart. Press lightly with your fingers to flatten each mound of cookie batter to about 1/2-inch thickness.

7. Bake 8 to 10 minutes. Cool on the baking sheet for a few minutes before transferring to a wire rack to cool completely.

Makes about 48 cookies

PEANUT BUTTER MR. CHIPS

THE AMALGAM of peanut butter and chocolate conjurs up those real cavity casualties of childhood: Reese's Peanut Butter Cups and Clark Bars. The following is a strictly adult version, with a highly subtle pairing of flavors. But, as the saying goes: Let the chips fall where they may!

1 1/4 cups cake flour

1 teaspoon baking powder

1/4 teaspoon salt

1/2 cup (1 stick) unsalted butter, softened

1 cup light brown sugar (packed)

1 large egg

1/2 cup chunky-style peanut butter

6 ounces (1 cup) semi-sweet chocolate chips

1. Preheat the oven to 350° F.

2. Sift the flour with the baking powder and salt into a bowl.

3. Beat the butter with the sugar in the large bowl of an electric mixer until light. Beat in the egg and peanut butter. Stir in the flour mixture; mix thoroughly. Stir in the chocolate chips.

4. Drop the batter by tablespoonfuls onto greased cookie sheets. Bake until lightly browned, 13 to 15 minutes. Cool on the baking sheet for a few minutes before transferring to a wire rack to cool completely.

Makes about 30 cookies

For the record, the cookie batter to which Mrs. Wakefield added her chopped chocolate was called Butter Drop Do. It was one of the most popular cookie recipes current in the 1930s and had been for some time. The Butter Drop Do, like its mighty successor, the Chocolate Chip, was an "Inn-ovation" invented in the 1700s at an inn along the King's Path (dirt road, actually) that ran between Philadelphia and New York. The original batter was made in the following manner: First, flour was sifted through fine muslin into a large bowl. Fresh cream was churned into sweet butter and added to the flour with freshly laid eggs. The batter was then whipped to a froth with birch twigs to give the "biskits" a soft, moist texture. Baked in a brick oven, these cookies caught on like wildfire in the colonies.

MRS. FIELD'S COOKIES?

A FRIEND in Kansas City sent me this recipe. It is reputedly the genuine article. However, since Debra Field's basic cookie formula is a close-guarded secret, it just may be an inventive soul's attempt to duplicate her whopper cookie. And if it really *is* the original? Well, then the secret's out.

1 1/2 cups rolled oats

1/2 cup (1 stick) unsalted butter, softened

1/2 cup sugar

1/2 cup light brown sugar (packed)

1 large egg

1 teaspoon vanilla

1 cup sifted all-purpose flour

1/2 teaspoon baking powder

1/2 teaspoon baking soda

1/4 teaspoon salt

6 ounces (1 cup) semi-sweet chocolate chips

2 ounces milk chocolate, chopped

1/2 cup chopped blanched almonds (about 1 1/2 ounces)

1. Preheat the oven to 375° F.

2. Place 1 1/4 cups rolled oats in the container of a food processor. Process 1 minute.

3. Beat the butter with both sugars in the large bowl of an electric mixer until smooth. Beat in the egg and vanilla.

4. Combine the processed oats with the flour, baking powder, baking soda, and salt. Slowly add to the butter mixture. Stir in the remaining 1/4 cup rolled oats, both chocolates, and the almonds.

5. Drop the cookie batter by tablespoonfuls on ungreased cookie sheets. Bake 10 minutes. Cool on the baking sheet for a few minutes before transferring to a wire rack to cool completely.

Makes about 40 cookies

DASTARDLY HASH

WHAT MAKES a chocolate chip cookie dastardly? The outright borrowing of a famous ice cream flavor: namely, chopped Heath Bars. This is a cookie with crunch, munch, and crackle (to bend another well-turned phrase toward the oven)—and was invented in Jackson Hole, Wyoming.

1 cup all-purpose flour

1/2 teaspoon baking soda

1/2 teaspoon salt

4 tablespoons (1/2 stick) unsalted butter, softened

1/4 cup vegetable shortening

3/4 cup sugar

1 tablespoon instant coffee powder

1 tablespoon boiling water

1 large egg

3 (1.2 ounces each) Heath Bars, chopped

3 ounces (1/2 cup) semi-sweet chocolate chips

1. Preheat the oven to 375° F.

2. Sift the flour with the baking soda and salt in a bowl.

3. Beat the butter and shortening with the sugar until creamy.

4. Stir the coffee powder with the boiling water in a small bowl until smooth. Beat into the batter. Beat in the egg. Stir in the flour mixture; mix well. Stir in the Heath Bars and chocolate chips.

5. Drop the cookie batter by tablespoonfuls onto greased cookie sheets. Bake 10 minutes. Cool on the baking sheet for a few minutes before transferring to a wire rack to cool completely.

Makes about 24 cookies

BROWN DIAMOND CHIPS

WE ALL KNOW that "diamonds are a girl's best friend," but these diamonds are everyone's friend. Made of soft wheat flour, the stuff dream desserts are made of, these cookies are utterly irresistible. Brown sugar in the devising adds a touch of caramel flavor to the batter. Neither over-crisp, nor under-soft, but happily betwixt and between. They are habit forming, so pass the milk!

1/2 cup (1 stick) unsalted butter, softened

1/4 cup dark brown sugar (packed)

2 large egg whites

Pinch of salt

1/2 teaspoon vanilla

3/4 cup cake or soft wheat flour

3 ounces (1/2 cup) semi-sweet chocolate chips

1/4 cup chopped nuts

1. Preheat the oven to 350° F.

2. Beat the butter with the sugar in the large bowl of an electric mixer until light. Beat in the egg whites and salt until mixed. Beat in the vanilla.

3. Add the flour to the mixture and beat on low speed until mixed. Stir in the chocolate chips and nuts.

4. Drop the cookie batter by rounded teaspoonfuls onto greased cookie sheets, placing them about 2 inches apart. Gently press down the tops. Bake until edges begin to brown, 8 to 10 minutes. Cool on the baking sheet for a few minutes before transferring to a wire rack to cool completely.

Makes about 18 cookies

CHOCOLATE CHIP MERINGUES

I HAVE a sneaking suspicion that the Kellogg's Company had a hand in developing the following formula, as a lot of people my age seem to have grown up with similar meringue cookies. Corn flakes is one of the main ingredients. Though it sounds high-blown, this is one of the most satisfying munchies for kids of all ages.

3 large egg whites

1/4 teaspoon salt

1/4 teaspoon vanilla

1 1/2 cups sugar

3 cups corn flakes, lightly crushed

6 ounces (1 cup) semi-sweet chocolate chips

1. Preheat the oven to 350° F.

2. Beat the egg whites with the salt and vanilla in the large bowl of an electric mixer until frothy. On high speed, beat in the sugar, 1 tablespoon at a time, until a stiff meringue is formed. Fold in the corn flakes and chocolate chips.

3. Drop the cookie batter by tablespoonfuls onto greased cookie sheets. Bake 12 to 15 minutes. Cool on the baking sheet for a few minutes before transferring to a wire rack to cool completely.

Makes about 36 cookies

RENO REFRIGERATOR
CHOCOLATE CHIPS

NO GAMBLE, this cookie is devised of rolled dough, crammed with chocolate, which is refrigerated before it is cut, sliced, and baked to sweet perfection. What makes a Reno, Nevada chocolate chip different from rank and file chips? Milk chocolate. You'll know they're high rollers at first nibble.

1 cup sifted all-purpose flour	1/2 cup sugar
1 teaspoon baking powder	1/2 teaspoon vanilla
1/4 teaspoon salt	3 tablespoons sour cream
1/4 cup vegetable shortening	4 ounces milk chocolate, chopped (do not use chips)

1. Sift the flour with the baking powder and salt into a bowl.

2. Beat the shortening with the sugar in the medium bowl of an electric mixer until light. Beat in the vanilla and sour cream. Stir in the flour mixture; mix well. Stir in the chopped chocolate. Refrigerate, covered, at least 1 hour or until ready to use. (The dough can be made up to a week in advance.)

3. Preheat the oven to 350° F.

4. Divide the cookie batter in half and roll each half on a lightly floured board until slightly more than an inch in diameter. Cut the roll into about 1/4-inch thick slices and place on lightly greased baking sheets.

5. Bake until the edges turn golden, 10 to 12 minutes. Cool on the baking sheet a few minutes before transferring to a wire rack to cool completely.

Makes about 48 cookies

CHIP MINTIES

When the mint is in the liquor and its fragrance on
     the glass,
It breathes a recollection that can never, never pass.
          —Clarence Ousley

THE MINT is in the liquor, but the "liqueur" is in the chocolate chip cookies. One of the world's favorite combinations of flavors—chocolate and mint— in one chewy bite.

1 cup plus 2 tablespoons all-purpose
    flour

1/2 teaspoon baking soda

1/4 teaspoon salt

1/2 cup (1 stick) unsalted butter,
    softened

3/4 cup sugar

1 large egg

2 tablespoons white crème de menthe

6 ounces (1 cup) semi-sweet chocolate
    chips

1. Preheat the oven to 350° F.

2. Sift the flour with the baking soda and salt into a bowl.

3. Beat the butter with the sugar in a large bowl until light. Beat in the egg and crème de menthe. Stir in the flour mixture; mix well. Stir in the chocolate chips.

4. Drop the cookie batter by rounded teaspoonfuls onto lightly greased baking sheets, about 2 inches apart. Press flat. Bake 8 minutes. Cool on the baking sheets for a few minutes before transferring to a wire rack to cool completely.

Makes 24 cookies

Chowders

Of soup and love, the first is best.
                                    —Old Spanish proverb

OF SOUP and chowder, however, the second is best. Because chowder is one soup that cannot be made without love.

The word *chowder* is a corruption of a French name for a huge copper vessel known as *la chaudière* in which all such creamy farragos were stirred up. Once upon a time, chowder was only made as a communal dish prepared by the wives of coastal fishermen in France as a thanksgiving offering to God for returning their husbands and sons from the sea. Each homecoming seaman threw a share of his catch into the pot and all friends and relatives within traveling distance were invited to share in the feast. Now that's definitely a dish with love as one of its ingredients.

Before long, communal chowders became an accepted form for expressing gratitude in France. In farm communities, for instance, a portion of each landowner's yield was voluntarily dispatched to the town's soup pot every fall—to celebrate another fruitful harvest. In time the custom made its way north.

Fishermen and farmers in England were simmering benediction chowders long, long before the first British colonists set foot in the Americas. When they did, the first arrivals were unfortunately neither fishermen nor farmers (nor hunters for that matter), and found themselves hard put to give thanks with any show of bounty. So the thanksgiving chowder went unstirred. That is until the local Indians taught the newcomers how to snare small fish with

169

nets and thicken their soups with "coarse corn siftings." It was not until the late seventeenth century, however, that the most famous of all American chowders (the ubiquitous clam) came into being.

As the story goes, a shipwreck was responsible for the invention. A band of Breton sailors, cast adrift when their vessel foundered off the coast of Maine, swam ashore to safety. Taking stock of the "beached" provisions, they discovered they had only ship's biscuits (hard crackers), some potatoes, and salt pork—but, as luck would have it, one of the big galley pots, *la chaudière,* came floating in as well. Being resourceful fellows (and French in the bargain), they placed the biscuits, potatoes, and salt pork in the pot over an open fire and improvised, digging fresh clams from the sand and picking savory onions and green herbs along the beach. Adding spring water, they stirred the pot in relays until the brew was ready. The happy end to this tale is not just the steaming bowl of *chaudres* they consumed before bedding down on the beach, but the celebration of a new and decidedly New World dish. Thanks were given then. And thanks are still being given for this wonderful soup by clam chowder lovers everywhere.

As progress moved, so did chowder. In time, dense clam and fish concoctions were joined by vegetable and even poultry fabrications. Everything that grew, flowered, or fattened in our native land found its place in the pot. A totally American chowder became our favorite mess of pottage; made and consumed with lots of *love,* needless to say.

Some Challenges For the Chowder Pot

In theory, a chowder is just a thickened soup devised of fish, seafood, or vegetable. But that's where the theory ends. Chowder must be slurpable, yet not watery. Thick, but not stewlike. Optimally, a chowder should have a smooth texture, whether it is thickened with crackers, potatoes, cream, rice, or even an occasional bean.

Though all early chowder recipes always included crackers or, more accurately, "biscuits" in the ingredient list, their use as a thickener now-a-days has become the exception, rather than the rule. Even those who insist on making the dish with absolute authenticity, must settle for the ubiquitous soda cracker instead of the hard-floury pilot or ship's biscuit of earlier times.

Basic techniques for their use, however, have not changed. Always soak the crackers first, whether in milk or water, before adding them to a chowder.

An 1871 version of chowder by Mary Cornelius that appeared in *The Young Housekeeper's Friend* cites one of the earliest prescriptions:

Fry three or four slices of salt pork, soak a dozen hard crackers, cut up four or five onions. When the pork is fried brown take it out, and lay in half of the crackers, and half the onions. Cut up the cod, and lay the pieces next, then the rest of the crackers and onions, season it with pepper and salt, pour boiling water enough into the kettle to cover the whole. Let it stew moderately an hour.

However you choose to make a pot of chowder, remember some serious cooking maxims. If the mixture becomes too thick as it simmers, merely add liquid (milk, water, broth) to thin it to a desired texture. If, on the other hand, the soup seems too diluted, the best means I know to give it body is the addition of what the French call *beurre manie*. Easier to produce than pronounce, it is a smooth paste composed of equal amounts of softened butter and flour, beaten together with a spoon until smooth. A tablespoon of this mixture will usually thicken 3 to 4 quarts of soup, but it should be added to the pot by teaspoons and stirred well after each addition. Raise the heat slightly so the *beurre manie* cooks and fuses into the body of the chowder.

Chowders, like most soups, benefit by being made the day before serving to allow the flavors to mingle. When making fish chowders in advance, it is advisable to add the fresh fish only after the chowder has cooked and the kettle removed from heat. The fish will cook as the soup cools, but will not be mushy when it is reheated.

GREAT DISHES have always stimulated the written word. And so it goes with chowder. Monumental essays on the subject have appeared in print over the years, but in my view, the definitive thoughts on this homely elixir are still the province of M.F.K. Fisher, originally published in *How To Cook A Wolf,* back in 1942:

> There are some proud boosters of regional cookery who say that a chowder made with anything but crumbled soda crackers is heinous and insulting. They can but ignore the potatoes, then, and substitute their chosen thickener, and feel happy.
>
> There is another well-worn controversy among chowder-lovers as to which is correct, the kind made with milk or the kind made with tomato and water. Long ago it may have been dependent on transportation and climate and so forth, so that in the winter when the cow was still fresh there was milk, and in the summer when the tomatoes were plump and heavy they were used . . .
>
> Who knows? Furthermore, who cares? You should eat according to your own tastes, as much as possible, and, if you want to make a chowder with milk and tomato, and crackers and potatoes, do it, if the result pleases you (which sounds somewhat doubtful, but possible).

Taking a leaf from Mrs. Fisher, I will confess that I hardly ever add crackers to chowder. To my tongue, crackers are a textural intrusion and in this cook's opinion, chowder should always be smooth based, even when it is studded with diverse ingredients and flavors. In any case, this is the quintessential comfort food in a bowl! To prove the point, have a dozen of the most comforting chowders I know.

PORTSMOUTH FISH CHOWDER

MY FIRST taste of a genuine East Coast chowder took place in a small waterfront seafood restaurant in Portsmouth, New Hampshire overlooking the Piscataqua River toward Maine. It was a rich, golden soup that I have never forgotten. This is my sense-memory recollection of that dish.

2 tablespoons unsalted butter
1 medium onion, finely chopped
1 clove garlic, minced
1/2 red bell pepper, finely chopped
1 medium carrot, diced
2 medium baking potatoes (about 1 pound), peeled, cubed
4 cups fish stock (see page 378)
2 teaspoons all-purpose flour

2 1/2 cups heavy or whipping cream
1 pound white fish fillets (cod, flounder, petrale sole), cut into 1-inch pieces
1/2 pound bay scallops
Dash of hot pepper sauce
Salt and freshly ground black pepper
2 egg yolks
Chopped fresh parsley

1. Melt 1 tablespoon butter in a large heavy saucepan or Dutch oven over medium-low heat. Add the onion; cook 1 minute. Add the garlic; cook 4 minutes longer. Stir in the bell pepper, carrot, and potatoes until well coated with the onion mixture. Add the fish stock. Heat to boiling; reduce the heat. Cook, covered, over medium-low heat until the vegetables are tender, about 20 minutes.

2. Mix the remaining 1 tablespoon butter with the flour until smooth. Stir into the chowder along with 2 cups of the cream. Heat to boiling; reduce the heat. Cook over medium-low heat 2 minutes. Add the fish and scallops; cook 4 minutes longer. Add the hot pepper sauce, and salt and pepper to taste. Reduce the heat to very low.

3. Whisk the egg yolks with the remaining 1/2 cup cream in a bowl. Whisk in 1/4 cup hot chowder. Slowly stir this mixture back into the chowder. Cook over low heat 2 minutes. Do not allow to boil. Sprinkle with parsley.

Serves 6

NEW ENGLAND CLAM CHOWDER

THE MONIKER should really be Gardiner's Bay Clam Chowder, for those waters off Long Island's East End provide the most succulent clams to be found anywhere along the Atlantic coast. And that's where I choose to live *and* make chowder.

1 1/2 to 2 quarts quahogs or chowder clams

1 teaspoon baking powder

1/4 cup diced salt pork

1/2 cup (1 stick) unsalted butter, softened

1 cup water

1/2 cup dry white wine

2 sprigs parsley plus chopped fresh parsley for garnish

1 bay leaf

1 small onion, whole, plus 1 large onion, finely chopped

1 large clove garlic, minced

1 rib celery, finely chopped

2 tablespoons minced green bell pepper

2 medium baking potatoes, peeled, diced

2 cups milk, scalded

2 tablespoons all-purpose flour

2 cups heavy or whipping cream

Dash of hot pepper sauce

Dash of Worcestershire sauce

1/4 teaspoon chopped fresh thyme, or a pinch of dried

Salt and freshly ground black pepper

1. Scrub the clams well and place in a large pot. Cover with cold water and stir in the baking powder. Let stand 30 minutes. Rinse under cold running water; drain. (The clams will expunge themselves of any sand.)

2. Meanwhile, cook the salt pork in boiling water 3 minutes. Drain.

3. Place the clams in a large pot. Add 2 tablespoons butter, the water, wine, parsley sprigs, bay leaf, and the whole onion. Cover and heat to boiling over high heat. Reduce heat to medium and cook, covered, until the clams begin to open, 3 to 5 minutes. Remove from heat. (Do not overcook—the clams will be open far enough to pry open with a knife if necessary.) Discard any unopened clams. Remove the clams from their shells over the pot, catching all the juices. If the clams are large, cut them in half. Cover and reserve. Strain the juices and keep warm.

4. Sauté the salt pork in a large heavy saucepan or Dutch oven over medium heat until golden, about 4 minutes. Drain all but 1 tablespoon fat from the pan and add 2 tablespoons butter. Add the chopped onion; cook 1 minute. Add the garlic, celery, and green pepper; cook 5 minutes. Add the potatoes, scalded milk, and clam juice. Heat to boiling; reduce the heat. Cook, covered, over medium-low heat until potatoes are tender, about 20 minutes.

5. Mix 3 tablespoons butter with the flour in a bowl until smooth. Stir into the chowder along with the cream. Heat to boiling; reduce the heat to medium-low; cook 5 minutes. Add the hot pepper sauce, Worcestershire sauce, thyme, and salt and pepper to taste. Continue to cook until the chowder is thickened, about 4 minutes. Add the reserved clams; cook 2 minutes longer. Stir in the remaining 1 tablespoon butter. Sprinkle with chopped parsley.

Serves 6 to 8

POTATO AND LEEK
SEAFOOD SLURP

"SOUP AND FISH explain half the emotions of life." So wrote British wit Sydney Smith (1771–1845). No further amplification needed, for the following combination represents two of the best ingredients nature has to offer. This result may have some English or French influences, but it is otherwise pure Schulz.

2 strips bacon

1 large leek, washed, finely chopped

1 large clove garlic, minced

1/2 teaspoon chopped fresh thyme, or a pinch of dried

1 medium rib celery, finely chopped

1 1/2 pounds potatoes (about 3 medium), peeled, cubed

3 1/2 cups chicken broth

1/4 pound medium shrimp, shelled, deveined, halved

1/2 pound thick fish fillets (cod, haddock, etc.), cubed

1/2 pound bay scallops

Salt and freshly ground black pepper

Chopped fresh parsley

1. Sauté the bacon strips in a large saucepan over medium heat until crisp. Drain on paper towels. Crumble and reserve.

2. Add the leek to the bacon drippings; cook over medium-low heat 1 minute. Add the garlic and thyme; cook 2 minutes longer. Stir in the celery; cook, covered, 10 minutes.

3. Add the potatoes and chicken broth to the leek mixture. Heat to boiling; reduce the heat. Cook, covered, over medium-low heat until the potatoes are very tender, about 20 minutes.

4. Transfer about 1 1/2 cups soup, mostly potatoes, to the container of a food processor. Process until smooth. Stir back into the soup and add the shrimp. Heat to boiling; reduce the heat; cook 1 minute. Stir in the fish and scallops; cook 3 minutes longer. Add salt and pepper to taste. Serve sprinkled with parsley.

Serves 4

SEATTLE SALMON CHOWDER

FRENCH FOOD writer James de Coquet wrote in *Le Figaro* (1975) that, "Salmon are like men: too soft a life is not good for them." Only salmon of fortitude—the kind that swim up the rivers of the Northwest yearly—are right for the following Washington State inspired chowder. It takes a rugged fillet to stand up to strong flavors such as tomato and dill.

2 tablespoons unsalted butter

1 large onion, finely chopped

1 clove garlic, minced

3 cups fish stock (see page 378)

1 cup chicken broth

1 can (8 ounces) tomatoes, crushed

1/2 teaspoon sugar

Pinch of dried thyme

1 large potato, peeled, cubed, rinsed in cold water

1 teaspoon lemon juice

Salt and freshly ground black pepper

10 ounces fresh salmon, cut into 1-inch cubes

3 tablespoons chopped fresh dill

1. Melt the butter in a large heavy saucepan over medium-low heat. Add the onion; cook 1 minute. Add the garlic; cover and cook 5 minutes longer. Remove cover and stir in the fish stock, chicken broth, tomatoes, sugar and thyme. Heat to boiling; reduce the heat. Simmer, uncovered, 5 minutes. Add the potatoes and lemon juice. Continue to cook, uncovered, until the potatoes are tender, about 12 minutes.

2. Gently stir the salmon into the chowder and cook until the fish flakes easily with a fork, about 7 minutes. Sprinkle with dill.

Serves 4

WINTER SQUASH AND
SHRIMP CHOWDER

ONE OF chowder's great gifts is its utter malleability. In the next Mid-Atlantic bequest, some totally alien ingredients (such as butternut squash, pepper, ham, and shrimp) form an unexpectedly delicate balance.

3 tablespoons unsalted butter

1 bunch scallions, green tops and white bulbs, finely chopped (about 1 1/3 cups)

1 large clove garlic, minced

1 small red bell pepper, seeded, finely chopped

1/4 cup chopped fresh parsley plus extra for garnish

2 tablespoons chopped fresh basil, or 1 teaspoon dried

1 butternut squash (2 pounds), peeled, seeded, diced

1 small ham bone, or 1/2 pound chunk of smoked ham

1 quart chicken broth

1/2 teaspoon ground allspice

1/4 teaspoon ground mace

Pinch of freshly grated nutmeg

2 medium potatoes (about 1 1/4 pounds), peeled, diced

1 cup heavy or whipping cream, at room temperature

1/2 pound fresh shrimp, shelled, deveined, cut into pieces

1. Melt the butter in a large pot or Dutch oven over medium-low heat. Add the scallions; cook 3 minutes. Stir in the garlic and bell pepper; cook 3 minutes longer. Add 1/4 cup parsley, the basil, squash, and ham bone or ham. Stir well and add the chicken broth. Sprinkle with allspice, mace, and nutmeg. Heat to boiling; reduce the heat. Simmer, partially covered, 25 minutes.

2. Add the potatoes and cream. Return mixture to boiling; reduce the heat. Simmer, partially covered, until the potatoes are tender, about 25 minutes longer. Remove ham, adding some meat if desired.

3. Add the shrimp to the chowder. Cook, uncovered, over low heat until the shrimp turn pink, about 3 to 4 minutes. Serve sprinkled with parsley.

Serves 6

VERMONT CHEDDAR CHOWDER

VERMONT is a cold weather state where kitchen ingenuity is a necessity to endure the long, hard winters. One of the rugged state's prime offerings is a white-gold cheddar cheese and the best, to my mind, is produced at the Cheese Factory in Grafton. This cheese is also the basis of a zesty chowder that will bring pride to any tureen on or off Vermont turf.

2 tablespoons unsalted butter

2 small onions, halved, sliced

2 teaspoons all-purpose flour

2 small potatoes (12 ounces), peeled, diced

1 cup chicken stock (see page 378)

4 cups milk

1/4 teaspoon celery seed

1/2 teaspoon English dry mustard

1/2 teaspoon Hungarian hot paprika

1 1/2 cups grated sharp cheddar cheese

Salt and freshly ground black pepper

Croutons (optional)

1. Melt the butter in a large saucepan over medium-low heat. Add the onion; cook 5 minutes. Sprinkle the onion with flour and stir in the potatoes, chicken stock, milk, and celery seed. Heat to boiling; reduce the heat. Cook, covered, over medium-low heat 25 minutes.

2. Stir the mustard and paprika into the chowder. Cook, uncovered, 5 minutes. Remove from heat, stir in the cheese, and season with salt and pepper to taste. Serve with croutons if desired.

Serves 6

Clam chowder controversies rage on and on. More precisely, contentious disputes over what is (and what is not) an appropriate ingredient in the chowder pot seem never to end.

Laws banning the use of the tomato in chowders have actually been proposed in certain New England states. A Maine politician once called tomato's intrusion into the pot, "The work of Reds," seeking to undermine "our most hallowed tradition," even going so far as to suggest that any housewife or chef caught with the offending member in their soup be forced "to dig a barrel of clams at high tide!"

Actually, the blame lies with Italian-American cooks. Manhattan clam chowder made its first appearance at New York Italian seafood restaurants in the 1930s. The soup was based on a gutsy Neapolitan speciality known as *zuppe di vongole*. The *zuppe*, however, did not survive the sea change, and ended up, in the words of the late James Beard, as a "rather horrendous soup . . . which resembles a vegetable soup that accidentally had some clams dumped into it." Despite the naysayers, fifty years later, Manhattan (or red) clam chowder remains as popular in the environs of the Empire State as its creamy counterpart does from Buzzard's Bay to Bar Harbor.

"NOT MANHATTAN"
TOMATO AND CLAM CHOWDER

EVEN A CHOWDERHEAD could not mistake the following pink amalgam for the tomato-clam source of James Beard's fulmination. This pacific elixir is one of the great soups of the world—and if Manhattanites don't agree, it's out of culinary chauvinism—or plain chagrin.

4 tablespoons (1/2 stick) unsalted butter
1 medium onion, finely chopped
1 large clove garlic, minced
4 allspice berries, crushed
1 teaspoon fennel seeds, lightly crushed
1 medium rib celery, finely chopped
12 large shucked clams with juice
    (about 2 pints)

Bottled clam juice, if necessary
2 tablespoons all-purpose flour
1 can (28 ounces) plum tomatoes,
    drained, chopped (about 2 cups)
3 cups light cream or half-and-half
2 teaspoons chopped fresh basil, or
    1/2 teaspoon dried
Freshly ground black pepper

1. Melt the butter in a large saucepan over medium-low heat. Add the onion; cook 1 minute. Add the garlic; cook 2 minutes longer. Add the crushed allspice, fennel seeds, and celery. Cook, covered, stirring occasionally, 15 minutes.

2. Meanwhile, drain the clams, reserving the juice. You should have about 1 3/4 cups juice. (Add bottled clam juice if you have less.) Chop the clams and set aside. (You should have about 1 3/4 cups.)

3. Sprinkle the vegetables with the flour. Stir in the clam juice and tomatoes. Heat to boiling; reduce the heat. Cook, covered, stirring occasionally, over medium-low heat 45 minutes.

4. Add the light cream, basil, and the clams to the chowder. Heat to boiling; cook 1 minute. Turn off the heat and let stand, covered, 5 minutes for the tastes to meld. Sprinkle with pepper before serving.

Serves 6 to 8

TOMATO AND SWEET POTATO CHOWDER

IT'S REALLY no surprise that New Jersey is called the Garden State, for the ripest, rosiest tomatoes in the nation grow there. The territory also yields a banner crop of sweet potatoes every fall. Here is a vegetable chowder devised of the dual bounty. It's rich, spicy, and pure Jersey gold on the spoon.

2 tablespoons unsalted butter
1 medium onion, chopped
1 large rib celery, minced
1 pound sweet potatoes, peeled, diced
1 cup beef broth
4 large ripe tomatoes (2 pounds),
    peeled, seeded, chopped

1 teaspoon sugar
1/2 teaspoon salt
1/8 teaspoon freshly ground black
    pepper
1/8 teaspoon ground cinnamon
Pinch of freshly grated nutmeg
2 tablespoons chopped fresh parsley

1. Melt the butter in a large saucepan over medium-low heat. Add the onion; cook 5 minutes. Stir in the celery and sweet potatoes. Cook 2 minutes longer.

2. Add the beef broth and tomatoes to the chowder and sprinkle with sugar. Heat to boiling; reduce the heat. Cook, covered, over medium-low heat 30 minutes.

3. Remove 1 cup of chowder from the pot and transfer to a blender container. Blend until smooth carefully, as the hot liquid will expand. Return the puréed mixture to the chowder and add the salt, pepper, cinnamon, and nutmeg. Cook, uncovered, 5 minutes. Sprinkle with parsley before serving.

Serves 4

SOUTHWESTERN CHEESE
AND CHILE CHOWDER

FROM NEW MEXICO, the following is a wonderful blending of all good things inherent to the Southwest. Although you can substitute Monterey Jack for the sharp cheddar cheese, I find that cheddar gives the chowder a more pronounced flavor and makes it more aesthetically appealing as well.

1 tablespoon olive oil

1 tablespoon unsalted butter

1 medium onion, chopped

1 large clove garlic, minced

1/4 teaspoon chopped fresh oregano, or a pinch of dried

1/4 teaspoon ground cumin

4 teaspoons all-purpose flour

1 jalapeño pepper, seeded, deveined, minced

1 large red bell pepper, seeded, chopped

1 can (4 ounces) mild green chiles, chopped

1 cup fresh corn kernels (from 2 large ears)

3 cups chicken broth

Salt and freshly ground black pepper

1 cup lightly packed sharp cheddar cheese

1 tablespoon chopped fresh cilantro (Chinese parsley)

1. Heat the oil with the butter in a large saucepan over medium-low heat. Add the onion; cook 1 minute. Add the garlic; cook 4 minutes longer.

2. Whisk the oregano, cumin, and flour into the onion mixture. Cook, stirring constantly, 2 minutes. Stir in the peppers, corn, and chicken stock. Heat to boiling; reduce the heat. Simmer, uncovered, 30 minutes.

3. Add salt and pepper to taste to the chowder and remove from the heat. Stir in the cheese, sprinkle with cilantro, and serve immediately.

Serves 4

CHICKEN, MUSHROOM, AND RICE CHOWDER

"CHOWDERATION" is what they say in polite Kentucky circles, when they mean to say "damn." I received this recipe from a soft-spoken Kentuckian (who lives in Covington) with the following amendment: "This is a real Bluegrass dish because everything in it is fresh, grown or raised within a five-mile radius. The only chowderation problem . . . finding a plump enough bird for leftovers the day after!"

1 whole chicken (2 1/2 to 3 pounds)

1 unpeeled onion, halved

1 large carrot, sliced

1 large rib celery, roughly chopped

1 parsnip, sliced

4 sprigs fresh parsley plus chopped fresh parsley for garnish

8 black peppercorns

6 cups chicken broth

2 cups water

6 ounces mushrooms, sliced

4 teaspoons lemon juice

2 tablespoons unsalted butter plus 1 teaspoon, softened

3 medium leeks, washed, sliced

1 clove garlic, minced

1/2 cup long grain rice

1 teaspoon all-purpose flour

1 cup heavy or whipping cream

Pinch of freshly grated nutmeg

Salt and freshly ground black pepper

1. Place the chicken in a large pot and add the onion, carrot, celery, parsnip, parsley sprigs, peppercorns, chicken broth, and water. Heat to boiling; reduce the heat. Simmer, covered, until chicken is tender, about 50 minutes.

2. Remove the chicken to a plate. Cool slightly and remove the meat from the bones. Return the skin and bones to the stock and continue to cook, uncovered, over medium heat until stock has reduced to about 6 cups, about 15 minutes. Strain. Chop enough of the chicken to make 1 cup. Reserve remaining chicken for use at another time.

3. Meanwhile, sprinkle the mushrooms with 1 tablespoon lemon juice. Let stand 10 minutes.

4. Melt 2 tablespoons butter in a large saucepan over medium heat. Add the mushrooms and cook, stirring constantly, until the mushrooms release their liquid and are lightly browned, about 5 minutes. Reduce heat to medium-low and stir in the leeks and garlic. Cook, stirring frequently, 5 minutes. Stir in the rice and add the 6 cups chicken stock. Heat to boiling; reduce the heat. Simmer, covered, 25 minutes.

5. Stir the flour with 1 teaspoon softened butter in a small bowl until smooth. Set aside.

6. Remove 1/2 cup of the mixture and transfer to a blender container. Add the cream. Blend until smooth being careful, as the hot liquid will expand. Pour this mixture back into the chowder. Stir in the flour mixture. Heat to boiling; reduce the heat. Gently simmer 10 minutes. Stir in the reserved chicken, the nutmeg, the remaining 1 teaspoon lemon juice, and salt and pepper to taste. Cook 3 minutes longer. Sprinkle with chopped parsley before serving.

Serves 4 to 6

MICHIGAN WHITE BEAN CHOWDER

MICHIGAN is the largest bean producing state in the country. A Michigan friend tells me that if you live in the northern half of the state where beans are grown, these legumes come to the table at every meal in one form or another—and no one complains, because beans keep them healthy, wealthy, and wise. One of the most beatific bean inventions I have ever sampled is the following Michigan chowder awash with fresh vegetables and nubbins of smoky pork. A veritable bean-bonanza.

1 pound dry white beans

2 tablespoons unsalted butter

4 tablespoons olive oil

4 medium leeks, washed well, chopped (about 1 1/2 cups)

4 large cloves garlic, minced

2 medium carrots, finely chopped

2 stalks celery, finely chopped

1 1/2 to 2 pounds smoked pork hocks, excess fat removed

4 cups beef broth

2 cups chicken broth

2 cups water

1/2 teaspoon chopped fresh sage, or 1/8 teaspoon dried

1 bay leaf

Chopped fresh parsley

1. Place the beans in a large pot and cover with cold water. Heat to boiling; boil 2 minutes. Remove from heat and let stand 1 hour. Drain.

2. Heat the butter with the oil in a large heavy pot or Dutch oven over medium-low heat. Add the leeks; cook 1 minute. Add the garlic, carrots, and celery; cook 5 minutes longer. Add the pork hocks, beans, beef broth, chicken broth, water, sage, and the bay leaf. Heat to boiling; reduce the heat. Simmer, covered, over medium-low heat until the beans are tender, about 1 1/2 hours. Remove from the heat and allow to cool slightly.

3. Discard the bay leaf. Remove the pork hocks and cut off the meat. Chop into pieces. Set aside.

4. Place 4 cups of the bean mixture, in two batches, in the container of a food processor. Process until smooth. Stir back into the chowder. Stir in the pork pieces and reheat over medium-low heat until warmed through. Sprinkle with parsley before serving.

Serves 6 to 8

GREAT LAKES CORN CHOWDER

THE IROQUOIS Indians tell a tale of a famine that once threatened their entire population. A killing drought seared the fields, dried the streams, and even withered the wild grasses they might have chewed for survival. Starving, they prayed to the gods for guidance. A spirit from the sky, taking pity on the Indian nation, came down to earth to walk in their lands. Wherever she trod, the earth grew soft and fertile, and corn stalks miraculously sprang forth in the marks of her moccasins. By the time her "walk" was over, the starving tribe was saved. To commemorate the blessing, corn has grown in abundance in the Great Lakes region from that day to this. And corn chowders (like the one that follows), bloom there as well.

6 medium ears corn

6 strips bacon

1 small yellow onion, finely chopped

1 small green bell pepper, seeded, finely
chopped

1 red cayenne pepper, seeded, deveined,
chopped

1 small rib celery, finely chopped

3 medium, peeled, seeded tomatoes,
finely chopped

1 teaspoon salt

1 teaspoon sugar

1/8 teaspoon ground allspice

1 small bay leaf

2 medium potatoes (about 1 pound),
peeled, diced

3 cups light cream or half-and-half at
room temperature

Freshly ground black pepper

Chopped fresh parsley

1. Cut the kernels from the corn cobs at about half their depth into a bowl. Then, with the back of the knife, scrape the cobs up and down to remove all "milk" from the cobs; add to the kernels. Set aside. The mixture will resemble scrambled eggs.

2. Sauté the bacon in a large heavy pot until crisp. Drain on paper towels. Crumble and set aside.

3. Discard all but 3 tablespoons bacon drippings from pot. Add the onion and cook over medium heat until golden, 4 to 5 minutes. Add the peppers and celery; cook 2 minutes longer.

4. Add the tomatoes to the onion/pepper mixture, scraping the bottom and sides of the pot with a wooden spoon. Add the salt, sugar, allspice, bay leaf, potatoes, and corn. Cook over medium heat until the mixture begins to sizzle. Reduce heat to low. Cook, covered, stirring occasionally, 30 minutes.

5. Stir the cream into the chowder and heat just to boiling. Remove from heat and add pepper to taste. Sprinkle with the crumbled bacon and chopped fresh parsley.

Serves 4 to 6

Cole Slaws

Cabbage, n: A familiar kitchen-garden vegetable about as large and wise as a man's head.

—Ambrose Bierce, *The Devil's Dictionary* (1911)

BLESS the "wise" man who turned the lowly cabbage into one of the most popular salads on earth!

Cabbage is as old as the hills. Older than some hills, actually. The queen of the *brassica* family, it was introduced into Britain by the Romans. The British brought cabbage with them to America. Or was it the Dutch? Or the Germans? Nobody seems to know for sure. But one thing is certain, both the Dutch and the Germans were eating cold cabbage salads long before the plant took root in the Colonies. The Dutch called their salad *koolsla* (cabbage salad), but the word *cole* is actually old English for the German *kohl*, which means "cabbage." To make matters more confusing, early American recipes generally referred to the dish as "cold slaw," which in turn gave rise to "hot slaw."

Salad sleuths say that the dish was known in America by 1792, but did not appear in cookbooks until the nineteenth century. One of the earliest cole slaw recipes appeared in *Directions for Cookery*, by Eliza Leslie, printed in Philadelphia in 1837. Miss Leslie is often credited with being one of a small cadre of cookery writers who logged recipes solely for American housewives—as opposed to those Anglophile anthologists who simply borrowed, sometimes word for word, prescriptions and formulas from earlier English works. Miss

Leslie recommended boiled dressing for her slaw. Hers involved warmed, beaten eggs and was the mainstay for not only cole slaw, but potato salad too, well into the twentieth century when commercial, bottled mayonnaise became widely available.

A boiled dressing, however, was not the only way "to coat a cabbage." Lettice Bryan, a much under-acknowledged pioneer in American cooking, published recipes for both "cold slaugh" and "warm slaugh" in the *Kentucky Housewife* in 1839. She sluiced her salads with cider vinegar, a practice that spread first to the Midwest, then the Southwest, where it is still a popular condiment-seasoning to this very day.

Cole slaw recipes are as diverse as the backgrounds of the cooks who toss them together. Dressings that seem to alter at state and even county borders reflect not only the lineage of a cook's forebears, but also a dogged sense of adaptability, making use of whatever ingredient was plentiful in one area and varying the mixture when pickings were slim in another. If food historians took a long hard look at cole slaw's evolution, I suspect they would come to the conclusion that necessity was not merely the mother of its invention, but a serious root in the cabbage's family tree.

Some Slaw Suggestions   Actually, the only controversy about cole slaw is *not* what ingredients are tossed together with cabbage in its making but, rather, how the cabbage itself is treated. Nothing mars a good slaw more than improperly cut "hunky" pieces of cabbage. In the late nineteenth century, cabbage for slaw was sliced with a razor-sharp cleaver into paper-thin shreds. Hard on the knuckles without a doubt, but every strand, after the cleavage, proved silky enough to mate with any dressing a homemaker had in mind. The mid-twentieth century, era of kitchen gadgetry, brought the four-sided grater into American kitchens. Awkward to be sure, some mighty fine shredding could still be effected by shaving a head of green against its sharp prestamped blades. And if any stray bit of epidermis sometimes seasoned the dish, who cared? Or even questioned? In the late 1960s, along came Carl Sontheimer, promoting a new multi-use kitchen-wiz gadget from France to the stars of the cooking world. That super-gadget was, of course, the Cuisinart.

So long cleaver, so long grater. Hello, minced cole slaw!

The Cuisinart food processor, and its kitchen look-alikes, unquestionably do a fine job shredding cabbage. But as someone who in the past spent countless hours in a city kitchen smaller than a newspaper stand, I find it more burdensome to rout out a machine from the detritus of a cabinet than to do it the old-fashioned way. To my mind, a sharp knife is still the best tool. I even use it in the country, in spite of the fact that my food processor is prominently placed on the kitchen counter. Why? Because it produces the least amount of waste. The secret to shredding cabbage? Trim the outer leaves of the head and discard them. Remove the core and then separate all the leaves. Stack the leaves on a cutting board, one on top of the other. Then, using a sharp, flat-bladed chef's knife, start slicing crosswise. If you prefer your cabbage finely chopped rather than in shreds, simply turn the board at a 90 degree angle and repeat the process. Zingo! Perfect every time.

You will note that some of the recipes in this chapter require the cabbage to be presoaked first in ice water. This is not done to remove any "cabbagy" taste, but rather to ensure that the cabbage remains crisp and unwilted when it is finally mixed with its dressing. Frankly, I feel it is the option of the person at the bowl. If you opt for a presoak, however, make certain all the slices are well drained and dried before proceeding with the recipe.

ONE OF THE main reasons cabbage was copiously eaten as salad in the old days is that heads are fairly easy to grow, and more to the point, store well after being harvested. Cabbage requires minimal, or no, refrigeration. Even today, for much the same reasons, cabbage ranks as one of the top produced vegetables in the world. But most importantly, cabbage salads have a positive effect on the human system. Cabbage is naturally high in potassium (163 milligrams per portion) and relatively low in calories (a scant 60 per cup). It is also loaded with natural fiber that inhibits and retards the growth of incipient cancer cells in the body. So, start chopping away!

GRANDMOTHERLY COLE SLAW

In the night the cabbages catch at the moon, the leaves drip silver, the rows of cabbages are series of little silver waterfalls in the moon.
—Carl Sandburg

DURING the day, the same cabbages catch at picnickers, cookout enthusiasts, and all manner of deep-dyed alfresco aficionados as they are converted into cole slaw from one end of the country to the other. For a single helping of some old-fashioned grandmotherly slaw always leads to two or three more. I learned this salad from Bert Greene in 1972, who learned it from his grandmother forty years before. It was a staple at every one of his summer outings—and I've never seen anyone pass a spoonful by. That's a real taste testimonial.

6 strips bacon
3 pounds red cabbage, cored, shredded
2 large carrots, shredded
1 green bell pepper, seeded, finely
　chopped

1/4 cup milk
1 1/2 tablespoons Dijon mustard
1 teaspoon bouillon powder
1/2 teaspoon chili powder
1/2 teaspoon salt

1 medium onion, finely chopped

2 cups mayonnaise

1/2 cup sour cream

1/4 teaspoon freshly ground black pepper

1 tablespoon chopped fresh parsley

1. Sauté the bacon in a heavy skillet until crisp. Drain the bacon on paper towels. Crumble and set aside. Reserve 3 tablespoons bacon drippings.

2. Combine the cabbage with the carrots, bell pepper, and onion in a large bowl.

3. Whisk the bacon drippings with half of the mayonnaise in a medium bowl. Whisk in the sour cream, milk, mustard, bouillon powder, chili powder, salt, and pepper. Whisk in the remaining mayonnaise. Pour over the cabbage mixture. Toss well. Sprinkle with parsley and serve at room temperature.

Serves 10

OKLAHOMA SLAW

ONE OF THE many offsprings of Lettice Bryan's original vinegary formula, the next recipe is probably somewhat sweeter than her straight-laced version, but in effect, creates a tantalizing sweet and sour salad. Note that the slaw must be made 6 to 8 hours prior to serving. Do not, however, make it the day before as the cabbage will become soggy.

1 pound green cabbage, cored, shredded, chopped

1/2 green bell pepper, minced

3 tablespoons minced onion

1 cup cider vinegar

2/3 cup sugar

1/2 teaspoon celery seed

1/2 teaspoon English dry mustard

1/4 cup water

Chopped fresh parsley

1. Combine the cabbage with the bell pepper and onion in a large bowl.

2. Combine the vinegar with the sugar, celery seed, and mustard in a medium saucepan. Heat, stirring frequently, to boiling; boil until thick, about

15 minutes. Remove from heat and whisk in the water. Immediately pour over the cabbage mixture. Toss well. Refrigerate, covered, 6 to 8 hours.

3. Just before serving, remove from refrigerator and drain some of the liquid from the cole slaw which will be quite wet. Sprinkle with parsley.

Serves 4 to 6

RUTH HENDERSON'S
CONNECTICUT YANKEE SLAW

RUTH HENDERSON, wife of Skitch Henderson and multi-talented creator of The Silo, a fabulous cooking school and cookware shop in New Milford, Connecticut, is not only a culinary dynamo, but a dynamite cole slaw maker as well. Her unusual recipe for a cole slaw that pairs unlikely pineapple with cabbage, follows:

2 pounds green cabbage, cored, shredded

1 large carrot, peeled, grated (about 1/2 cup

1 medium onion, finely chopped

1 small red bell pepper, seeded, finely chopped

1 can (8 ounces) pineapple chunks packed in juice

1 cup mayonnaise

1/4 cup sour cream

1 1/4 teaspoons tarragon vinegar

1/4 teaspoon crushed dried hot red peppers

1 slice dried pineapple, slivered (about 1/3 cup)

Thinly sliced green bell pepper rings (optional)

1. Combine the cabbage with the carrot, onion, and bell pepper in a large bowl.

2. Drain the pineapple, reserving 1/4 cup juice. Chop the pineapple and add to the cabbage mixture. Toss well.

3. Combine the mayonnaise with the sour cream in a medium bowl.

Whisk in the reserved pineapple juice, the vinegar, and hot peppers. Pour over the cabbage mixture. Toss well. Garnish with slivered dried pineapple and the pepper rings if you so desire. Serve slightly chilled.

Serves 8 to 10

NEW ENGLAND SLAW
WITH BOILED DRESSING

THE "CLASSIC," a recipe that dates back to Colonial America, or maybe beyond. Sure-handed cooks will whip up the dressing for this salad in a small, heavy-duty saucepan. The secret, however, is to cook the dressing quickly, yet not let the eggs clot. The addition of the vinegar will add a slight curdle to the sauce after it is cooked, giving it a golden "boiled" look. Boiled dressing is best made, and the cabbage dressed, several hours before it is to be served.

1 pound green cabbage, cored, shredded, chopped

1 small onion, grated

1/4 teaspoon caraway seeds

1/2 teaspoon English dry mustard

1/2 teaspoon all-purpose flour

1/2 teaspoon salt

1 tablespoon sugar

2 large egg yolks

1/2 cup milk, hot

3 tablespoons cider vinegar

1. Place the cabbage in a large bowl of ice water. Let stand 1 hour.

2. Drain the cabbage and squeeze dry. Combine with the onion and caraway seeds in a large bowl.

3. Combine the mustard, flour, salt, and sugar in the top of a double boiler. Whisk in the egg yolks and hot milk. Cook, stirring constantly, over boiling water until thick, about 5 minutes. Remove from heat and whisk in the vinegar. Pour over the cabbage mixture. Toss well. Allow to cool slightly and then refrigerate, covered, at least 1 hour.

Serves 4 to 6

"STOP HERE" SLAW

AN UNRECONSTRUCTED member of the '60s generation, I am most aware of my allegiance to that decade in terms of the music of the time. Recently, when I found myself free and footloose in Kansas City, I spent almost 2 hours trying to place where "12th Street and Vine" intersected because a song "Kansas City, Kansas City, Here I come" had pointedly informed the kids of my generation that "they've got some crazy little women there, and I'm gonna get me one." Unfortunately, the crazy little women obviously moved on to greener pastures elsewhere. But that section of Kansas City still offers some of the best barbecue and tantalizing slaws in the Midwest. The one below came with a hand-lettered sign in the window that sums up the entire situation: "Stop Here! Ribs and Slaw!"

1 pound green cabbage, cored, shredded, chopped

1 large carrot, finely grated

1 stalk celery, finely chopped

1/2 cup small radishes, cut into thin rounds

1 tablespoon minced red onion

1/2 teaspoon celery seed

1 clove garlic, crushed

1/2 teaspoon salt

1 teaspoon Dijon mustard

1/4 cup vegetable oil

1/4 cup V-8 juice or Bloody Mary mix

2 teaspoons red wine vinegar

Pinch of Hungarian hot paprika

1/8 teaspoon freshly ground black pepper

1. Combine the cabbage, carrot, celery, radishes, red onion, and celery seed in a large bowl. Toss well.

2. Mash the garlic with the salt in a small bowl with the back of a spoon. Whisk in the remaining ingredients and pour over the cabbage mixture. Toss well. Serve at room temperature or slightly chilled.

Serves 4 to 6

MADELINE'S RED HOT SLAW

"HE WHO has plenty of pepper will pepper his cabbage," said Publilius Syrus boldly. In this case, it is "She," Madeline Rogers, a great cook and former editor at the New York *Daily News,* who has a gift for peppering a dish without any perceptible pain to the taste buds. Like her personality, her recipe is spicy, unorthodox—yet totally wholesome and unhackneyed. Use as much crushed dried hot red pepper as you dare.

1 pound cabbage, cored, shredded, chopped

1 small white turnip, peeled, finely shredded

1 small carrot, peeled, finely shredded

5 small red radishes, trimmed, chopped

1 small red onion, minced

1/4 cup chopped fresh parsley

2 tablespoons chopped fresh dill

4 tablespoons cider vinegar

6 tablespoons mayonnaise

1/2 teaspoon salt

1/4 teaspoon freshly ground black pepper

1/4 teaspoon crushed dried hot red peppers, or more to taste

1. Combine the cabbage, turnip, carrot, radishes, onion, parsley, and dill in a large bowl. Toss well.

2. Whisk the vinegar with the mayonnaise, salt, ground pepper, and crushed hot peppers in a small bowl. Pour over the cabbage mixture. Toss well. Serve well chilled.

Serves 4 to 6

ROASTED PEPPER SLAW

Such epithets, like pepper,
    Give zest to what you write;
And, if you strew them sparely,
    They whet the appetite:
But if you lay them on too thick,
    You spoil the matter quite!

—Lewis Carroll

WHEN THE peppers are roasted and toasted red, green, and yellow bells, one can never lay them on too thick. For this slaw is dependent on unbridled pepper flavor.

1 small red bell pepper
1 small green bell pepper
1 small yellow bell pepper
1 pound green cabbage, cored and shredded
1 large shallot, minced
1 large clove garlic, peeled
1 jalapeño pepper, seeded, deveined, chopped

2 scallions, chopped
1 large tomato, peeled, seeded, chopped
3 tablespoons white wine vinegar
5 tablespoons olive oil
Good dash of hot pepper sauce
Salt and freshly ground black pepper
3 tablespoons chopped fresh cilantro (Chinese parsley)

1. Roast the peppers over a gas flame or under a broiler until charred all over. Carefully wrap the peppers in paper towels and place in a plastic bag. Let stand 5 minutes, then rub the skin from the peppers with paper towels. Core the peppers and cut into thin strips.

2. Combine the cabbage, peppers, and shallot in a large bowl. Toss well.

3. With the motor running, drop the garlic into the feed tube of a food processor. Drop in the hot green pepper and scallions. Process until fairly smooth. Add the tomato, vinegar, and oil. Process until smooth. Add hot pepper sauce and salt and pepper to taste. Pour over the cabbage mixture. Toss well. Serve at room temperature or slightly chilled, sprinkled with cilantro.

Serves 4 to 6

WICHITA "RUSSIAN" COLE SLAW

THE "RUSSIAN" who lent his nationality to the next cole slaw's dressing is long since forgotten, but every good cook in Wichita, Kansas, and a twenty-mile radius knows how to whip a batch together. Russian cole slaw can be made in 5 minutes flat, but note that it should stand 30 minutes or longer in a cool place before serving so the flavors properly meld. Refrigerate this dish if you plan to make it farther in advance. One to 2 hours is the ideal time to let the slaw sit.

1 pound red cabbage, cored, shredded, chopped

4 scallion bulbs, minced

1/2 cup mayonnaise

1 tablespoon sweet pickle relish

1/4 cup prepared chili sauce

Salt and freshly ground black pepper

1. Combine the cabbage and scallion bulbs in a large bowl. Toss well.

2. Beat the mayonnaise with the relish and chili sauce in a medium bowl. Pour over the cabbage mixture. Toss well, adding salt and pepper to taste. Let stand at least 30 minutes before serving.

Serves 4 to 6

TUNA SLAW

IF "eating fish will make a man spring," then eating fish combined with wonderfully healthful cabbage will make his *heart* soar and his tastebuds vibrate. This dish is of Italian origin (from Genoa), but I came upon it in Provincetown, Massachusetts—Portuguese-American territory.

1 pound red cabbage, cored, shredded, chopped

1 small red onion, minced

1 can (6 1/4 ounce) tuna, packed in olive oil

4 anchovy fillets, finely chopped

6 tablespoons olive oil

2 tablespoons red wine vinegar

4 teaspoons heavy cream

1/4 teaspoon freshly ground black pepper

1 tablespoon chopped fresh parsley

1. Combine the cabbage with the onion in a bowl.

2. Drain the tuna, pouring off the oil into a small bowl. Flake the tuna and add to the cabbage mixture.

3. Mash the anchovies with the reserved oil until smooth. Whisk in the olive oil, vinegar, cream, and pepper. Pour over the cabbage mixture. Toss well. Sprinkle with parsley and serve at room temperature.

Serves 4 to 6

Cole slaw has a habit of appearing on every hamburger plate, sandwich platter, and even "blue plate" special in family run businesses around the country. Sad to say, in big city eateries it is usually made far from the kitchen in a large steel drum by a commercial purveyor and sold bottled to the restaurant—with no taste and very little texture. But this was not always the case.

In *The Grapes of Wrath,* John Steinbeck remembers the multitude of hamburger stands and luncheonettes that dotted the way from Oklahoma and Arkansas to California along Route 66. " 'Al & Susy's Place,' 'Carl's Lunch,' 'Will's Eats,'—Board and bat shacks. Two gasoline pumps in front, a screen door, a long bar, stools and a footrail." He noted that every special was served with a saucer or a fluted paper cupful of cole slaw that was refillable on request—though the pickle relish was not. In counter-man parlance, cole slaw cost less than 3 cents a portion, but bought ten times the good will—even if an odd customer sometimes left most of it on his plate.

Impressions last, Depressions come and go. Good cole slaw goes on forever.

MARY SURINA'S WILTED SLAW

MY DEAR friend Mary Surina of San Pedro, California, sent me the next recipe, which has been in her family for years. Mary wrote that this cole slaw is part of her Yugoslavian heritage. A heritage she was born into, paradoxically, in Tacoma, Washington. What's so unusual about Mary's slaw is the combination of cabbage and hot cooked potatoes. It's like nothing you will ever eat, I promise!

1 large potato, peeled, cubed	1/3 cup olive oil
1 clove garlic, minced	1 pound green cabbage, cored, shredded
1 teaspoon salt	Freshly ground black pepper
2 1/2 tablespoons white wine vinegar	Chopped fresh parsley

1. Cook the potato in boiling salted water until tender, about 15 minutes.

2. Meanwhile, mash the garlic with the salt in a small bowl with the back of a spoon until a paste is formed. Whisk in the vinegar and oil.

3. Place the cabbage in a large bowl. Drain the potato and immediately mash the potato into the cabbage. The cabbage will wilt slightly. Pour the dressing over the cabbage mixture. Toss well. Add pepper to taste, sprinkle with parsley, and serve immediately.

Serves 4 to 6

SACKS' SOHO SLAW

IN NEW YORK City's SoHo, there is a small food shop on Prince Street called simply Donald Sacks. Mr. Sacks is something of an eclectic with salads. The following I do declare to be one of his best. An interesting sidelight about this vaguely Oriental cole slaw is a mild pickling process which removes a major dose of the onion's acidity and the cabbage's sting.

1 1/2 pounds green cabbage, cored, shredded

3 tablespoons coarse salt

4 medium red onions, thinly sliced

2-inch piece gingerroot, peeled, minced

3/4 cup lemon juice

1/3 cup olive oil

1 tablespoon fennel seeds, crushed

1/4 teaspoon freshly ground black pepper

1 1/2 cups chopped fresh dill

1. Toss the cabbage with 2 tablespoons salt in a large bowl; let stand 4 hours. Cover with cold water and let stand 1 hour longer.

2. Meanwhile, toss the onions with the remaining 1 tablespoon salt in a medium bowl; let stand 1 hour. Cover with cold water and let stand 1 hour longer.

3. Rinse the cabbage and onions, separately, under cold running water. Drain well and gently squeeze dry. Combine the cabbage and onions in a large bowl.

4. Press the gingerroot in a fine-mesh sieve over a small bowl to extract all the juice. Discard the pulp. Whisk the lemon juice, oil, fennel seeds, and pepper into the ginger juice. Pour over the cabbage mixture. Toss well. Add the fresh dill and toss once more. Serve well chilled.

Serves 6 to 8

DREAMY WHIPPED SLAW

... cabbages, whose heads, tightly folded see and hear nothing of this world, dreaming only on the yellow and green magnificence that is hardening within them.

—John Haines

WHO WOULDN'T dream of this Iowan specialty? A cole slaw of such rarity, it incorporates whipped cream in the dressing. Don't be afraid of the calories;

the cabbage itself is not only good for you, but low-tabbed enough to offset the dressing.

1 pound green (or red) cabbage, cored, shredded, chopped

1 small red onion, minced

1 small green bell pepper, finely chopped

3 tablespoons red wine vinegar

2 tablespoons sugar

1/2 teaspoon salt

1/4 cup mayonnaise

1/2 cup heavy or whipping cream

1. Combine the cabbage with the onion and pepper in a large bowl. Toss well.

2. Whisk the vinegar with the sugar, salt, and mayonnaise in a small bowl until smooth.

3. Beat the cream in a large bowl until very stiff. Beat in the mayonnaise mixture. Pour over the cabbage mixture. Toss well. Serve at room temperature or slightly chilled.

Serves 4 to 6

Fried Chicken

Only a *Southerner* knows how to fry a chicken. *Period!*
—An anonymous Chicken Fryer

THE "PERIOD" in that sentence is somewhat of a wry joke. Since it was a *southerner* who founded the most berated fried chicken franchise of all time, "Kentucky Fried." And in many parts of this country, the late Colonel Sanders is still held in a thrall reserved only for Santa Claus, Uncle Sam, and the Pillsbury Doughboy. But not (no, never) in the South, where the mere mention of the man's name and image of his glistening visage raises hackles from Virginia to Mississippi, including his home state where outspoken Louisville cooks claim that his saturated animal fat deep-fried, not-so-finger-lick'n-good-for-you product has done as much to disinter the reputation of honest fried chicken as "whatchamacallit's McNuggets!" That may seem a harsh judgment to anyone not born and bred "below the Line," but after all, fried chicken *did* have its roots in the South.

The classic American dish is generally assumed to have evolved from the traditional fricassee (sometimes called "frigasee" in the old days) that was served in homes all over the South in the latter half of the eighteenth century. Most early fricassee recipes called for the chicken to be fried in some kind of fat, most often lard, before it was gently stewed to tenderness. Who first decided that it might be a great idea to fry the chicken and eliminate the liquid is not known. But, it was Mrs. Mary Randolph who first published a recipe for fried chicken in *The Virginia Housewife* in 1824. Her instructions follow:

Cut them (chickens) up as for the fricassee, dredge them well with flour, sprinkle them with salt, put them into a good quantity of boiling lard, and fry them a light brown; fry small pieces of mush and a quantity of parsley nicely picked, to be served in the dish with the chickens, take half a pint of rich milk, add to it a small bit of butter, with pepper, salt, and chopped parsley; stew it a little, and pour it over the chickens, and then garnish with the fried parsley.

Mrs. Randolph, incidentally, was one of the first cookbook writers who paid particular attention to the dredging process. She wrote:

Fish, and all other articles for frying, after being nicely prepared, should be laid out on a board and dredged with flour or meal mixed with salt; when it becomes dry on one side, turn it and dredge the other.

Edna Lewis, a notable southern food writer of today, always lets her chicken rest for an hour after dredging, to ensure crispness. But that is her personal caveat and personal caveats are what fried chicken is all about.

Fried Chicken . . . A Personal Affair Ask ten (no make that ten thousand!) cooks how to fry a chicken and you're likely to receive ten million different answers. Some presoak the chicken in milk, or buttermilk, or water, or vinegar and water; others don't bother. There are those who insist on only bacon drippings or lard for frying; and there is the butter-only crowd. Health-minded fryers use safflower or corn oil; but a few cheat and admit to adding a tablespoon of bacon drippings or butter to the oil for flavor. Whether a chicken piece is skinned or left as is before it is coated is yet another point of disagreement. And coatings? Depending on their locales, chicken fryers are highly prejudiced in the matter of what crusts a bird. In the South, flour, seasoned with salt, freshly ground pepper, and cayenne pepper or even freshly grated nutmeg on occasion, is the only viable option. In other parts of the country, cornmeal, bread crumbs, bran, and even crushed corn flakes will blanket a breast or drumstick. The correct way to dredge the pieces, however, is one point generally agreed on. Not in a bowl, not in a plastic Zip-Lock, but in a *brown paper bag. "Period!"*

The "right" skillet in which to fry chicken is never really an issue, since the vast majority of practiced chicken fryers overwhelmingly prefer an old-time cast-iron skillet, one that has been seasoned with long use. What *is* an issue, however, is whether chicken should be fried covered, or partially covered, or is it best to let the pieces spatter (uncovered) to Kingdom Come? Not to mention the stove, sink, and ceiling.

Regardless of one's inclinations, there are a few basic rules to keep in mind. For starters, always use a large enough skillet, 12 to 14 inches (for 1 chicken) so the pieces are not crowded. If such a size skillet is not available, it is far better to use two than to cramp the chicken, for it will never turn crusty in an undersized pan. The oil, butter, lard, shortening, or whatever, should never come more than a third up the sides of the chicken pieces—it is not meant to be "deep-fried." Always start frying chicken at medium-high heat, and then reduce the heat to medium, turning the chicken only once, until it is golden brown. Turn the pieces with tongs; never use a fork or you will pierce the flesh and lose natural juices. After a chicken is fried, it must be drained. Once again, a brown paper bag is the best bet because it is highly absorbent and leaves the chicken pieces crisp. Paper towels have a tendency to turn the pieces soggy.

Perhaps a word on the chicken itself is in order. Since more and more Americans are demanding *taste* and quality in their foods, "farm raised" chickens ("free range" is a misnomer for most of these birds) are becoming increasingly available at markets. If you haven't tried one as yet, do yourself a favor and look for a source. Mass-produced counterparts don't even come close to the flavor and texture of the true barnyard variety that are not plumped up on hormones and are permitted to wander and develop naturally. Some investigation might be necessary, but it is well worth the time and trouble. The first place to start is with kosher butchers. Kosher law insists that chickens must be fed only pure grains and be killed humanely only hours before they are sold. Failing that, look in the Yellow Pages under the wholesale section for "fresh poultry and eggs." You'll be amazed how many chicken breeders are willing to supply your local needs. But be forewarned—because of the extra effort and time, barnyard birds do cost a few dollars more than the supermarket brands.

*I*N CASE you didn't notice, Mrs. Randolph, in her recipe, instructed the cook to pour cream gravy *over* the fried chicken. A notion that makes a Southerner's gorge rise at the very thought. Below the Mason-Dixon Line, not even a drop of gravy is permitted to touch crisply fried chicken. After all, why go through the toil and trouble of making chicken crisp if you're going to douse it with a sauce? Gravy, they say, is meant to be poured in a puddle over a mound of whipped potatoes—and that is that. But whether you make cream gravy or not, always serve fried chicken warm, *never* piping hot; the juices need to settle before a diner's fork pierces the crusty skin.

America's mighty fine fried chicken makers influenced the following collection of fried chicken recipes, using odd-fellow ingredients or techniques. And, even if you're of the school that holds to the line that the only way to fry a chicken is your own (Southerner or no), all I can suggest is "try it, you might like it."

OLD DOMINION FRIED CHICKEN
WITH CREAM GRAVY

Two people never lit a fire without disagreeing!
—Irish proverb

PARTICULARLY, that is, under a pan of spattering chicken! To throw ourselves right into the fray, let's start with a controversial recipe. This genuine Virginia family recipe was literally handed down from a Black slave kitchen "Mammy" through passing generations—and is still prepared the same way today. Unorthodox by any standards, it calls for the chicken to be totally skinned before it is dredged, fried in butter, and "finished" in a warm oven. And the cream gravy is really made with cream *and* bourbon, too! Hardly traditional, but then a dish that's undeniably *wonderful* rarely is.

1 chicken (about 4 pounds), cut into
    serving pieces
1/2 cup all-purpose flour
Salt and freshly ground black pepper
Pinch of ground allspice
1/8 teaspoon freshly grated nutmeg

1/2 cup (1 stick) unsalted butter
2 tablespoons vegetable oil
1 cup chicken stock (see page 378)
1 cup heavy or whipping cream
1 teaspoon bourbon
Chopped fresh parsley

1. Remove the skin from the chicken pieces. Combine the flour, 1/2 teaspoon salt, 1/4 teaspoon pepper, the allspice, and nutmeg in a large paper bag. Place the chicken, a few pieces at a time, in the bag and shake to coat evenly with the flour mixture. Set aside 2 tablespoons leftover flour mixture.

2. Preheat the oven to 275° F.

3. Melt the butter with 1 tablespoon oil in a large, heavy (cast-iron preferred) skillet over medium-low heat. Gently place the chicken in the skillet. Do not crowd the pieces; use two skillets if necessary. Sauté the chicken over medium-low heat until golden brown. This should take 12 to 15 minutes per side. Reduce heat if the chicken is cooking too fast. Add more oil if needed.

4. When the chicken is crisp, drain on a paper bag. Transfer to a shallow

heatproof serving platter and place uncovered, for at least 30 minutes, but no longer than 1 hour, in the preheated oven.

5. Meanwhile, drain all but 2 tablespoons drippings from the skillet. Stir in the reserved flour and cook, stirring constantly, over medium-low heat 2 minutes. Whisk in the chicken stock, scraping the bottom and sides of the skillet with a wooden spoon. Whisk in the cream and cook, stirring occasionally, 20 minutes. Add salt and pepper to taste. Stir in the bourbon.

6. To serve, spoon some of the cream gravy over the chicken and sprinkle the chicken with parsley. Pass the remaining gravy on the side.

Serves 4

KANSAS CITY FRIED

THERE MAY be more than one fried chicken produced in the golden mean that stretches from Missouri to Kansas, but even the best of those pale before the following creation. It was the inspiration of the late "Chicken Betty" Lucas who became somewhat of a legend in her time. Working most of her life for others, she always made her chicken in heavy cast-iron skillets. No matter how many batches she cooked up in a night, she would never, ever use a deep-fryer. "Chicken Betty" did, however, go against the rules— she partially covered her frying pieces and turned them as often as she felt like it.

1 large egg

2/3 cup milk

1 chicken (about 4 pounds), cut into serving pieces

Salt and freshly ground black pepper

1 teaspoon chicken bouillon powder

2 cups plus 1 1/2 tablespoons all-purpose flour

1 cup lard

1 cup vegetable shortening

2 cups light cream or half-and-half

1. Whisk the egg with the milk in a shallow bowl until light. Dip the chicken pieces into this mixture. Allow excess liquid to drain off. Place the chicken on a large plate. Sprinkle both sides generously with salt, pepper, and the bouillon powder.

2. Place 2 cups flour on a large plate. Roll the chicken pieces in the flour, pressing and pounding the flour into the chicken.

3. Preheat the oven to 250° F.

4. Heat the lard with the vegetable shortening in a large heavy (cast-iron preferred) skillet. Add the chicken pieces to the skillet; they may be close together but should not touch. Fry the chicken over medium-high heat until golden brown, about 7 minutes per side. Reduce the heat to medium-low. Cover the skillet about two-thirds of the way. Cook, turning the chicken several times until crisp and the juices run yellow when pricked with a fork, about 20 minutes. The chicken will be deep copper in color. Reduce heat if the cooking is going too fast. Drain the chicken pieces on a paper bag. Keep warm in the preheated oven.

5. Drain all but 2 tablespoons drippings from the skillet. Stir in 1 1/2 tablespoons flour. Cook, stirring constantly, over low heat, 2 minutes. Whisk in the light cream. Heat to boiling, stirring the bottom and sides of skillet with a wooden spoon. Boil until thickened. Add salt and pepper to taste. Serve with the chicken.

Serves 4

ATLANTA-STYLE FRIED CHICKEN

ATLANTAN'S do not all have typical southern tastebuds. Perhaps it was the city's burning during the Civil War that left them with a taste for fiery things. The following eclectic fried chicken is first soaked in ice water, then dredged in flour that is liberally spiked with both cayenne and hot paprika before it is fried. It's not meant for your mild-appetited Aunt Minnie, but everyone else will drool. Incidentally, cold beer puts out the fire!

1 chicken (about 3 1/2 pounds), cut
    into serving pieces
Ice water
1/2 cup all-purpose flour
1 tablespoon cayenne pepper

1 tablespoon Hungarian hot paprika
1 teaspoon salt
1/2 teaspoon freshly ground black
    pepper
1 1/2 cups vegetable oil

1. Place the chicken in a glass or ceramic bowl. Cover with ice water, including the ice. Let stand, covered, 1 hour. Drain and pat dry.

2. Combine the flour with the cayenne pepper, paprika, salt, and freshly ground pepper in a paper bag. Place the chicken, a few pieces at a time, in the bag and shake to coat evenly with the flour mixture. Place the coated chicken on a plate. Let stand 15 minutes.

3. Heat the oil in a large, heavy (cast-iron preferred) skillet over medium heat until hot but not smoking. Add the dark meat of the chicken and cook, partially covered, 5 minutes. Turn the chicken over and cook, partially covered for 5 minutes longer. Add the white meat of the chicken and continue to cook, partially covered, 12 minutes. Turn all the pieces over and cook, partially covered, until crisp and the juices run yellow when pricked with a fork, about 12 minutes longer. Drain on a paper bag.

Serves 2 to 4

HONEY AND BACON FRIED CHICKEN
WITH LEMON GRAVY

MATCHLESS recipes stem from unlikely places. This recipe was uncovered in a "bed-and-breakfast" establishment not far from Nashville, Tennessee. For a minor increment fried chicken was served at lunch at this small and tidy place. When the meal was praised to the heavens, the owner confessed the recipe was not exactly her own. Her grandmother brought a honey-baked chicken as part of her dowry when she sailed from Scotland to America in the late nineteenth century. In the intervening years, she altered her chicken to its present sensational rendition. After I ate extra portions for two days, she generously donated the formula.

1 chicken (about 4 pounds), cut into
    serving pieces
1/4 cup honey
2 tablespoons white wine vinegar
4 strips bacon
1/2 cup vegetable shortening
3 tablespoons all-purpose flour
3 tablespoons whole wheat flour

Salt and freshly ground black pepper
1/4 cup chicken stock (see page 378)
1 cup heavy or whipping cream
1 teaspoon lemon juice
Dash of hot pepper sauce
1 teaspoon chopped fresh chives

1. Place the chicken in a shallow glass or ceramic bowl. Combine the honey with the vinegar and pour over the chicken, turning the pieces to coat with the mixture. Let stand, covered, 2 hours.

2. Sauté the bacon in a 12- to 15-inch cast-iron skillet until crisp. Drain on paper towels. Crumble and set aside.

3. Add the vegetable shortening to the bacon drippings. Heat over medium-low heat until hot.

4. Meanwhile, remove the chicken pieces from the marinade and pat dry. Combine the flours with salt and pepper to taste on a plate. Coat the chicken pieces well with the flour mixture. Set aside 1 tablespoon of the flour mixture.

5. Gently place the floured chicken skin-side down in the hot grease. Slowly fry the chicken pieces until crisp and the juices run yellow when pricked with a fork, about 20 minutes per side.

6. Preheat the oven to 375° F.

7. Drain the chicken pieces on a paper bag and place on a shallow heatproof serving platter. Place in the oven 12 to 15 minutes.

8. Meanwhile, discard all but 1 tablespoon drippings from the skillet. Stir in the reserved 1 tablespoon flour mixture. Cook, stirring constantly, 2 minutes. Whisk in the chicken stock and cream, scraping the sides and the bottom of the skillet. Cook over medium heat until thickened, about 5 minutes. Reduce heat to low and stir in the lemon juice and hot pepper sauce. Add salt and pepper to taste. Stir in the chives.

9. Spoon some of the gravy over the chicken pieces and sprinkle with the reserved bacon. Pass the remaining gravy on the side.

Serves 4

TROPIC BUTTERMILK BATTERED CHICKEN

Good friends, good food, good wine, and good weather—doth a good picnic make.

—Anonymous

THIS RECIPE might be subheaded "The Perfect Picnic Chicken," for the golden skin stays remarkably crisp and crunchy—even after a long day's stint in the refrigerator. The very special rendering is adapted from Joyce LaFray Young's *Tropic Cooking* (10-Speed Press, 1987), virtually a treasury of Southern Florida and Caribbean specialities that are a magnet to the kitchen.

1 chicken (about 3 1/4 pounds), cut into pieces
1 1/2 cups self-rising flour
1 cup buttermilk

Salt and freshly ground black pepper
Freshly grated nutmeg
1 1/2 to 2 cups vegetable shortening

1. Roll the chicken in flour and dip in buttermilk. Shake off the excess buttermilk and roll the pieces once more in the flour. Transfer to a plate, skin-side up. Sprinkle generously with salt, pepper, and nutmeg. Let stand 15 minutes.

2. Melt the shortening in a 12-inch heavy (preferably cast-iron) skillet over medium heat. Gently add the chicken pieces. (The shortening should come at least halfway up the chicken.) Cook covered 10 minutes. Remove cover and continue to fry the chicken, turning once, until crisp and the juices run yellow when pricked with a fork, about 25 minutes longer. Drain on a paper bag.

Serves 2 to 4

FRIED CHICKEN AND HAM
WITH RED-EYE GRAVY

HAM WITH red-eye gravy is generally attributed to the state of Tennessee, but my favorite story is that it came to light during the California Gold Rush days when some hard-drinking forty-niner's pan of fried ham caught on fire. Having nothing at hand but bourbon and a cup of coffee he put out the blaze with both. The resulting dish caught fire too, and inspired hundreds of variations on the theme. The following rendering from unlikely Natchez may be the hands down winner.

1/2 cup all-purpose flour

1/2 teaspoon salt

1/8 teaspoon freshly ground black
    pepper

1/8 teaspoon Hungarian hot paprika

Pinch of freshly grated nutmeg

1 chicken (3 1/2 to 4 pounds), cut into
    pieces

1/2 pound lard

1/2 pound ham steak, cut into 1- by
    3-inch pieces

1/4 cup chicken stock (see page 378)

1/2 cup strong coffee

1/2 teaspoon sugar

1/4 cup milk

1/4 cup heavy or whipping cream

1 1/2 tablespoons bourbon

Chopped fresh parsley

1. Combine the flour with the salt, pepper, paprika, and nutmeg in a medium paper bag. Add the dark meat of the chicken and shake until well coated.

2. Heat the lard in a large, heavy, 2-inch deep skillet until hot. Add the dark meat of the chicken, skin-side down. Cover and cook over medium-low heat 15 minutes. Remove cover, taking care not to drip any liquid into the skillet, and turn the chicken over. Cook, covered, 10 minutes longer. The chicken should be crisp, but light golden in color. Reduce heat if cooking too fast. Drain well on a paper bag.

3. Repeat the flouring process with the white meat of the chicken. Cook, covered, 8 minutes per side. Drain on a paper bag. Allow the pan to cool slightly. Set aside 2 teaspoons of the flour mixture.

4. Preheat the oven to 375° F.

5. Transfer the chicken to a heatproof shallow baking dish. Bake in oven until the juices run yellow when pricked with a fork, about 15 minutes.

6. Meanwhile, drain all but 1 tablespoon drippings from the pan. Place over medium heat. Sauté the ham pieces until lightly browned, about 2 minutes per side. Add to the chicken; bake 10 minutes longer.

7. Reduce the heat under the skillet and stir in the reserved 2 teaspoons flour mixture. Cook, stirring constantly, 1 minute. Add the chicken stock and coffee, scraping the bottom and sides of the skillet. Heat to boiling and add the sugar, milk, cream, and bourbon. Reduce the heat. Simmer, uncovered, until thickened. Spoon some of the gravy over the chicken and ham, then sprinkle with parsley. Pass the remaining gravy on the side.

Serves 4

CAROLINA FRIED

There is but an hour a day between a good housewife and a bad one.
—English proverb

ANOTHER southern rendition, this one from Asheville, North Carolina, can be prepared in less than an hour and guarantees raves as not only a good housewife, but the best "frier" on the block. The chicken pieces in the following recipe are marinated in a combination of honey and apple cider vinegar before being dredged in whole wheat flour and fried in a mixture of vegetable and peanut oil. The delicate balance of flavors is further enhanced by a touch of orange in the gravy. Gravy *on* the chicken, please.

1 chicken (about 3 1/2 pounds), cut
   into pieces
1/2 cup honey
1/4 cup apple cider vinegar
1/2 cup whole wheat flour
Salt and freshly ground black pepper
1/2 cup vegetable oil
1/2 cup peanut oil

1 tablespoon unsalted butter
1 teaspoon slivered orange peel
1 cup chicken broth
1/3 cup heavy or whipping cream
1/8 teaspoon freshly grated nutmeg
Chopped fresh parsley

1. Place the chicken pieces in a shallow glass or ceramic dish. Combine the honey and vinegar in a bowl. Pour over the chicken. Let stand, covered, turning the chicken occasionally, 2 hours.

2. Combine the flour with 1 teaspoon salt and 1/2 teaspoon pepper on a plate. Remove chicken from marinade and roll in the flour mixture to coat. Set aside 2 tablespoons marinade and 1 tablespoon leftover flour.

3 Preheat the oven to 250° F.

4. Heat the oils in a large heavy skillet over medium heat. Fry the chicken pieces, turning often, until crisp and the juices run yellow when pricked with a fork, about 30 minutes. Reduce the heat slightly if the chicken browns too quickly. Drain on a paper bag. Keep warm in the preheated oven.

5. Discard all the grease from the skillet. Add the butter and orange peel. Cook over low heat, stirring often with a wooden spoon, 5 minutes.

6. Sprinkle the orange peel with the reserved 1 tablespoon of flour. Cook 2 minutes. Whisk in the reserved 2 tablespoons marinade, the broth and cream. Heat to boiling; reduce the heat. Cook until thickened, about 3 minutes. Add the nutmeg and salt and pepper to taste. Spoon some of the gravy over the chicken and sprinkle with parsley. Pass the remaining gravy on the side.

Serves 2 to 4

If you think fried chicken partisans are exclusive to the South, disabuse yourself of the notion, please.

In his book, *Third Helpings* (Ticknor and Fields, 1983), Calvin Trillin chronicles what he calls the "fried chicken wars" of Crawford County in southeast Kansas. The nub of this dispute was a small case of rivalry between two local fried chicken emporiums, Chicken Annie's and Chicken Mary's. Fat hit the fire when a local politico sought to have the county road that interfaces both establishments renamed "Chicken Annie's Road." In response, the owners of Chicken Mary's demanded a road sign of their own and hinted that it be altered to read, "Chicken Mary's This Way!" What ensued was a feud. A European feud by Kansas standards, but Balkan unmistakably, since both ladies came from Hungary and retained memories of such conflict in their blood, beside the collections of fine chicken dishes in their heads.

The odd aspect of the Crawford County "fried chicken wars" was that it was mostly talk, bad mouthing, and harmless gossip. And, as it turned out, the feudin' and fussin' had little effect on Crawford County appetites. Though some people ate only at Chicken Mary's and some only at Chicken Annie's prior to the hostilities, everyone seemed to patronize the two interchangeably afterwards. For this is one war that had a happy ending.

Chicken Annie's grandson fell in love with Chicken Mary's granddaughter; both restaurants threw the wedding bash. To return the favor, the young couple opened a fried chicken restaurant of their own, conveniently out of the family bailiwick in Pittsburgh. But if you ask whose recipe they use, don't expect an answer.

FRIED CHICKEN À LA PAPRIKASH

CHICKEN PAPRIKASH is one of the landmark dishes of Austro-Hungary. This rendering comes from Reading, Pennsylvania. How did it get there? One can only surmise in some immigrant's "heckel and peokel" (duffle bag). The recipe is actually a far cry from the original, but then so is Vienna from Reading.

1 chicken (about 3 1/2 pounds), cut into pieces

1/2 lemon

Salt and freshly ground black pepper

1 1/2 teaspoon Hungarian sweet paprika

1/4 cup all-purpose flour

2 tablespoons unsalted butter

2 tablespoons vegetable oil

1 small onion, minced

1/2 cup chicken broth

1/2 teaspoon tomato paste

1/2 cup heavy or whipping cream

1. Rub the chicken pieces with the lemon. Sprinkle with salt, pepper, and 1 teaspoon paprika. Let stand 30 minutes.

2. Roll the chicken pieces in the flour. Transfer to a plate. Set aside 1 tablespoon leftover flour.

3. Preheat the oven to 350° F.

4. Heat the butter with the oil in a large heavy skillet over medium-high heat. Fry the chicken pieces, half at a time, until golden brown on both sides, about 10 minutes. Drain on a paper bag. Transfer to an ovenproof serving dish. Place in the oven until the juices run yellow when pricked with a fork, about 30 minutes.

5. Meanwhile, discard all but 1 tablespoon of the drippings from the skillet. Add the onion and cook over medium-low heat 5 minutes. Sprinkle the onion with the reserved 1 tablespoon flour. Cook, stirring constantly, 2 minutes. Whisk in the chicken broth, tomato paste, remaining 1/2 teaspoon paprika, and the cream. Heat to boiling; reduce the heat. Simmer over medium heat until slightly thickened, about 4 minutes. Add salt and pepper to taste. Spoon sauce over the chicken. Pass the remaining sauce on the side.

Serves 2 to 4

SUNSET FRIED CHICKEN

Poultry is for the cook what canvas is for the painter.
—Brillat-Savarin

FROM TUCSON, where the sun always shines brightly, comes a pink-gold dispensation. The chicken rests for an hour in a tomatoey marinade and then is rolled in a lightened cornmeal coating. It fries to the shade of a painted desert sunset.

1 chicken (about 3 1/2 pounds), cut
    into pieces
1/2 cup V-8 juice
1/4 cup sour cream
1/3 cup plus 1 tablespoon all-purpose
    flour
1/3 cup yellow cornmeal
1/4 teaspoon Hungarian hot paprika

1/8 teaspoon English dry mustard
Salt and freshly ground black pepper
3 tablespoons unsalted butter
1 tablespoon vegetable oil
3/4 cup milk
Dash of hot pepper sauce

1. Place the chicken in a shallow glass or ceramic dish. Combine the V-8 juice and the sour cream. Pour over the chicken. Let stand, covered, turning the pieces once, 1 hour. Remove chicken from the marinade; set aside the marinade.

2. Preheat the oven to 325° F.

3. Combine 1/3 cup flour with the cornmeal, paprika, mustard, and salt and pepper to taste on a large plate.

4. Heat the butter with the oil in a large heavy skillet over medium heat.

5. Coat the chicken pieces with the flour/cornmeal mixture and fry, about half at a time, until golden on both sides, 5 to 8 minutes per side. Drain on a paper bag. Transfer to a shallow baking dish. Place in the oven until the juices run yellow when pricked with a fork, about 30 minutes.

6. Meanwhile, drain all but 1 tablespoon drippings from the skillet. Sprinkle with the reserved 1 tablespoon flour and cook, stirring constantly, over medium heat until the flour begins to turn golden, about 4 minutes. Whisk in the milk and cook until the mixture thickens, 2 to 3 minutes. Reduce

heat to low and whisk in 3 tablespoons of the reserved marinade and the hot pepper sauce. Cook 1 minute. Add salt and pepper to taste. Pass the sauce with the chicken.

Serves 2 to 4

BUFFALO WINGS

THE NEXT recipe is an original. Straight from the Anchor Bar & Grill in Buffalo, New York, where wings made their leap to immortality in the 1960s. There are lots of chicken wing recipes in common currency, but in all the versions I have seen, the hot sauce is brushed on immediately after deep-frying, reducing the bite. It occurred to me that if they were marinated first and fried later, they'd be a heck of a lot zingier. They are, too. As Chaucer said, "Woe to the cook whose sauce has not sting!" So don't stint on the cayenne! And don't forget the celery and blue cheese adjuncts; they help cool the palate.

1 cup cider vinegar

2 teaspoons English dry mustard

1 1/2 teaspoons cayenne pepper

2 teaspoons Worcestershire sauce

1 tablespoon ketchup

1 tablespoon vegetable oil

20 to 24 small chicken wings

Oil for frying

4 stalks celery, cut into 3-inch-long, 1/4-inch-thick strips

Creamy Blue Cheese Dressing (recipe follows)

1. Combine the cider vinegar with the mustard, cayenne pepper, Worcestershire sauce, ketchup, and vegetable oil in a medium saucepan. Slowly heat to just below the boiling point. Let stand 2 hours.

2. Cut the tips off the chicken wings and set aside for use in stocks. Cut the remaining wings in half at the joint. Place in a large bowl and pour the vinegar marinade over the top. Let stand, covered, 3 to 4 hours. Drain; pat dry.

3. Heat enough oil in a heavy pot to deep fry the wings until hot but not smoking. Add the wings. Fry until crisp and the juices run yellow when pricked with a fork, about 12 minutes. Drain on a paper bag and serve immediately with the celery sticks and individual bowls of blue cheese dressing.

Serves 4

CREAMY BLUE CHEESE DRESSING

2 tablespoons minced onion

1 clove garlic, crushed

1/4 cup chopped fresh parsley

1 cup mayonnaise

1/2 cup sour cream

1 tablespoon lemon juice

1 tablespoon white wine vinegar

6 ounces blue cheese, cut into pieces

Salt and freshly ground black pepper to taste

Whisk all ingredients together in a bowl until smooth. Chill well before serving.

Makes about 2 1/2 cups

SOMBRERO FRIED CHICKEN WITH HOMINY AND SALSA RANCHERA

It is not really an exaggeration to say that peace and happiness begin, geographically, where garlic is used in cooking.

—X. Marcel Boulestin

THIS definitive, garlicky, geographic rendering of fried chicken originated in Albuquerque. The chicken is marinated in garlicky salsa before it is fried and then baked, layered on peppery hominy. And yes, the hominy is zapped with more garlic. It's a dish you won't forget.

Salsa Ranchera (recipe follows)

1 chicken (3 1/2 to 4 pounds), cut into
    serving pieces

1 green Cubanelle or Italian (or small
    green bell) pepper

1 red Cubanelle or Italian (or small red
    bell) pepper

1 jalapeño pepper

Vegetable oil or shortening for frying

1/4 cup all-purpose flour

3 tablespoons unsalted butter

1 medium onion, chopped

2 large cloves garlic, minced

1 tomato, seeded, chopped

1 can (29 ounces) white hominy,
    drained, rinsed

1/2 cup grated Monterey Jack cheese

2 teaspoons chopped fresh cilantro
    (Chinese parsley)

1. Make the Salsa Ranchera.

2. Toss the chicken pieces with 1/3 cup of the salsa. Cover the chicken and marinate 2 hours. Set aside remaining salsa.

3. Meanwhile, roast all the peppers over a gas flame or under a preheated broiler until charred all over. Carefully wrap each pepper in paper towels and place in a plastic bag for 5 minutes to cool. Rub off the charred skin with the paper towels. Seed and finely chop the Cubanelle (or bell) peppers. Seed, devein, and mince the chile pepper. Set aside.

4. Heat 1/2-inch oil or shortening in a heavy skillet. Roll the chicken pieces in flour and fry, half at a time, over medium-low heat until golden, about 8 minutes per side. Drain on a paper bag.

5. Preheat the oven to 300° F.

6. While the chicken is frying, melt the butter in a large heavy skillet over medium-low heat. Add the onion; cook 1 minute. Add the garlic and cook until golden, about 4 minutes longer. Add the tomatoes; cook 1 minute. Add the reserved roasted peppers and cook 2 minutes longer. Toss in the drained hominy, remove from heat, and allow to cool slightly.

7. Toss the cheese and the cilantro into the hominy mixture. Spread over the bottom of a shallow buttered baking dish. Add the chicken pieces, tucking gently into hominy mixture. Bake in the preheated oven until chicken juices run yellow when pricked with a fork and the hominy turns a tawny shade, about 40 to 45 minutes. Serve with remaining salsa on the side.

Serves 4

SALSA RANCHERA

1 shallot, minced

1 large clove garlic, minced

1 or 2 jalapeño peppers, seeded (but not deveined), minced

1 medium Anaheim pepper, seeded, finely chopped

1 large fresh tomato, seeded, diced

1 1/2 tablespoons chopped fresh cilantro (Chinese parsley)

1 teaspoon chopped fresh basil, or a pinch of dried

1 tablespoon lime juice

1/4 teaspoon salt

1/4 teaspoon freshly ground black pepper

Combine all ingredients in a bowl. Mix well.

Makes about 1 1/4 cups

OMAHA OVEN FRIED

CONTROVERSIAL beginnings deserve controversial endings. I happen to think oven-fried chicken is delicious—and it certainly keeps the stove top clean. The secret to crisp, crackly chicken is to locate a rack (I use cake racks) over the top of a roasting pan so that the chicken sits over the pan and is thus heated from all sides. Broiler trays have a tendency to turn the chicken soggy. This is a solid Midwestern contribution; another of Nebraska's joys of the larder.

1 chicken (about 3 1/2 pounds), cut into serving pieces

1 1/2 cups milk

2 teaspoons hot pepper sauce

2 teaspoons soy sauce

1/2 cup bran flakes, crushed

1/4 cup all-purpose flour

1/2 teaspoon salt

1/4 teaspoon freshly ground black pepper

1/8 teaspoon ground allspice

1/2 cup (1 stick) unsalted butter

1/2 cup water

1. Place the chicken in a shallow glass or ceramic dish. Combine the milk, hot pepper sauce, and soy sauce in a bowl. Pour over the chicken pieces. Let stand, covered, turning once, 3 hours.

2. Preheat the oven to 375° F.

3. Drain the chicken pieces and pat dry. Combine the crushed bran flakes with the flour, salt, pepper, and allspice in a paper bag. Place the chicken pieces, a few at a time, in the bag and shake to coat evenly with bran/flour mixture. Place the coated chicken, skin-side down, on an oiled rack in a roasting pan. Bake 5 minutes.

4. Meanwhile, melt the butter with the water in a small saucepan. Baste the chicken with the butter mixture. Continue to bake the chicken, basting every 5 minutes, for 25 minutes. Turn the chicken over and continue to bake, basting every 5 minutes with butter mixture and pan juices, until crisp and the juices run yellow when pricked with a fork, about 30 minutes longer.

Serves 2 to 4

Hash

Take hares and hew them to gobbets . . .
Take conies (rabbits) and smite them to pieces . . .
Take chickens and ram them together . . .

A RATHER violent beginning for pacific hash, these somewhat graphic instructions first appeared in *The Forme of Cury* (The Art of Cookery) published around 1390 by the royal cooks who served Richard II. Since average weekend fare at the King's castle consisted of 50 swans, 110 geese, 72 hens, 5 herons, 6 kids, 72 rabbits, 120 peacocks, 60 pullets for jelly plus 132 for roasting, besides assorted cranes, curlews, and other "wilde fowle," the chefs obviously had plenty of leftovers for creative hash-making during the rest of the week.

Hash (from the French *hacher*, meaning "to chop") is, in its simplest form, nothing more than cut up cooked meat or fish warmed in a creamy sauce or gravy. In early Colonial America, hash was made in footed cast-iron pots set over hot coals, and most often appeared at the breakfast table. Very few hash recipes have been passed down through the ages, because using what was on hand was the only prerequisite in making the dish.

Hash became a standard menu item at the "All-U-Kan-Eat-For-a-Nickel" lunch counters that sprang up in the late 1800s, and continued in popularity at diners into the early 1900s. But by the mid-1930s, Depression-minded clientele began to question what actually went into the hash served at these eateries. The term "hash house" became a pejorative description and the dish itself fell from grace in the public view.

Hash's return to glory can be traced, believe it or not, to a Frenchman. When chef Louis Diat was hired to head up the kitchen at the austere Ritz-Carlton Hotel in New York, he included a creamed chicken hash on his menu. To be sure, the rendition was totally French, but hash gained new gastronomic favor with diners under his surveillance, this time with elitist implications. Prior to World War II, it was a legend in literary lunch circles that an aspiring author knew an editor was *really* interested in his work once he was urged to try the Ritz Chicken Hash, most likely because it was the most expensive item on the restaurant's à la carte menu. A version of Diat's classic dish is, to this day, still made at New York's "21" Club. A handful of other restaurants with "serious" kitchens also offer fine hash, if for far more than a nickel.

Hashing it Out   One early recorded recipe for hash is a prescription that has been credited far and wide as an original of Martha Washington's daughter by her first marriage, Nelly Custis Lewis. However, as we live in revisionist times, some food authorities now claim that all recipes credited to Ms. Lewis were stolen outright from Martha herself. Regardless of who the inventor actually was, the recipe is quite basic in its preparation, and worth noting seriously two hundred some years after the fact.

> Cut your meat very thin, and set it on the fire, put to it a few capers and liquor, 2 or 3 ounions, a little spinnage, mint or what other hearbs you please, put in a little vinegar water, gravie and some butter, soe let it stew 2 houres before you serve it up.

As you will discover, methods for making hash are as motley as the leftovers that go into the communal pan. Some hashes use partially cooked vegetables to speed up the cooking process. Others may call for raw vegetables cooked in stock or vegetable juice until soft—but never mushy. Onions and peppers should always be finely chopped to make sure they cook properly. Potatoes, and other vegetables, should be cut into pieces approximately the size of the meat you are basing the hash on. Half-inch cubes are generally your best bet. Bear in mind that a hash is a *fusion* of all the ingredients, so time all your vegetables accordingly.

A practiced hand at making hash insists on using a cast-iron skillet to ensure a crispy crust around the bottom and sides of the hash. You can either flip the hash over and then crisp the other side, or take the easy way out and run the cooked hash under a broiler until the top is nicely browned.

"THE ART of using up leftovers is not to be considered as the summit of culinary achievement."—*Larousse Gastronomique*. The summit, perhaps not, but it is certainly high on anyone's improvisational achievement list, as far as I'm concerned. After all, it does require significant "artistry" to determine what flavors will comingle into a totally new and satisfying meal. Among hashes some are dry and crisp to the tongue, others smooth and creamy. The former type, such as red flannel hash, is generally served with poached eggs. The latter, such as ultimate chicken hash, can be served over toast points. Since the making of hash depends on what the cook has husbanded away in his or her refrigerator, the recipes that follow are meant as guides. Let your imagination (and good taste) be your sole culinary counsel.

ROAST BEEF HASH

It may not be a dish for every occasion, but when it comes to those American foods that somehow always evoke casual warmth, wholesome relaxation, and goodwill, a toothsome hash served with green salad, fresh bread, and premium beer is still pretty hard to beat.

—James Villas

ONE SUCH toothsome dish follows. The recipe is reputed to be the handiwork of one of Brigham Young's wives.

2 1/2 tablespoons unsalted butter

1 medium onion, chopped

1 large clove garlic, minced

1/2 green bell pepper, seeded, finely chopped

1 small rib celery, finely chopped

2 medium potatoes (about 1 pound), unpeeled, cut into 1/2-inch cubes

2 cups chopped leftover roast beef

1/2 teaspoon crushed dried hot red peppers, or more to taste

1 teaspoon chopped fresh basil, or 1/4 teaspoon dried

1/3 to 1/2 cup beef broth

1/2 teaspoon Worcestershire sauce

1/2 teaspoon salt

1/4 teaspoon freshly ground black pepper

Pinch of ground allspice

2 teaspoons cider vinegar

Chopped fresh parsley

1. Melt the butter in a large cast-iron skillet over medium-low heat. Add the onion; cook 1 minute. Add the garlic; cook 4 minutes longer. Add the pepper and celery. Continue to cook 5 minutes.

2. Slowly stir the potatoes and roast beef into the vegetable mixture. Add the hot peppers, basil, 1/3 cup beef broth, the Worcestershire sauce, salt, pepper, and allspice. Mix well. Cook, uncovered, tossing occasionally, 30 minutes. Add more beef broth if mixture is dry.

3. Preheat the oven to 325° F.

4. Transfer the skillet to the oven and bake 30 minutes.

5. Preheat the broiler.

6. Sprinkle the hash with the vinegar and place under the broiler until the hash is very crisp. Sprinkle with parsley.

Serves 4 to 6

WOONSOCKET RED FLANNEL HASH

IN NEW ENGLAND, the classic rendering of this dish is always in dispute. Purists insist the dish be composed of nothing other than bacon, potatoes, and beets. More flexible cooks allow that since the dish was invented to use up leftover corned beef, potatoes, and carrots from a Sunday New England boiled dinner, any ingredient that boiled with the beef was admissable to the sauté pan. This Rhode Island version has all of the above, but is further enriched with a poached egg. It is traditional (no, make that obligatory) to pass chili sauce on the side.

1/2 pound beets, trimmed

2 medium potatoes (about 1 pound), unpeeled

3 cups cooked cubed corned beef

2 carrots, finely chopped

1 small green bell pepper, seeded, finely chopped

1 large onion, finely chopped

1 small clove garlic, minced

3 tablespoons chopped fresh parsley

2 strips thick bacon, chopped

1 teaspoon Worcestershire sauce

1 teaspoon hot pepper sauce

1/4 cup tomato juice (approximately)

Salt and freshly ground black pepper

4 to 6 poached eggs

Prepared chili sauce (optional)

1. Place the beets in a saucepan; cover with cold water. Heat slowly to boiling; reduce the heat. Simmer the beets until barely tender, about 35 minutes. Rinse under cold running water; drain. Remove the skins from the beets. Cube the beets and place in a large bowl.

2. Meanwhile, cook the potatoes in boiling salted water 10 minutes. Drain. Cook slightly and cut into cubes.

3. Lightly toss the potatoes with the beets and add the corned beef, carrots, bell pepper, onion, garlic, and parsley. Toss well.

4. Sauté the chopped bacon in a large cast-iron skillet until crisp. Transfer the bacon to the hash mixture with a slotted spoon. Mix well.

5. Spoon the hash into the skillet with the bacon drippings, pressing the hash down. Cook, uncovered, over medium-low heat 5 minutes. Stir in the

Worcestershire sauce, hot pepper sauce, tomato juice, and salt and pepper to taste. Cook, without stirring, 30 minutes.

6. Preheat the oven to 350° F.

7. Using two large spatulas, turn the mixture over in the pan. (Or flip into a second cast-iron skillet.) Place in the oven and bake until the potatoes are tender and the top is very browned, about 30 minutes. Sprinkle with more tomato juice if the mixture seems too dry. Serve from the skillet, topped with poached eggs. Serve with chili sauce if desired.

Serves 4 to 6

CORINTH HAM AND APPLE HASH

ALONG THE roads and byways of rural Vermont, business booms at smoke houses and local markets from June to November. Hams, smoked over corn cobs, are a Vermont specialty, and as noted elsewhere, some of the crispest apples grown north of the Massachusetts border are found at Vermont farmstands. Late September and early October is the time when thousands of "leafers" (Vermontese for fall tourists who come to witness the season's changes) descend on the state and then ultimately depart with hams and apples in tow. They might do well to come away with the following recipe too. It's yet another wonderful Vermont franchise.

2 large potatoes (about 1 1/2 pounds), unpeeled

3 tablespoons unsalted butter

1 medium onion, chopped

1 clove garlic, minced

2 cups diced cooked ham

1 small red bell pepper, seeded, finely chopped

2 small tomatoes, finely chopped

1/8 teaspoon ground mace

1/2 teaspoon salt

1/4 teaspoon freshly ground black pepper

Pinch of sugar

1 small apple

Juice of 1/2 lemon

3/4 cup prepared chili sauce

3 tablespoons Vermont maple syrup

1. Cook the potatoes in boiling salted water until just barely tender, about 20 minutes. Rinse under cold running water. Cool slightly. Peel and cut into 1/2-inch cubes.

2. Melt the butter in a 12-inch cast-iron skillet over medium heat. Add the onion; cook 1 minute. Add the garlic; cook 4 minutes longer. Add the ham and continue to cook, stirring frequently, until lightly browned, about 5 minutes longer. Reduce the heat.

3. Add the bell pepper and tomatoes to the ham mixture. Sprinkle with mace, salt, pepper, and sugar. Cook over medium-low heat 5 minutes.

4. Meanwhile, peel, core, and dice the apple. Sprinkle with the lemon juice. Combine the chili sauce and maple syrup in a small bowl.

5. Preheat the broiler.

6. Stir the apple into the ham mixture. Cook 1 minute. Add the cooked potatoes and toss gently until well mixed and heated through. Place under the preheated broiler to lightly brown the top. Serve with the chili sauce mixture.

Serves 4 to 6

GLOUCESTER FISH HASH

Of all the fish that swim or swish
In Ocean's deep autocracy,
There's none possess such haughtiness
As the codfish aristocracy.
—Wallace Irwin

THOSE WORDS are highly befitting to the next recipe: a Massachusetts' hash of "fried cod" and "frizzled" vegetables—delicately thickened with mayonnaise and, in the Yankee maverick tradition, served with tartar sauce on the side.

2 medium potatoes (about 1 pound),
   unpeeled
3 tablespoons all-purpose flour
1/3 cup milk
1/4 cup fresh bread crumbs
1/2 pound cod fillets
4 tablespoons (1/2 stick) unsalted butter
1 tablespoon vegetable oil
1 small bunch scallions, white bulbs
   and green tops, chopped separately
1 small rib celery, finely chopped

1/2 yellow bell pepper, finely chopped
1/2 red bell pepper, finely chopped
Pinch of dried thyme
Pinch of crushed dried hot red peppers
3/4 teaspoon salt
1/8 teaspoon ground white pepper
1/4 cup mayonnaise
2 tablespoons chopped fresh dill
Tartar Sauce (recipe follows)

1. Cook the potatoes in boiling water until just tender, about 20 minutes. Rinse under cold running water; drain. Peel the potatoes and cut into 1/4-inch cubes. Set aside.

2. Place the flour on a plate. Place the milk in a shallow bowl. Place the bread crumbs on another plate. Dip the fish fillets in flour, then the milk, and finally in the bread crumbs.

3. Heat 1 tablespoon butter with the oil in a large skillet over medium heat. Sauté the breaded fish fillets until golden brown on both sides, 2 to 3 minutes per side. Cut the cooked fish into 1/2-inch pieces. Set aside.

4. Melt the remaining 3 tablespoons butter in a large heavy skillet over medium-low heat. Add the scallion bulbs; cook 5 minutes. Add the celery, the bell peppers, thyme, and crushed hot peppers. Cook, stirring frequently, 5 minutes. Stir in the potatoes, sprinkle with salt and pepper, and continue to cook, stirring frequently, 8 minutes. Toss in the scallion ends; cook 2 minutes longer.

5. Stir the mayonnaise into the hash mixture. Add the cooked fish and toss gently until warmed through, about 1 minute. Sprinkle with dill and serve with Tartar Sauce.

Serves 4

TARTAR SAUCE

1 cup mayonnaise

1 tablespoon Pernod liqueur

1/4 cup sour cream

1/2 teaspoon Dijon mustard

1 small shallot, minced

2 small sour pickles, finely chopped

1 teaspoon lemon juice

1 teaspoon chopped fresh parsley

1 tablespoon chopped fresh dill

Dash of hot pepper sauce

Salt and ground white pepper to taste

Whisk all ingredients together in a medium bowl. Serve chilled.
Makes about 1 1/2 cups

MOLDED LAMB HASH
WITH EGG SAUCE

SHEEP WERE raised in great numbers in Shaker communities throughout the Northeast in the 1800s both for clothing and food. The "Shaking Quakers," as they were called, believed that waste of any kind was abhorrent and an affront to God. So it is no surprise that mutton hash was a specialty to their vast communal kitchens. The following recipe, baked like a custard and served with an egg sauce, also demonstrates the sophistication of Shaker cookery. It can be traced back to the Hancock Shaker Village in Massachusetts, which was founded in 1790 and existed, surprisingly enough, until 1960. The village is today maintained as a kind of "living museum" of Shaker customs and crafts.

For the lamb hash

1 medium eggplant (about 3/4 pound), finely chopped

Salt

2 small potatoes (1/2 to 3/4 pound), unpeeled, diced

3 tablespoons unsalted butter

2 tablespoons vegetable or olive oil

1 medium onion, finely chopped

1 large clove garlic, minced

2 cups finely chopped leftover lamb

1/4 teaspoon freshly ground black pepper

1/4 teaspoon ground mace

1 tablespoon finely chopped fresh basil, or 1/2 teaspoon dried

2 tablespoons unsalted butter	1/2 cup heavy or whipping cream
2 tablespoons all-purpose flour	2 large hard-cooked eggs, chopped
1/2 teaspoon English dry mustard	1 tablespoon chopped fresh parsley
1 cup milk, hot	Salt and freshly ground black pepper

1. Place the eggplant in a colander. Sprinkle generously with salt. Let stand 30 minutes. Rinse under running water; squeeze dry.

2. Preheat the oven to 375° F.

3. Cook the potatoes in boiling salted water until tender, 10 to 15 minutes. Drain. Peel the potatoes and cut into 1/4-inch cubes. Set aside.

4. Heat the butter with the oil in a large heavy skillet over medium-low heat. Add the onion; cook 1 minute. Add the garlic; cook 4 minutes longer. Stir in the eggplant and continue to cook until the eggplant changes color, about 5 minutes. Stir in the lamb and potatoes. Add 1/2 teaspoon salt, the pepper, mace, and basil. Cook until soft, about 10 minutes.

5. Spoon the hash mixture into 6 well-buttered custard cups. Place the cups in a roasting pan and add boiling water to the pan to come halfway up the sides of the cups. Bake in the preheated oven for 35 minutes. Let stand 5 minutes before unmolding.

6. Meanwhile, to make the egg sauce: Melt the butter in a medium saucepan over medium-low heat. Stir in the flour and the mustard. Cook, stirring constantly, 2 minutes. Whisk in the milk and cream. Cook until slightly thickened. Add the eggs, parsley, and salt and pepper to taste. Spoon over the unmolded hash.

Serves 6

FIFTIETH STATE HASH

SWEET POTATOES and pork. Two Hawaiian specialties that were obviously destined to end up in the same pot. Throw in some pineapple juice for good measure, a jot of brown sugar for color, plus a splash of vinegar to cut any excessive sweetness and you have "Fiftieth State Hash," one of the Islands' great contributions to American cuisine.

2 large sweet potatoes (about 1 1/2 pounds), unpeeled
1/4 cup raisins
1/4 cup boiling water
4 tablespoons (1/2 stick) unsalted butter
1 tablespoon vegetable oil
2 cups cubed cooked pork
1 small onion, finely chopped

1 clove garlic, minced
Pinch of ground cinnamon
2 tablespoons dark brown sugar
3 tablespoons pineapple juice
1 teaspoon red wine vinegar
Salt and freshly ground black pepper
Chopped fresh parsley

1. Cook the potatoes in boiling water until just tender, about 25 minutes. Rinse under cold running water to cool; drain. Peel and cube the potatoes.

2. Meanwhile, soak the raisins in the boiling water in a small heatproof bowl until soft. Drain.

3. Heat 1 tablespoon butter with the oil in a large heavy skillet over medium heat. Add the pork cubes and sauté, stirring frequently, until browned. Transfer to a plate with a slotted spoon. Add 1 tablespoon butter to the skillet. Add half the potato cubes and cook, stirring frequently, until browned. Transfer to the plate with the meat. Add another tablespoon butter and the remaining potatoes. Cook, stirring frequently, until browned. Add to the potatoes on the plate. Reduce the heat under the skillet to medium-low.

4. Add 1 more tablespoon butter to the skillet. Add the onion; cook 1 minute. Add the garlic and sprinkle with cinnamon. Cook 4 minutes longer. Stir in the meat and potatoes. Sprinkle with the sugar and cook, tossing gently, 5 minutes. Sprinkle with the pineapple juice and vinegar. Continue to cook 5 minutes longer. Add salt and pepper to taste. Sprinkle with parsley.

Serves 4

There is a somewhat raffish book called *Bull Cook and Authentic Historical Recipes and Practices* that I wouldn't think of using at the stove, but affords me no end of reading pleasure away from it. A quasi-authoritative tome, it was compiled by George and Berthe Herter, two iconoclasts who live in Waseca, Minnesota. The Herters have written dozens of books on a wide variety of decidedly offbeat subjects. To name but a few: *How to Live with a Bitch*, *Herter's Professional Course in the Science of Modern Taxidermy*, and *How to Make the Finest Wines at Home in Old Glass or Plastic Bottles and Jugs for as Little as 10¢ a Gallon*. In "Bull Cook," their culinary loins girded, they tell of a famous chicken hash that was invented in Virginia. Originally called "chicken muddle," this dish was first offered at church sales to raise money for building more churches, of course. Since the hash outsold any cakes, pies, and candies the church ladies had to offer, it soon became known as "church builder chicken." And, it is claimed by the Herters, that thousands of churches were financed by this dish alone. The recipe calls for just 1 chicken to 1/2 pound bacon, 3 large onions, 4 pounds potatoes, 5 cans lima beans, 2 cans corn, and 5 cans of tomatoes; the mixture cooked till fork tender and the chicken obviously somewhat miniscule in that muddle.

ULTIMATE CHICKEN HASH

NO MUDDLE this, the following recipe is actually a combination of Louis Diat's quintessential Ritz original with a few flourishes borrowed from the version served up with equal panache at the "21" Club in New York City. Ultimate Chicken Hash is an extremely elegant brunch/lunch/midnight supper offering. I serve it over toast triangles with no other accompaniment other than a green salad. A glass of champagne would not be an inappropriate quaff, but remember to tilt the goblet in Diat's direction, please.

2 tablespoons unsalted butter

2 tablespoons plus 2 teaspoons
   all-purpose flour

1 1/4 cups chicken stock (see page 378)

Salt

2 tablespoons dry sherry

2 cups diced cooked chicken

1 small white onion, halved, sliced thin

2/3 cup light cream or half-and-half

1/4 teaspoon freshly ground black
   pepper

2 large egg yolks

2 tablespoons freshly grated Parmesan
   cheese

1. Preheat the oven to 300° F.

2. Melt 4 teaspoons butter in a heavy skillet over medium-low heat. Stir in 2 tablespoons flour. Cook, stirring constantly, 2 minutes. Whisk in the chicken stock and cook until thick, about 5 minutes. Add 1/4 teaspoon salt, and the sherry. Stir in the chicken. Spoon the mixture into a shallow flame-proof serving dish. Keep warm in the oven.

3. Melt the remaining 2 teaspoons butter in a small saucepan over medium-low heat. Add the onion; cook 5 minutes. Stir in 2 teaspoons flour. Cook, stirring constantly, 2 minutes. Whisk in the cream, 1/4 teaspoon salt, and the pepper. Cook until slightly thickened, about 4 minutes. Remove from heat.

4. Preheat the broiler.

5. Beat the egg yolks in a small bowl and slowly beat in 1/4 cup of the hot cream mixture. Beat this mixture back into the saucepan and stir over low heat until thickened. Do not allow to boil. Stir in the cheese and spoon over the chicken hash. Place the hash under the broiler to lightly brown the top before serving.

Serves 4

SHEEPHERDER'S HASH

"HOW SWEET is the Shepherd's sweet lot!" Particularly when he was well fed—at home and in the fields. The following is a distant cousin of an old "blighty" standby, shepherd's pie. Made with beef in this rendering, this dish was originally prepared of leftover lamb, baked and taken straight from the fiery oven and carried off by shepherds to the high meadows in leather rucksacks which kept the noonday meal reasonably warm. For the record, this is one hash dish that can stand up to a wide variety of disparate vegetables (string beans, carrots, corn, parsnips, etc.), so feel free to experiment. Shepherds' wives certainly did!

2 medium potatoes (about 1 pound), peeled, quartered

5 tablespoons unsalted butter plus 2 tablespoons melted butter

3 tablespoons heavy or whipping cream

1 onion, finely chopped

1 medium rib celery, finely chopped

1/2 pound carrots, finely chopped

1 1/2 tablespoons all-purpose flour

1/2 cup strong beef stock

1/8 teaspoon ground allspice

1/4 teaspoon hot pepper sauce

2 cups chopped leftover roast beef

1 cup fresh peas, blanched, or 1 cup frozen peas, thawed

Salt and freshly ground black pepper

2 tablespoons freshly grated Parmesan cheese

1. Cook the potatoes in boiling salted water until tender, about 20 minutes. Drain. Rice the potatoes and mash with 3 tablespoons butter and the cream until smooth. Set aside.

2. Melt 2 tablespoons butter in a medium saucepan over medium-low heat. Add the onion; cook 2 minutes. Add the celery and carrots. Cover and cook until the vegetables are almost tender, about 8 minutes. Remove the cover and sprinkle the mixture with flour. Stir in the stock, allspice, and hot pepper sauce. Cook until very thick, about 5 minutes. Toss in the roast beef, peas, and salt and pepper to taste.

3. Spoon the hash into a shallow ovenproof baking dish. Spread the mashed potatoes in a thin layer over the top. Sprinkle with cheese and drizzle with the melted butter. Bake 15 minutes.

4. Preheat the broiler.
5. Place the hash under the broiler to lightly brown the top before serving.

Serves 4

CHINESE-AMERICAN HASH

FIRST YOU bake potatoes, then scoop out the insides and "fry" the skins under the broiler. It doesn't sound Chinese. Matter of fact, it doesn't even sound like hash. Yet, what makes the following dish a "hash" is that the vegetables are cooked longer than any typical stir-fry. The meat is seared quickly and the potato chunks pull the whole thing together. A splash of soy sauce sets it off. It's not only unusual, but incredibly delicious, too. The recipe came my way from a young woman who was born and raised in Stockton, California, and has an irreversible streak of culinary invention in her nature. Her ancestors wouldn't approve of her "not-so" Chinese-American Hash, but you will.

2 medium baking potatoes (about 1 pound), unpeeled

1 medium carrot, cut into thin strips about 1-inch long

3 tablespoons unsalted butter

Salt

1 1/2 tablespoons vegetable oil

2 cups leftover rare roast beef or steak strips (about 12 ounces)

1 bunch scallions, white bulbs and green tops, thinly sliced (about 1 cup)

1 large clove garlic, minced

1/2 red bell pepper, cut into thin strips

1/2 yellow bell pepper, cut into thin strips

2 tablespoons beef broth

2 teaspoons soy sauce

1/2 teaspoon anchovy paste

1 cup cherry tomatoes (about 5 ounces), halved and seeded

Freshly ground black pepper

3 tablespoons chopped fresh basil

1. Preheat the oven to 350° F.

2. Wash the potatoes and bake in the oven until tender, about 1 hour. Cool completely. Cut the potatoes in half lengthwise. Using a teaspoon, scoop out the insides of the potato halves in rough ball shapes, leaving about 1/8-inch potato covering the skin. Set aside. Cut the potato skins into long strips; cut each strip in half.

3. Cook the carrot strips in boiling salted water 3 minutes. Drain.

4. Preheat the broiler.

5. Melt 2 tablespoons of the butter in a large heavy skillet over low heat. Add the potato skins and toss until well coated with the butter. Transfer the skins to a flameproof pan. Sprinkle with salt and place under the broiler until crisp on both sides. Set aside.

6. Add the oil to the skillet and heat over medium-high heat until hot. Sauté the beef strips, 1/2 cup at a time, until well browned on both sides. Transfer to a plate. Allow the skillet to cool.

7. Melt the remaining 1 tablespoon butter in the skillet over low heat. Add the scallions; cook 1 minute. Add the garlic; cook 4 minutes longer. Add the peppers; cook, stirring occasionally, 4 minutes. Add the carrots and continue to cook 10 minutes longer. Add the scooped out potato pieces; cook, tossing frequently, 5 minutes.

8. Combine the beef broth, soy sauce, and anchovy paste in a small bowl. Whisk until smooth.

9. Raise the heat under the skillet to medium. Toss in the tomatoes; cook 1 minute. Toss in the beef and pour the broth/soy mixture over the top. Sprinkle with salt and pepper to taste. Toss until warmed through, about 4 minutes. Toss in 2 tablespoons of the basil. Remove from heat and toss in the potato skins. Sprinkle with the remaining 1 tablespoon basil and serve immediately.

Serves 4

ROAD TO GALVESTON HASH

Nothing helps scenery like ham and eggs.
—Mark Twain

EVEN BETTER when the ham is added to a hash and the eggs are served sunny-side up. This dish was uncovered at a roadside stand between Houston and Galveston some while back. The sign on the lunch counter read: Vegetable Hash. When it was ordered, the Mexican chef apologized at once. "Yesterday, it was vegetarian," he said. "Today, not quite." To flesh out his hash, he'd simply added chopped chorizos (Spanish sausages) and strips of smoky ham. It won't pass muster with the healthfood crowd, but sure as heck pleased the folks who stopped in.

2 tablespoons olive oil
1 tablespoon unsalted butter
1 large onion, chopped
2 cloves garlic, minced
1/8 teaspoon ground allspice
1/4 pound lean ham, diced
2 Spanish sausages (chorizos), chopped
1 medium potato (about 1/2 pound), peeled, cubed

1 red bell pepper, seeded, chopped
3 medium ripe tomatoes, peeled, seeded, chopped
Pinch of sugar
2 small zucchini, diced
1 package (10 ounces) frozen lima beans, thawed
Salt and freshly ground black pepper
1 cup grated Monterey Jack cheese

1. Heat the oil with the butter in a large heavy cast-iron skillet over medium heat. Add the onion; cook 1 minute. Add the garlic and sprinkle mixture with allspice; cook until golden, about 4 minutes longer. Stir in the ham and sausages. Cook 2 minutes. Add the potato and red pepper. Continue to cook over medium heat, scraping the bottom of the skillet occasionally, until the potatoes take on a golden hue, about 10 minutes.

2. Stir the tomatoes into the hash mixture and sprinkle with sugar. Stir in the zucchini, and lima beans. Reduce the heat to medium-low and cook, stirring often, until the vegetables are tender, 20 to 25 minutes. Add salt and pepper to taste.

3. Preheat the broiler.

4. Sprinkle the cheese over the vegetable mixture and place under the broiler to melt the cheese. Serve immediately.

Serves 4 to 6

BLACK OLIVE AND MINTED LAMB HASH

WHAT FOLLOWS is originally a Basque dish that obviously went through several sea changes by the time I came upon it in Kern County, California, where ripe black olives grow in profusion. The folks of Kern (not all Basques, needless to say) are always on the lookout for ways to cook the local harvest. This is one of the best of their olive amalgams to my tongue.

3 medium baking potatoes (about 1 1/2 pounds), unpeeled

2 tablespoons unsalted butter

2 tablespoons olive oil

1 large onion, finely chopped

2 cloves garlic, minced

2 cups diced, cooked lamb

1/3 cup chopped black olives

1 small red bell pepper, seeded, chopped

1 small jalapeño pepper, seeded, deveined, minced

2 tablespoons chopped fresh mint, or 1 teaspoon dried

2 tablespoons soy sauce

1/4 cup beef broth

Salt and freshly ground black pepper

3 tablespoons freshly grated Parmesan cheese

1. Cook the potatoes in boiling water until just tender, about 20 minutes. Rinse under cold running water; drain. Peel the potatoes and cut into 1/2-inch cubes. Set aside.

2. Heat the butter with the oil in a large heavy skillet over medium-low heat. Add the onion; cook 1 minute. Add the garlic; cook until golden, about 4 minutes longer. Push the onion to the edges and add the lamb to the center of the skillet. Cook, tossing gently, until lightly browned, about 4 minutes.

3. Add the potatoes to the skillet and mix well. Stir in the olives, peppers,

mint, and soy sauce. Cook over medium heat, stirring occasionally, until the potatoes begin to brown, about 10 minutes. Sprinkle the mixture with the beef broth. Add salt and pepper to taste. Lightly press the hash down and cook, without stirring, 10 minutes.

4. Preheat the broiler.

5. Sprinkle the cheese over the hash mixture and place under the broiler until the top is crisp.

Serves 4 to 6

HAPPILY EVER AFTER
SHRIMP AND SCALLOP HASH

Love does not dominate; it cultivates.
—Goethe

THE NEXT recipe is traditional wedding breakfast fare cultivated for newlyweds in Jonesport, Maine, where some of the sweetest scallops are plumbed from the icy waters. There this dish is made to celebrate the tying of a nuptial knot. Don't save it for weddings only—it's too good to be ritualized. Besides, every mouthful bespeaks a happy ending at the table year round.

6 tablespoons unsalted butter (3/4 stick)

1 tablespoon olive oil

1 small white onion, finely chopped

2 cloves garlic, minced

2 medium baking potatoes (about 1 pound), peeled, cubed

1/2 pound bay scallops or sea scallops

3 tablespoons all-purpose flour

1/2 pound raw shrimp, shelled, deveined, roughly chopped

4 scallions, white bulbs and green tops, chopped

1 tablespoon lemon juice

1 teaspoon finely slivered lemon peel

1/2 cup chopped fresh parsley

1/4 teaspoon crushed dried hot red peppers

Salt and freshly ground black pepper

1. Heat the butter with the oil in a large heavy skillet over medium-low heat. Add the onion; cook 1 minute. Add the garlic, cook 4 minutes. Stir in the potatoes. Cook, stirring constantly, until the potatoes are light gold in color and almost tender, about 10 minutes.

2. Pat the scallops dry and dust lightly with flour. Stir the scallops and shrimp into the potato mixture, along with the scallions, lemon juice, and lemon peel. Cook, stirring frequently, until the potatoes are tender, about 6 minutes. Toss in the parsley and hot red peppers. Add salt and pepper to taste.

Serves 4

Meat Loaves

EVER SINCE Man had his first taste of flesh (with its ensuing rush of protein energy), eating *meat* became synonymous with *strength*. This was especially true in Roman times. Athenaeus went so far as to proclaim that vegetables, fish, and fowl were not to be eaten, "because eating these is a sign of greed," and in turn, "unseemly, . . . beneath the level of heroic and godlike deeds . . ." Even Shakespeare touched on the symbolism in *Julius Caesar*. When Cassius was recruiting Brutus to do in Caesar, he wrote, "Upon what meat doth this our Caesar feed, that he is grown so great?"

Perhaps, Caesar's "meat" was the forerunner of pâté. Both the Greeks and Romans were eating crude forms of meat loaves, if you will, long before the pâté was invented. (And for the record, by definition a *pâté* is enclosed in crust; while a *terrine* is made in a mold, sans crust, although common usage uses these terms more loosely and sometimes interchangeably.) Apicius, the well-known Roman epicure, is credited with the first recipe for a fish-shaped, molded liver terrine. As James Villas reports in *American Taste* (1982), Apicius called the dish *salsum sine salso,* or fish without fish, suggesting a thrift that to this day is inherent in the making of meat loaves of all kinds. And while pâté became popular with the elite, and still is, of course, meat loaf was always peasant food, usually made from finely chopped leftover meats that may very well have included badger, porcupine, and dormouse. But then, as Socrates said, ". . . the true creator is necessity, who is the mother of our invention."

Early English (and subsequently American), meat loaves were generally made with veal. A recipe in *Beeton's Book of Household Management*, originally published in a monthly series in 1859, calls for minced cold roast veal, minced raw bacon, minced lemon peel, chopped onion, salt, pepper, and pounded mace—bound together by a slice of toast soaked in milk and an egg. This mixture was then placed in a mold, baked, and served with brown gravy. This was a fairly standard recipe for the time.

In the late 1800s, meat loaf, like hash, began appearing on menus at "All-U-Kan-Eat-for-A-Nickel" lunch counters. Only now *raw* veal was the principle ingredient and crackers the binder. In some cases, customers were hard put to find the meat for the crackers. Diners grew wary of eating meat loaf away from home.

Some food authorities say it was a Southerner who first added raw pork to the veal mixture, hoping for juicier results. However, the Germans had long been adding raw pork to their ham loaves for just the very same reason. In the 1900s, beef began replacing veal in many a favorite family recipe.

The Meat of the Matter Using pure beef alone in the meat mixture results in a somewhat dry loaf. It is best to use a combination of beef, veal, and pork. For three pounds of raw meat (which assures leftovers in my house), an appropriate ratio is 1 1/2 pounds ground beef, 1 pound ground veal, and 1/2 pound ground pork. However, a tasty meat loaf can also be made from lamb, ham, and even turkey.

Every able-bodied man, woman, and child at the stove has his or her favorite meat loaf recipe it seems—and almost always with a "secret ingredient!" This secret ingredient, nine times out of ten, turns out to be rolled oats, instead of bread crumbs, as a binder and "stretcher." But crackers, popular in the eighteenth century, can be used as well as wheat germ, bran cereal, and, a new twist, crushed tortilla chips.

Indiscriminate cooks throw just about everything *but* the kitchen sink into their loaves. That is your option, but when it comes to onions, I, for one, prefer to sauté them lightly before they go into the mixture. It is my opinion that nothing ruins a good meat loaf like an overwhelming blast of undercooked onions.

A meat loaf, most commonly baked in a loaf pan, can take any shape. I generally form the meat mixture into an oval and bake it on a shallow baking dish. If you wish to get really fancy, however, consider making the loaf in a round mold. But a word to the wise; for easy unmolding, use a nonstick pan (or a nonstick spray on the pan) before adding the meat mixture. To adapt a recipe for any mold, the standard rule of thumb is to allow a pound of meat per two cups of mold. In any case, do not fill the pan completely or the juices will run over the top. A round, molded loaf of about 3 pounds will bake in less time than your average loaf; about 50 to 60 minutes.

A thing is better for being shared.
—Scottish proverb

MEAT LOAF is probably one of the most "shared" of all dishes in the history of food. Whether it is served for Sunday supper, at a family picnic, or a casual brunch, a meat loaf symbolizes a closeness of those partaking in the meal. A time of no pretenses or formalities; just sharing in old-fashioned goodness. The possibilities are endless—a mere dozen follow.

GLAZED MEAT LOAF

FROM SACRAMENTO, this fairly standard recipe for a basic meat loaf is removed from the realm of "everyday" with a glaze of mustard and duck sauce. The end result is a crusty exterior with just a hint of "sweet and sour."

1 1/2 teaspoons unsalted butter

2 medium shallots, minced

1 1/2 tablespoons minced celery

1 1/2 tablespoons minced red bell
    pepper

1 1/2 pounds ground beef

1 pound ground veal

1/2 pound ground pork

1 tablespoon minced fresh basil, or
    1 teaspoon dried

1 tablespoon minced fresh parsley

2 large eggs, lightly beaten

1/2 cup milk

1/2 cup fresh bread crumbs

1 teaspoon soy sauce

1 teaspoon prepared chili sauce

1/2 teaspoon salt

Freshly ground black pepper

1/3 cup duck sauce (Chinese sweet and
    sour sauce)

2 teaspoons Dijon mustard

Chopped fresh parsley

    1. Preheat the oven to 400° F.

    2. Melt the butter in a medium skillet over medium-low heat. Add the shallots; cook 2 minutes. Add the celery and bell pepper; cook 3 minutes longer. Remove from heat.

3. Combine the beef, veal, and pork in a large bowl. Mix well. Add the shallot mixture, the basil, parsley, eggs, milk, bread crumbs, soy sauce, chili sauce, salt, and 1/4 teaspoon pepper. Mix thoroughly. Form into a loaf on a shallow baking dish.

4. Combine the duck sauce with the mustard in a small bowl. Spread evenly over the top and sides of loaf. Sprinkle with more pepper. Bake 1 1/4 hours. Let stand 5 minutes before serving, sprinkled with parsley.

Serves 6 to 8

MEAT LOAF WITH CRISPED POTATOES

SMOKY HAM in the meat mixture gives this loaf its character. The potato wedges, roasted in the same pan, turn crisp and golden brown. If you wish, you can add sliced carrots for a hearty "one-dish" dinner.

2 strips bacon, chopped

1 white onion, minced

1 small clove garlic, minced

3 tablespoons unsalted butter

1 1/2 pounds ground beef

3/4 pound ground veal

1/2 pound ground smoky country-style cooked ham

1 large egg, lightly beaten

1/2 cup fresh bread crumbs

1 teaspoon English dry mustard

1/2 teaspoon salt

1/8 teaspoon freshly ground black pepper

3/4 cup beef broth

3 medium baking potatoes, cut into sixths, lengthwise

1 teaspoon tomato paste

1/4 cup dry red wine

Chopped fresh parsley

1. Preheat the oven to 375° F.

2. Sauté the bacon in a heavy skillet over medium heat until almost crisp. Add the onion; cook 1 minute. Add the garlic; cook until golden, about 4 minutes. Remove from heat and stir in 1 tablespoon butter.

3. Combine the beef, veal, and ham in a large bowl. Mix well. Add the

bacon/onion mixture, the egg, bread crumbs, mustard, salt, pepper, and 1/2 cup beef broth. Mix thoroughly. Form into a loaf in a lightly buttered shallow roasting pan. Place the potato wedges, skin-side down, around the meat loaf.

4. Melt the remaining 2 tablespoons butter in a small saucepan. Whisk in the tomato paste, wine, and remaining 1/4 cup broth. Spoon over potatoes and meat. Bake, basting the meat and potatoes occasionally with pan juices, 1 1/4 hours. Let stand 5 minutes before serving, sprinkled with parsley.

Serves 6 to 8

POMPEY'S HEAD

"FOR UNKNOWN foods, the nose acts always as a sentinel and cries, Who goes there?" This remark by Brillat-Savarin is appropriately applied to this next recipe of unknown origin. Its roots lie in the South, but it is indeed a most unusual dish. The meat mixture is formed into a mound on a baking pan; a hole then poked in its center. A sprinkling of flour gives the loaf a very crusty top. And note, the onions, a rather generous amount, are *not* precooked. Your "sentinel" sense of smell will not be disappointed, however. Be sure to use the juices in the hole, as well as in the pan, when basting.

1 pound ground beef

1 pound ground veal

1/2 pound pork sausage meat

2 onions, finely chopped

1 tablespoon Dijon mustard

1/4 teaspoon chopped fresh sage, or a pinch of dried

1/4 teaspoon chopped fresh thyme, or a pinch of dried

1/4 cup chopped fresh parsley

1/4 teaspoon crushed dried hot red peppers

2 large eggs, lightly beaten

1 1/4 cups beef broth

All-purpose flour

7 tablespoons unsalted butter

Chopped fresh parsley

1. Preheat the oven to 500° F.

2. Combine the beef, veal, and sausage in a large bowl. Mix well. Add the onions, mustard, sage, thyme, parsley, hot peppers, eggs, and 1/2 cup beef broth. Mix thoroughly. Form into a ball.

3. Place about 1/3 cup flour in a shallow bowl. Roll the ball of meat in the flour. Place on a lightly buttered shallow baking dish and press down gently. Make a 1-inch circular depression halfway through the center. Bake 10 minutes.

4. Meanwhile, melt 6 tablespoons of the butter. Remove the meat from the oven and reduce the oven heat to 350° F. Drizzle the loaf with melted butter, adding some to the hole in the center. Bake 10 minutes longer.

5. Remove the meat once more and sprinkle lightly with flour. Return to oven and bake, basting every 15 minutes with pan juices, 1 hour longer. Transfer to a serving platter; keep warm. Remove the scum from the baking dish and degrease the juices.

6. Melt the remaining 1 tablespoon butter in a medium saucepan over medium-low heat. Add 1 tablespoon flour. Cook, stirring constantly, 2 minutes. Whisk in the meat juices and the remaining 3/4 cup beef broth. Simmer until slightly thickened. Sprinkle the loaf with parsley and pass the gravy on the side.

Serves 6 to 8

MICHIGAN MIDDLE-EASTERN
MEAT LOAF

FROM THE Detroit area, the next loaf's main ingredient is ground lamb, much like the keftas of the Middle-Eastern countries. But cinnamon, normally kefta's essential spice, is reserved here for the glaze.

2 1/2 teaspoons unsalted butter

1 medium onion, minced

2 cloves garlic, minced

1 1/2 pounds ground lean lamb

1 pound ground lean beef

1/2 cup bread crumbs

1/4 cup cold water

1 large egg, lightly beaten

1/2 teaspoon salt

1/4 teaspoon freshly ground black
   pepper

1/4 teaspoon crushed allspice berries

1/2 teaspoon English dry mustard

1/2 teaspoon crushed hot red peppers

1/8 teaspoon Hungarian hot paprika

2 tablespoons chopped fresh parsley

1/3 cup prepared chili sauce

2 teaspoons honey

1/4 teaspoon ground cinnamon

Chopped fresh parsley

1. Preheat the oven to 400° F.

2. Melt 1 1/2 teaspoons butter in a medium skillet over medium-low heat. Add the onion; cook 1 minute. Add the garlic; cook 4 minutes longer. Remove from heat.

3. Combine the lamb with the beef in a large bowl. Mix well. Add the onion mixture, the bread crumbs, water, egg, salt, pepper, allspice, mustard, hot peppers, paprika, and parsley. Mix thoroughly. Form into a loaf on a shallow baking dish. Bake 15 minutes.

4. Meanwhile, melt the remaining 1 teaspoon butter in a small saucepan over medium heat. Stir in the chili sauce, honey, and cinnamon. Raise heat to high and cook until thick, about 4 minutes. Remove from heat.

5. After 15 minutes, remove meat loaf from oven and spread evenly with the chili sauce mixture. Return loaf to oven. Bake 1 hour longer. Let stand 5 minutes before serving, sprinkled with parsley.

Serves 4 to 6

POCATELLO 'TATER LOAF

NEEDLESS to say, a meat loaf recipe from Idaho wouldn't be authentic without grated potatoes in the mix. The potatoes in this case take the place of bread crumbs (or other binders) and keep the loaf moist for days, in the bargain.

1 1/2 pounds ground beef

1 pound ground veal

1/2 pound ground pork

1 teaspoon salt

1/4 teaspoon freshly ground black pepper

1/4 teaspoon ground mace

1/3 cup plus additional chopped fresh parsley

2 tablespoons chopped fresh basil, or 1 teaspoon dried

1/3 cup chopped scallions

3 tablespoons minced green bell pepper

2 large eggs, lightly beaten

2/3 cup light cream or half-and-half

1 cup grated, peeled Idaho potatoes, squeezed dry (about 1 medium)

2 teaspoons Dijon mustard

2 strips thick-cut bacon

1/2 cup beef broth

1 tablespoon unsalted butter

1 tablespoon all-purpose flour

1/4 cup heavy or whipping cream

1. Preheat the oven to 400° F.

2. Combine the beef, veal, and pork in a large bowl. Mix well. Add the salt, pepper, mace, the 1/3 cup parsley, the basil, scallions, bell pepper, eggs, light cream, and grated potatoes. Mix thoroughly. Form into a loaf on a shallow baking dish. Spread the mustard evenly over the top and sides of loaf. Lay the bacon strips over the top. Bake 1 1/4 hours.

3. Transfer the meat to a serving platter. Cover loosely with foil and let stand 10 minutes.

4. Meanwhile, remove excess fat from the pan juices and stir in the beef broth, scraping the sides and the bottom of the dish.

5. Melt the butter in a medium saucepan over medium heat. Stir in the flour. Cook, stirring constantly, until lightly browned, about 3 minutes. Whisk in the meat juices and heavy cream. Cook until thickened, 3 to 4 minutes. Sprinkle the loaf with parsley and pass the gravy on the side.

Serves 6

CLARA ARMSTRONG'S HAM LOAF

Plain cooking cannot be entrusted to plain cooks.
—Countess Morphy

I DISAGREE! The next recipe is the best old-fashioned ham loaf one could ever hope to find. It was passed on by a friend whose mother always made it for special occasions. She was a "plain cook" who made "plain cooking" taste like haute cuisine.

1 cup fresh bread crumbs

1/2 cup light brown sugar (packed)

2 teaspoons Dijon mustard

1 1/2 pounds uncooked smoked ham, ground

1 1/2 pounds ground pork

1 cup milk

2 large eggs, lightly beaten

1/4 teaspoon salt

1/4 teaspoon freshly ground black pepper

1. Preheat the oven to 350° F.

2. Combine the bread crumbs and brown sugar in a medium bowl. Toss with a fork until well mixed. Add the mustard and mix with your fingers until crumbly. Remove 1/2 cup of this mixture and reserve.

3. Add the remaining ingredients to the remaining bread crumb mixture. Mix thoroughly. Form into a loaf in a shallow baking dish. Sprinkle the reserved crumb mixture over the top, gently pressing into the meat. Bake 1 hour and 10 minutes. Serve warm, at room temperature, or well chilled.

Serves 8

TEXAS BORDER-TOWN MEAT LOAF

AS PRIORLY noted, just about anything that can be crushed or ground can take the place of bread crumbs in a meat loaf. This Texas specialty with all the right seasonings (chiles, cilantro, and cumin) is loaded with crushed tortilla chips, which hold the amalgam together. It's a Lone Star winner.

2 teaspoons unsalted butter

1 small red onion, minced (about 3 tablespoons)

1/2 red bell pepper, seeded, minced

2 cups tortilla chips

1 1/4 pounds ground beef

3/4 pound ground veal

1/4 pound ground pork

1 large egg, lightly beaten

1 can (4 ounces) mild green chiles with liquid, roughly chopped

1 teaspoon chopped fresh cilantro (Chinese parsley)

1 teaspoon chili powder

1/2 teaspoon ground cumin

1/4 teaspoon freshly ground black pepper

1/2 cup beef broth

1/3 cup prepared chili sauce

1 tablespoon light brown sugar

1 1/2 teaspoons red wine vinegar

Chopped fresh parsley

1. Preheat the oven to 375° F.

2. Melt the butter in a medium skillet over medium-low heat. Add the onion and bell pepper. Cook until softened, about 5 minutes. Cool slightly.

3. Place the tortilla chips in the container of a food processor. Process until the texture of cornmeal.

4. Combine the beef, veal, and pork in a large bowl. Mix well. Add the onion mixture, the ground tortilla chips, the egg, mild green chiles, cilantro, chili powder, cumin, black pepper, and beef broth. Mix thoroughly. Form into a loaf on a shallow baking dish or roasting pan.

5. Combine the chili sauce, brown sugar, and vinegar in a small bowl. Spread over the top and sides of the loaf. Bake 1 1/4 hours. Let stand 5 minutes before serving, sprinkled with parsley.

Serves 6

SARATOGA "SURPRISE" LOAF

THIS RECIPE is a version of a meat loaf I tasted many years ago at a diner on the road to Saratoga Springs in New York. The loaf, striped with green and red peppers, had a secret ingredient according to the chef. You guessed it—oatmeal. The peppers went unroasted in those days, but the mixture is far better for it.

1 small red bell pepper
1 small green bell pepper
1 teaspoon olive oil
1 small shallot, minced
1 pound ground beef
2/3 pound veal
1/3 pound ground pork
1 large egg, lightly beaten
2/3 cup rolled oats
3/4 cup plus 1 teaspoon spicy Bloody
    Mary mix

1/2 teaspoon salt
1/4 teaspoon freshly ground black
    pepper
Pinch of dried thyme
1 tablespoon Dijon mustard
1/4 teaspoon soy sauce
1 tablespoon dark brown sugar
Chopped fresh parsley

1. Roast the peppers over a gas flame or under a broiler until charred all over. Carefully wrap the peppers in paper towels and place in a plastic bag. Let stand 5 minutes. Rub the skins from the peppers with paper towels. Seed and cut into strips.

2. Preheat the oven to 375° F.

3. Heat the oil in a small saucepan over medium-low heat. Add the shallot; cook until lightly browned, about 4 minutes. Remove from heat.

4. Combine the beef, veal, and pork in a large bowl. Mix well. Add the shallot, egg, rolled oats, 3/4 cup Bloody Mary mix, the salt, pepper, and thyme. Mix thoroughly.

5. Divide the meat mixture into three parts. Form a loaf with the first portion in the bottom of a shallow baking dish. Press flat. Layer half the peppers over the meat, lengthwise, leaving 1/2 inch around the edges. Press the second portion of meat mixture over the peppers. Layer the remaining peppers on top. Cover with the remaining meat mixture and form into a loaf, pressing the edges smoothly together.

6. Combine the mustard, soy sauce, the remaining 1 teaspoon Bloody Mary mix, and brown sugar in a small bowl. Spread over the top and sides of the meat loaf. Bake 1 1/4 hours. Let stand 5 minutes before serving, sprinkled with parsley.

Serves 6

SPINACH LOAF

THE FOLLOWING veal loaf is equally delicious hot, cold, or at room temperature. This is one recipe that deserves to be included on your next buffet table. It is always at home on mine, excellent served with a thick homemade tomato sauce.

1 package (10 ounces) frozen chopped spinach, thawed
1 1/2 tablespoons unsalted butter
1 teaspoon vegetable oil
1 small onion, finely chopped
1 clove garlic, minced
1 pound ground beef
1/2 pound ground veal
1/4 pound pork sausage meat
1/4 teaspoon ground allspice
1/4 teaspoon ground mace

1/8 teaspoon freshly grated nutmeg
1/2 teaspoon salt
1/4 teaspoon freshly ground pepper
1 tablespoon Madeira
2 large eggs, lightly beaten
Dash of hot pepper sauce
3/4 cup fresh bread crumbs
1/3 cup plus 1/4 cup freshly grated Parmesan cheese
2 teaspoons Dijon mustard
1 teaspoon prepared chili sauce

1. Preheat the oven to 375° F.

2. Cook the spinach in boiling salted water 1 minute. Drain, pressing out all liquid with the back of a spoon.

3. Heat the butter with the oil in a medium saucepan over medium-low heat. Add the onion; cook 1 minute. Add the garlic; cook 4 minutes. Stir in the spinach and raise the heat. Cook, stirring constantly, until all the moisture has evaporated.

4. Combine the beef, veal, and sausage in a large bowl. Mix well. Add the spinach mixture, the allspice, mace, nutmeg, salt, pepper, Madeira, eggs, hot pepper sauce, bread crumbs, and 1/3 cup cheese. Mix thoroughly. Form into a loaf on a shallow baking dish.

5. Mix the mustard with the chili sauce in a small bowl. Spread over the top and sides of loaf. Bake 1 hour. Sprinkle the loaf with the remaining 1/4 cup cheese and bake until golden brown, 15 to 20 minutes longer. Let stand 5 minutes before serving.

Serves 4 to 6

In eighteenth-century England, there lived a woman who called herself "housekeeper to Lady Warburton." Elizabeth Raffald was something more than just a housekeeper, to be sure. For one thing, she also managed to operate a confectionery shop, two successful inns, a domestic agency—plus a cooking school. *And* at the same time, "bore sixteen daughters." If that wasn't enough, she also wrote a cookbook which was published in 1769. In a recipe for a meat loaf, she called for a topping of cooked macaroni, tossed in butter and cream until "thick enough to stick where it lands." The topping was spread over the cooked loaf, sprinkled with grated Italian cheese and browned under a hot fire. Oh yes, the name of her book: *The Experienced English Housekeeper*.

BRAN AND MUSHROOM MEAT LOAF

MORE WISE words from Shakespeare: "Give them great meals of beef and iron and steel, they will act like wolves and fight like devils." No iron or steel here, but bran cereal sets the stage for this mushroom enhanced energy booster. It's one way to get your daily dose of bran and be grateful for it!

3 1/2 tablespoons unsalted butter
1 medium onion, finely chopped
1 small clove garlic, minced
1/2 pound mushrooms, stems removed, finely minced (about 1/2 cup)

3/4 cup chopped fresh parsley
1 tablespoon chopped fresh basil, or
    1 teaspoon dried
1/4 teaspoon ground allspice

Juice of 1 lemon
1 1/2 cups All Bran cereal
1 1/4 pounds ground beef
1 pound ground veal
3/4 pound ground pork
2 large eggs, lightly beaten
1 cup chicken stock (see page 378)

1/8 teaspoon crushed dried hot red peppers
Salt and freshly ground black pepper
3 strips bacon
1 tablespoon all-purpose flour
2 tablespoons heavy or whipping cream
Chopped fresh parsley

1. Preheat the oven to 375° F.

2. Melt 1 1/2 tablespoons butter in a large heavy skillet over medium-low heat. Add the onion; cook 1 minute. Add the garlic; cook 2 minutes longer. Stir in the mushrooms and lemon juice. Raise the heat to high and cook, stirring constantly, until all the liquid has evaporated. Set aside. Wipe out the skillet.

3. Place the bran in the container of a food processor and process until it is the texture of coarse bread crumbs. Melt 1 tablespoon butter in the skillet over medium heat and sauté the processed bran, stirring constantly, until golden, about 4 minutes. Cool slightly.

4. Combine the beef, veal, and pork in a large bowl. Mix well. Add the onion mixture, the toasted bran, the eggs, 1/2 cup chicken stock, the parsley, basil, allspice, hot red peppers, 1/2 teaspoon salt and 1/4 teaspoon ground pepper. Mix thoroughly. Form into a loaf on a shallow baking dish. Place the bacon strips over the top. Bake 1 hour. Reduce the heat to 350° F. and bake 15 minutes longer. Transfer to a serving platter; keep warm. Degrease the pan juices.

5. Melt the remaining 1 tablespoon butter in a medium saucepan over medium low heat. Add the flour. Cook, stirring constantly, 2 minutes. Whisk in the pan juices and the remaining 1/2 cup chicken stock. Cook until thickened. Whisk in the cream. Sprinkle the loaf with parsley and pass the gravy on the side.

Serves 6 to 8

SILVERTON RHUBARB LOAF

SILVERTON, in my home state of Colorado, is not only known for its incredible scenery, but its prodigious rhubarb crop as well. Every July 4 there is a rhubarb festival that benefits the public library, which, believe it or not, was first funded in this out-of-the-way silver-mining mountain town by Andrew Carnegie in 1905. This rhubarb studded, and rhubarb topped, loaf would take first prize at any festival.

For the topping

1/2 cup diced fresh rhubarb (1 medium rib)

3 tablespoons dark brown sugar

1 tablespoon water

1 tablespoon Dijon mustard

For the loaf

1 pound ground cooked ham

1 pound ground beef

1/2 pound pork sausage meat

1 large egg, lightly beaten

3/4 cup rolled oats

1/4 cup wheat germ

1/2 cup water

2 tablespoons unsalted butter

1 small onion

2 1/2 tablespoons dark brown sugar

1 teaspoon Dijon mustard

1/4 teaspoon soy sauce

1/2 teaspoon red wine vinegar

1/2 cup diced fresh rhubarb (1 medium rib)

1 jalapeño pepper, seeded, deveined, minced

1 teaspoon salt

1/4 teaspoon freshly ground black pepper

1/4 teaspoon ground allspice

    1. To make the topping: Combine the rhubarb, brown sugar, and water in a small saucepan. Heat to boiling; reduce the heat. Cook, covered, over low heat until the rhubarb is very soft, about 10 minutes. Remove from heat. Let stand 10 minutes and stir in the mustard.

    2. Preheat the oven to 400° F.

    3. To make the meat loaf: Combine the ham, beef, and sausage meat in a large bowl. Mix well. Add the egg, oats, wheat germ, and water. Mix well.

4. Melt the butter in a medium skillet over medium-low heat. Add the onion; cook until well browned, 8 to 10 minutes. Stir in the sugar, mustard, soy sauce, and vinegar. Remove from heat and stir in the rhubarb and jalapeño pepper. Add to the meat mixture along with the salt, pepper, and allspice. Mix thoroughly. Form into a loaf on a shallow baking dish.

5. Spread the topping over the top and the sides of the loaf. Bake 1 hour and 15 minutes. Let stand 5 minutes before serving.

Serves 6 to 8

HERBED AND CRUSTED
TURKEY LOAF

I am a great lover of secondary causes, and I believe firmly that the whole gallinaceous race was created for the sole purpose of filling our larders and enriching our banquets.

—Brillat-Savarin

WHEN YOU taste turkey, in one of its finest guises, you won't argue the point. Ground turkey these days is readily available in supermarkets everywhere. Rice is used as a binder in this rendering of turkey loaf, while bread crumbs are relegated to the topping, forming a crisp-crunchy layering one can sink one's teeth into.

2 1/2 pounds fresh ground turkey

1/4 pound thinly sliced cooked ham, finely chopped

1 small shallot, minced

1 teaspoon salt

1/4 teaspoon freshly ground black pepper

2 large eggs, lightly beaten

1 cup cooked rice

2/3 cup light cream or half-and-half

2 tablespoons plus additional unsalted butter, softened

1 small clove garlic, bruised

1/2 cup fresh bread crumbs

(ingredients continued)

1/8 teaspoon freshly grated nutmeg

2 tablespoons minced fresh parsley

1 tablespoon minced fresh basil, or 1 teaspoon dried

1/2 teaspoon minced fresh sage, or a pinch of dried

Dash of hot pepper sauce

1/2 cup sour cream, at room temperature

Salt and freshly ground black pepper

1. Preheat the oven to 350° F.

2. Combine all the ingredients through the light cream in a large bowl. Mix thoroughly.

3. Rub a shallow baking dish with butter. Rub the dish with the bruised garlic. Form the turkey mixture into a loaf on the dish and lightly rub the loaf with the garlic.

4. Mix the 2 tablespoons butter with the bread crumbs in a small bowl until smooth. Add the hot pepper sauce and spread carefully over the loaf, making sure no crumbs fall into the dish. Bake 1 1/2 hours.

5. Remove the drippings (there will be only a small amount) from the dish and transfer to a bowl. Cover the loaf loosely with foil; let stand 10 minutes.

6. Meanwhile, stir the sour cream into the drippings and season with salt and pepper to taste; pass on the side.

Serves 6 to 8

Pancakes

*I*F YOU happen to be driving through Liberal, Kansas, on Shrove Tuesday (the day before lent), you might very well think the whole town has taken leave of its collective senses. For on that day, the ladies of Liberal hold their annual competition with their sister city, Olney, England. A most unusual event, like something out of Dogpatch, the competition consists of a footrace. But no ordinary contest, the rules of this sprint require that each entrant (fifteen is the maximum) hold a cast-iron skillet in her hand, flip a pancake at the beginning of the race, hold it in place to the finish, and flip it yet again as she crosses the line. This contest, which began in 1950 has become such an event in Liberal that the day has become known as Pancake Day, featuring not only the flapjack marathon, but pancake eating contests and flipping matches as well. Of course, if you get hungry, some of the best pancakes anywhere can be had for a pittance. Incidentally, at this writing, Olney leads twenty to nineteen.

Pancakes were actually the first form of bread. Originally a mixture of pounded grain and water, the batter was spread upon hot rocks to dry. Ancient Hebrews upgraded the cooking of the batter to a stone griddle, and seasoned it with salt. The Romans added yet another dimension; they ate their early pancakes flavored with pepper and sweetened with honey syrup. The Mexican tortilla, the Scots' oatcake, the Indian chapati, and the Chinese egg roll wrapper (made with egg batter) are all descendants of this most ancient form of bread, as were the *piki* (paper bread) of the Pueblo Indians and the first truly American pancake, the Jonnycake.

Although European settlers introduced pancakes of every shape, size, and flavoring to our culinary heritage, it was the native Indians of what is now Rhode Island who brought Jonnycakes to the American table. Basically a flat bread, the Indians used nothing but water and ground dried "maize" (cornmeal) in their device. Early homesteaders substituted milk for water and eventually added eggs to the batter as well, but purists decry such embellishment, even to this day.

The breakfast pancake as we know it, slaked with melting butter and maple syrup, would seem to be a purely American innovation. Not so. While "hot cakes," "flapjacks," and "griddlecakes" are most decidedly all-American tags, the pancake cognomen actually came to us from Holland. Food sleuths tell us that *pannekoeken* cooked in heavy skillets over open fires were a favored food of Netherlanders as far back as the sixteenth century and were probably brought to New Amsterdam by some gastronomic (and homesick) Dutch settler.

Pancakes were not purely a lowland prerogative; Anglo-Saxons, according to the same pundits, consumed them with relish in pre-Elizabethan England. Indeed they were so popular as Lenten fare that, according to Shakespeare, the peasantry dubbed Shrove Tuesday "Pancake Tuesday." Known as "shriving cakes," these wafers were eaten in conjunction with confession; the offenders being "shriven" of their iniquities after a single bite. The flour in the cakes is said to represent the staff of life; the salt, wholesomeness; the eggs, the Lenten spirit; and the milk, pure innocence.

Flipping Your Flapjacks Cooking pancakes is easy. All you need is the right pan or griddle. Soapstone (nature's answer to man-made nonstick surfaces) is the ideal surface for pan-cakery. After a preliminary scouring with salt, this organic utensil requires no grease or seasoning whatsoever before it is used. More to the point, a soapstone griddle is well tempered for a most even distribution of heat—and makes even the stickiest flapjacks unflappable. Unfortunately, while soapstone griddles were everyday kitchen adjuncts in Colonial kitchens, they are somewhat pricier today.

Cast-iron skillets or griddles, on the other hand, besides being a good deal less expensive and fragile than soapstone, maintain even heat as well. However, cast-iron must be seasoned well (in advance and after each use) to keep foods from sticking to its porous surface. To season a cast-iron skillet properly, scour the surface of a new utensil (which looks silver-gray, by the way) with a nonsoapy steel wool pad; rinse and wipe dry. Rub the pan liberally with vegetable oil and place it in a 350° F. oven for 2 hours. After the pan cools down, wipe out the excess oil.

If you do not wish to make the financial commitment to soapstone or the investment of time required by cast-iron, consider a nonstick skillet or even an electric frypan for your next pancake spree. But remember, treated metal surfaces (such as Teflon) absorb heat rapidly and will brown a pancake faster than you can say, "Where's the syrup?" In any event, it is important to bear in mind that pancakes are "baked" on a stovetop—not fried. Never use more shortening to "whet" the griddle than absolutely necessary. Butter or oil can be used—or do as the Shakers did and keep a chunk of smoky ham fat on hand for just such amenities.

Pancakes can be made small, like silver dollars, or man-handler size. Whatever its size, the pancake should be turned only when the edges brown slightly and bubbles form on top of the batter. Use a flat wide spatula for a soapstone grill, a metal-eyelet flipper for cast-iron griddles, and a heavy-duty plastic spatula for nonstick griddles.

Always keep the heat under griddle or pan at *medium* (as pointed out earlier, the heat under nonstick surfaces might have to be adjusted lower). High temperature will cause the cakes to cook too quickly and leave the surface blotchy—rather than the desired golden—and the inside raw. And though the cakes are absolutely best when consumed "hot off the griddle," they will suffer no great loss in either taste or texture if they are kept warm in a 200° F. oven until a whole batch is finished—but no longer than that.

WHETHER ONE calls them pancakes (made in a pan) or griddle-cakes (made on a griddle), pancakes are an extremely popular food; and there are as many pancake recipes today as there are pancake makers. Some batters require advance preparation; others can be whipped up just prior to the pan. The varieties are endless. There are whole wheat cakes, buckwheat cakes, cornmeal cakes, rice cakes, bread crumb cakes, wheat germ cakes, and hominy cakes. Moreover, there are thin cakes, fat cakes, breakfast cakes, vegetable cakes, and dessert cakes. All one needs is a little imagination.

Pancakes can be served plain or buttered, sprinkled with confectioners' sugar and maple syrup (Vermont *is* the best), caramel syrup (see New Orleans Praline Pancakes, p. 278), or with any fruit syrup. A favorite jelly, jam, or preserve can also be thinned with fruit juice or water and served as well.

The following recipes are for some personal favorites. All American, though ethnic spoons have certainly stirred up some of these batters, they are as varied and unique as the parts of the country from which they were collected.

THE CLASSIC BREAKFAST PANCAKE

SIR ALAN PATRICK HERBERT once wrote, "The critical period in matrimony is breakfast-time." It needn't be; just serve up a batch of the following pancakes. Flexible in nature, the batter can be whipped up at the last moment or made in advance and refrigerated overnight. If making in advance, do not add the egg whites until the last minute. Whole wheat flour, wheat germ, or even hominy, can be substituted in part for the all-purpose flour. Moreover, fresh fruit, such as sliced strawberries or blueberries, can be sprinkled over the surface of the cakes as soon as the batter hits the griddle.

3 large eggs, separated
1 tablespoon sugar
2 cups buttermilk

4 tablespoons (1/2 stick) unsalted butter, melted
2 cups all-purpose flour
1 teaspoon baking soda

1. Beat the egg yolks with the sugar in a large bowl until light. Whisk in the buttermilk, butter, flour, and baking soda.

2. Beat the egg whites until stiff; fold into the batter.

3. Heat a lightly greased griddle or heavy skillet over medium heat. Pour about 1/3 cup batter for each cake on the griddle and cook until the underside is golden brown and the top is bubbly, about 2 minutes. Turn the pancake over and lightly brown the other side. Keep warm in a low oven while preparing the remaining pancakes.

Makes about 12 pancakes

BRIDGE CREEK HEAVENLY HOTS

MARION CUNNINGHAM, well known for her work on the recent Fannie Farmer cookbooks, devised these delicacies for the Bridge Creek Restaurant in Berkeley. Her latest book, *The Breakfast Book* (Knopf, 1987), is simply wonderful. Her "hots," simply genius.

2 large eggs	2 tablespoons cake or soft wheat flour
1/4 teaspoon salt	1 cup sour cream
1/4 teaspoon baking soda	1 1/2 tablespoons sugar

1. Lightly whisk the eggs in a medium bowl. Whisk in the remaining ingredients.

2. Heat a lightly greased griddle or heavy skillet over medium heat. Spoon small spoonfuls of batter (the pancakes should be no more than 2 1/2 inches across) for each cake on the griddle and cook until the underside is golden brown and the top is bubbly, about 1 minute. Turn the pancake over and cook it briefly on the other side. Keep warm in a low oven while preparing the remaining pancakes.

Makes about 25 small pancakes

OLD-FASHIONED BUCKWHEAT CAKES

Then [Pa sat] down, as they urged him, and lifting the blanket cake on the untouched pile, he slipped from under it a section of the stack of hot, syrupy pancakes . . . The pancakes were no ordinary buckwheat pancakes . . . the cakes were light as foam, soaked through with melted brown sugar.

Words from Laura Ingalls Wilder's *The Long Winter*. What made the pancakes light as "foam" was a yeast starter, much like that used in the sour dough bread of the time. Buckwheat cakes are not only substantial, but nourishing—and delicious, as the following recipe more than proves. Buckwheat flour can be purchased at natural food stores around the country.

2 1/2 cups milk

2 tablespoons molasses

1 1/2 teaspoons dry yeast

1 1/3 cups buckwheat flour

2/3 cup all-purpose flour

1/2 cup fine cornmeal

1/2 teaspoon salt

1 teaspoon sugar

1 teaspoon baking soda

1/2 cup lukewarm water

2 tablespoons unsalted butter, melted

2 large egg yolks, lightly beaten

3 large egg whites

1. The night before serving: Scald the milk and stir in the molasses. Cool to lukewarm. Stir in the yeast; let stand 10 minutes. Transfer to a large bowl.

2. Add the buckwheat flour, all-purpose flour, cornmeal, and salt to the yeast mixture, beating with a wooden spoon until smooth. Cover and let stand at room temperature overnight.

3. The next morning, dissolve the sugar and baking soda in the lukewarm water. Stir into the batter mixture along with the melted butter and egg yolks.

4. Beat the egg whites until stiff; fold into the batter.

5. Heat a lightly greased griddle or heavy skillet over medium heat. Pour about 1/3 cup batter for each cake on the griddle and cook until the underside is golden brown and the top is bubbly, about 2 minutes. Turn the pancake over and lightly brown the other side. Keep warm in a low oven while preparing the remaining pancakes.

Makes about 18 pancakes

COLORADO SURPRISE CAKES

THE NOTION of adding curds of cottage cheese to pancakes originated in Brittany. The traditional method calls for sour cream in the batter, but unflavored yogurt makes the following version special. This formula stems from Colorado where no leavening is required because of the altitude. A teaspoon of baking powder can be added at the cook's discretion, but truly, I prefer it sans leavening even at sea level!

4 large eggs, separated
2 tablespoons sugar
1 cup California-style cottage cheese

1 cup plain yogurt
1 1/2 teaspoons vanilla
3/4 cup all-purpose flour

1. Beat the egg yolks with the sugar in a large bowl until light. Whisk in the cottage cheese, yogurt, vanilla, and flour.
2. Beat the egg whites until stiff; fold into pancake batter.
3. Heat a lightly greased griddle or heavy skillet over medium heat. Pour about 1/3 cup batter for each cake on the griddle and cook until the underside is golden brown and the top is bubbly, about 2 minutes. Turn the pancake over and lightly brown the other side. Keep warm in a low oven while preparing the remaining pancakes.

Makes about 12 pancakes

WICHITA VANILLA OAT CAKES

The oat is the Horatio Alger of cereals, which progressed, if not from rags to riches, at least from weed to health food.

—Waverley Root

AND NOBODY ever said that health food had to *taste* like health food. The following Kansas device for a vanilla-flavored oat cake is proof positive.

3 large eggs, separated
1/2 cup sour cream
1 cup milk
2 tablespoons unsalted butter, melted
1 teaspoon vanilla

1 cup all-purpose flour
1/2 cup quick rolled oats
1 tablespoon baking powder
1/2 teaspoon salt

1. Beat the egg yolks in a large bowl until light. Whisk in the sour cream, milk, butter, vanilla, flour, oats, baking powder, and salt.

2. Beat the egg whites until stiff; fold into the batter.

3. Heat a lightly greased griddle or heavy skillet over medium heat. Pour about 1/4 cup batter for each cake on the griddle and cook until the underside is golden brown and the top is bubbly, about 2 minutes. Turn the pancake over and lightly brown the other side. Keep warm in a low oven while preparing the remaining pancakes.

Makes about 12 pancakes

LACE CAKES

LACE CAKES, or lacy-edged cakes as they are sometimes known, are direct prandial descendants of the aforementioned Rhode Island Jonnycake. The batter for this somewhat more refined rendering is so thin, it *runs* into the griddle forming a very respectable lace edge in the process that snares the syrup as it is poured.

2 large eggs
1 teaspoon sugar
2 cups milk

6 tablespoons (3/4 stick) unsalted
    butter, melted
1 cup fine cornmeal
1/2 teaspoon salt

Like the ladies of Liberal, Kansas, and Olney, England, brave souls may want to "flip" their skillet cakes. But before doing so, they would do well to follow the advice of Martha Bradley in her cookbook, *The British Housewife: Or, the Cook, Housekeeper's and Gardiner's Companion* printed back in 1770.

This is a Thing very easy to a bold Hand, but which a timerous Person will never be able to do well; for such a one, she is to know that the first Thing to be done is to get rid of her Fear, and then a little Practice will make it quite familiar.

The Best Way to learn it is this:

Let a Kitchen Table Cloth be spread upon the Ground at a small distance from the Fire, and when the first Pancake is ready for turning let the Cook try to toss it over the Cloth; if it falls in right it is very well, and if not there is no harm done, it will be catched clean, and may do for the Servants Table.

When there is not the Danger of throwing them into the Fire the Cook will have less Fear, and as we said before, the less Fear the more Likelihood of Success.

The Way is to hold the Pan very steady, and toss the Pancake with a sudden Jerk.

Practice is all: for as the Children play at Bilbecket till they can catch the Ball every Time for many Minutes together, in the same Manner the Cook will be able to toss a hundred Pancakes without missing once, when she is accustomed to the Method of it.

1. Beat the eggs with the sugar in a large bowl until light. Whisk in remaining ingredients.

2. Heat a lightly greased griddle or heavy skillet over medium heat. Pour about 3 tablespoons batter for each cake on the griddle and cook until the underside is golden brown and the pancake is well set. Carefully turn the pancake over and lightly brown the other side. Keep warm in a low oven while preparing the remaining pancakes.

Note Beat the batter well before making each cake as the cornmeal will thicken. Add more milk if batter becomes too thick.

Makes about 12 pancakes

BANANA PANCAKES

BANANAS are full of potassium and make the perfect breakfast pancake— or dessert, for that matter. The next banana-studded recipe is adapted from Dorien Leigh Parker's charming book *Pancakes* (Clarkson N. Potter, 1987). Chop the bananas only after the whole batter is made, and fold them into the batter as you cut them, so they won't turn color.

4 large eggs, separated

3 tablespoons sugar

1 1/4 cups buttermilk

1/4 cup orange juice

2 tablespoons unsalted butter, melted

1 teaspoon vanilla

2 teaspoons finely grated orange peel

1 1/2 cups cake or soft wheat flour

1 teaspoon baking powder

1/2 teaspoon baking soda

1/2 teaspoon ground cinnamon

2 cups diced bananas (about 3 large bananas)

1. Beat the egg yolks with the sugar in a large bowl until light. Whisk in the buttermilk, orange juice, butter, vanilla, orange peel, flour, baking powder, baking soda, and cinnamon. Stir in the bananas.

2. Beat the egg whites until stiff; fold into the pancake batter.

3. Heat a lightly greased griddle or heavy skillet over medium heat. Pour about 1/4 cup batter for each cake on the griddle and cook until the underside is golden brown and the top is bubbly, about 2 minutes. Turn the pancake over and lightly brown the other side. Keep warm in a low oven while preparing the remaining pancakes.

Makes about 20 medium pancakes

VERMONT CHEDDAR CAKES

Nothing is more gentle than smoke . . . Smoke rising through the trees may signify the most charming thing in the world, the hearth . . .

—Victor Hugo

THESE OLD-TIME cheddar cakes were served at church suppers all over Vermont in the 1800s—and were always made over an open fire. I, myself, have had the opportunity to make the following cakes in an authentic Colonial fireplace equipped as cooking hearths once were. It was indeed an enlightening experience and the taste of the food, smoky good. But be assured these are equally delicious made on a modern griddle.

2 large egg yolks

1/2 cup sour cream

2 tablespoons all-purpose flour

1/4 teaspoon salt

Pinch of freshly ground black pepper

1/8 teaspoon freshly grated nutmeg

1/2 teaspoon baking powder

1/2 teaspoon finely grated lemon peel

3/4 cup roughly grated cheddar cheese

1. Beat the egg yolks in a large bowl until light. Beat in remaining ingredients.

2. Heat a lightly greased griddle or heavy skillet over medium heat. Spoon a large teaspoonful or more (depending on how large you want the cakes to be) of batter for each cake on the griddle and cook until the underside is nicely browned, about 2 minutes. Turn the pancake over and lightly brown the other side. Keep warm in a low oven while preparing the remaining pancakes.

Makes 16 small pancakes

SPINACH STUFFED FLANNELS

PANCAKE STACKS were dubbed "flannel cakes" in early lumbering camps; possibly to honor the layers of flannel worn by the lumberjacks in the cold weather pursuits—or perhaps because the cakes themselves were as chewy as damp flannel. No matter, the following are decidedly more digestible; and their lightness suggests rolling and filling rather than stacking. Much like fat crêpes, these flannel cakes can be wrapped around fresh fruit and served with syrup for dessert, or as in this case, filled with a creamy vegetable and offered as an unorthodox accompaniment for roast meat or broiled chicken.

For the filling

1 tablespoon unsalted butter
1 large shallot, minced
1 tablespoon all-purpose flour
1 cup chicken broth

1 pound spinach, trimmed, washed
Pinch of freshly grated nutmeg
Salt and freshly ground black pepper

For the pancakes

2 large eggs
1 cup sour cream
1/2 cup milk

1/2 cup all-purpose flour
1 teaspoon finely grated lemon peel

1. To make the filling: Melt the butter in a medium saucepan over medium-low heat. Add the shallot; cook 5 minutes. Add the flour. Cook, stirring constantly, 2 minutes. Whisk in the chicken broth until smooth. Cook, stirring constantly, until thick, 4 to 5 minutes. Cool.

2. Cook the spinach in boiling salted water until tender. Drain, squeezing out all the excess liquid with the back of a spoon.

3. Chop the spinach and stir into the cooled sauce. Add nutmeg and salt and pepper to taste.

4. To make the pancakes: Beat the eggs in a large bowl until light. Beat in the remaining ingredients.

5. Heat a lightly greased griddle or heavy skillet over medium heat. Pour about 1/4 cup batter for each cake on the griddle and cook until the underside is golden brown and the top is bubbly, about 2 minutes. Turn the pancake over and lightly brown the other side. Place a large spoonful of filling on the underside of each pancake and roll up. Place on a lightly buttered baking dish. Reheat, in a preheated 350° F. oven, for about 15 minutes before serving.
Makes 8 filled pancakes

NEW YORKERS'
POTATO PANCAKES

IT TOOK ME a long time in life to love potato pancakes. It took longer to learn how to make them. I discovered the following method, quite by accident. Having volunteered to make them for an informal gathering, I *roughly* grated the potatoes in a food processor, and left them to stand in ice water. When it was pointed out to me that potatoes for pancakes should be *finely* grated, I merely drained the potatoes, squeezed them dry, and reprocessed them with the steel blade in place. Consequently, most of the starch went down the drain, and the pancakes were feather light. Serve them with pot roasted meats and applesauce.

Juice of 1 lemon (about 3 tablespoons)
1 1/2 pounds baking potatoes
1 small onion, finely grated
1 large egg, lightly beaten

2 tablespoons all-purpose flour
2 teaspoons baking powder
Salt and freshly ground black pepper
Vegetable shortening

1. Add the lemon juice to a large bowl of cold water. Peel the potatoes and roughly grate them into the bowl. Let stand 30 minutes.

2. Drain the potatoes and squeeze dry with your hands. Place the potatoes in the container of a food processor fitted with the steel blade, and process, using the pulse switch, until fairly smooth but not wet, not quite a purée. Transfer to a large bowl and add the onion, egg, flour, baking powder, and salt and pepper to taste. Stir until smooth.

3. Heat a large cast-iron skillet over medium heat. Film the bottom of the skillet with shortening. Spoon the batter, using about 1 large tablespoon for each cake, into the skillet. Do not crowd. Cook until the underside is golden brown and the cakes puff up slightly, about 1 minute. Turn the pancakes over and lightly brown the other side. Place on a rack and keep warm in a low oven while preparing the remaining pancakes.

Makes about 20 small pancakes

STRAWBERRY PAPER PANCAKES
WITH STRAWBERRY-ORANGE SAUCE

A POPULAR dessert in Colonial times was a *Quire of Paper Pancakes*. Thin cakes, like crêpes, these "paper pancakes" were stacked and sprinkled with sugar. The following pancakes are similarly crêpelike. Strawberries in the batter turn the "paper" pink, and more strawberries are stewed with orange juice for a filling and topping. If you wish, you can stack the cakes, spread the topping between each layer, and create your own *quire*.

For the sauce

1/2 pint strawberries, trimmed, cleaned, finely chopped

1 cup orange juice

1/2 cup sugar

For the pancakes

1/2 pint strawberries, trimmed, cleaned

3 tablespoons sugar

2 large eggs

6 tablespoons cornstarch

1 tablespoon vegetable oil

1 teaspoon baking powder

Pinch of salt

3 or 4 tablespoons water, if needed

1. To make the sauce: Combine the strawberries, orange juice, and sugar in a medium saucepan. Heat to boiling; reduce the heat. Simmer, uncovered, 15 minutes. Cool.

2. To make the pancakes: Place all the ingredients, except the water, in the container of a blender. Blend until smooth. The mixture should be quite thin. If the berries aren't juicy enough, add 3 to 4 tablespoons water.

3. Line a plate with two sheets of paper towels and set aside. Lightly rub a crêpe or omelet pan (preferably with a nonstick surface) with a buttered cloth. Place the pan over medium heat until hot. Remove the pan from the heat and pour about 3 tablespoons batter into the center of the pan. Quickly tilt the pan in all directions to coat the bottom evenly. Return the pan to the heat and cook until the edges of the pancake are brown, about 1 minute. Carefully turn the pancake over with the aid of a spatula and your fingers; cook the second side 15 seconds. Flip out onto the paper-towel lined plate. Cover the pancake with another paper towel. Lightly grease the pan once more and continue the process until all the batter is used up, placing paper towels between the finished pancakes.

4. Flip the stack of pancakes over. Spoon about 2 tablespoons sauce over each pancake and roll up. Place the rolled pancakes in a lightly buttered shallow baking dish.

5. Before serving, reheat the remaining sauce over low heat and place the rolled pancakes in a 400° F. oven for 5 minutes. Serve with the sauce.

Makes 10 to 12 rolled pancakes

NEW ORLEANS PRALINE CAKES
WITH CARAMEL SYRUP

"Same old slippers,
Same old rice,
Same old glimpse of
Paradise."
—William G. Lampton

HOWEVER, when the rice ends up in a praline pancake drizzled with caramel sauce in a New Orleans kitchen, the diner gets more than just a glimpse of Paradise: he'll think he's in heaven. A dessert pancake, this is also eminently suitable for breakfast.

For the syrup

1 cup sugar
2/3 cup hot water

2 teaspoons vanilla

For the pancakes

4 large egg yolks
2 tablespoons sugar
1 1/2 cups milk
4 tablespoons (1/2 stick) unsalted
  butter, melted
1 teaspoon vanilla
2 teaspoons brandy

1 cup all-purpose flour
1/2 teaspoon salt
2 teaspoons baking powder
1/8 teaspoon ground cinnamon
1/2 cup coarsely chopped pecans
1 cup cooked rice, cold

1. To make the syrup: Heat the sugar in a medium heavy skillet over medium heat until it starts to melt and turn golden. Continue to cook, stirring constantly, until caramelized. Carefully add the hot water all at once and stir until all lumps are dissolved. Remove from heat and stir in the vanilla. Set aside.

2. To make the pancakes: Beat the yolks with the sugar in a large bowl until light. Beat in the remaining ingredients.

3. Heat a lightly greased griddle or heavy skillet over medium heat. Pour about 1/4 cup batter for each cake on the griddle and cook until the underside is golden brown and the top is bubbly, about 2 minutes. Turn the pancake over and lightly brown the other side. Keep warm in a low oven while preparing the remaining pancakes. Serve drizzled with caramel syrup.

Makes about 16 pancakes

Potato Salads

Pray for peace and grace and spiritual food,
For wisdom and guidance, for all these are good,
But don't forget the potatoes.

—John Tyler Pettee

GOOD ADVICE for a church picnic—potatoes are transformed into a miraculous creamy salad for just such a profound occasion. God, fresh air, and good food are a combination not to be taken lightly. Particularly since one bit of historical trivia credits Sir John Hawkins with the introduction of the tuber to Europe in 1565 after returning from Venezuela in his ship, the *Jesus of Lubeck*. Of course, that is only one of many theories.

The potato is indigenous to Central and South America. It was cultivated more than four thousand years ago in mountainous regions and has been found growing in areas up to fifteen thousand feet in altitude. The name actually derives from the Caribbean Indian word for the sweet potato, *batata,* which was corrupted to *patata* by the Spaniards; then, of course, to *potato* by the British. The vegetable was introduced into England and Ireland by 1610, but did not take hold on the Continent until the late 1700s. Rumor had it that the potato caused leprosy, which delayed its acceptance.

It is said the potato had to cross the Atlantic five times to "make it" in the American Colonies. The first productive crossing *and* successful cultivation (after earlier attempts in Virginia) took place near Londonderry, New Hampshire, when a group of Irish Protestants brought it over in 1719. Even then it took a while for this important food crop to take root with local taste buds.

By the 1800s, the potato had taken its rightful place in food history and each of the potato-consuming countries had added its own distinctive recipes to the world's larder. All of which eventually ended up on our shores with immigrants from all over. The Teutonic countries, particularly Germany, are credited with the invention of a cooked potato *salat,* served tossed with vinegar, oil, and seasonings.

Some Potato Salad Savvy For the most part, potato salads can be divided into two categories; those tossed with vinaigrette-style dressings and the ones with slightly higher calorie counts, blanketed with mayonnaise-based sauces. The type of potato to use in a potato salad has long been a point of contention with potato salad aficionados. Mealy versus waxy. Mealy potatoes (such as Idaho or Maine), considered best for baking and mashing, are "mealy" because their cells tend to separate when cooked. Waxy potatoes (like Early Rose and Green Mountain), on the other hand, are more cohesive and therefore do not absorb as much. I often use the mealy type for vinaigrette-based dressings because they do absorb, and waxy for mayonnaise concoctions because they do not. But, as far as I'm concerned, it's entirely up to the cook. If *you* are scrupulous, however, but aren't sure about the texture of the potato you have in hand, an old wives' tale has it that if you place a potato in a brine made of one part salt to eleven parts water and it floats, it is waxy. Mealy potatoes are denser and thus will sink.

Potatoes, no matter which type suits you best, should always be cooked unpeeled in boiling water until *just* tender. Overcooked potatoes disintegrate into pieces when tossed with a dressing. A medium potato cooks in about 20 minutes. One sure-fire way to test a potato's readiness is to insert a small sharp knife into the center. There should be a slight resistance to the point halfway through. The center will continue to cook as the potato cools. It is advisable to quickly douse the cooked potatoes with cold running water to cool the outer portions. When choosing potatoes, pick specimens of equal size for even cooking.

> There is hardly a vegetable which is not used, either cooked or raw, in salad, the usual dressing being one third or fourth vinegar, and two thirds or three fourths oil, with, of course, salt and pepper.
>
> —Maria Parloa (*Home Economics,* 1898)

AS SIMPLE as that. What else goes in, as well as what goes on, a potato salad is the prerogative of the salad tosser. Some not-quite-so-simple recipes follow.

OLD-FANGLED POTATO SALAD

> IT IS generally supposed that the water in which potatoes are boiled is injurious; and as instances are recorded where cattle having drunk it were seriously affected, it may be well to err on the safe side, and avoid its use for any alimentary purpose.
>
> —*Beeton's Book of Household Management*

Obviously, Mrs. Beeton would shudder if she knew that a very famous potato diet consists of nothing but drinking the water in which "potatoes in their jackets" are boiled. Whether you drink potato water or throw it down the drain can be your secret, but do not keep this classic potato salad to yourself.

4 medium baking potatoes (about 2 pounds)
1/2 cup finely chopped celery

2 teaspoons Dijon mustard
1 teaspoon Hungarian sweet paprika

(ingredients continued)

1/2 cup chopped dill pickles

4 hard-cooked eggs, peeled, roughly chopped

1 large clove garlic, minced

1/2 teaspoon salt

1/8 teaspoon cayenne pepper

2 tablespoons lemon juice

1/4 cup olive oil

2/3 cup mayonnaise

Chopped fresh parsley

1. Cook the potatoes, unpeeled, in boiling water until just barely tender, about 20 minutes. Rinse under cold running water and drain. Allow to cool.

2. Peel the potatoes and cut each in half lengthwise. Cut each half into 1/4-inch-thick slices. Combine the potatoes with the celery, pickles, and eggs in a large bowl.

3. Mash the garlic with the salt in a small bowl until a paste is formed. Stir in the mustard, paprika, and cayenne pepper. Whisk in the lemon juice, oil, and mayonnaise. Pour over the potato mixture. Gently toss to mix. Sprinkle with parsley and serve at room temperature or slightly chilled.

Serves 4 to 6

SPECK'S FAMOUS
HOT POTATO SALAD

A RECIPE with a reputation, this hot German potato salad was one of the specials at the now-vanished restaurant Speck's in St. Louis. The bacon and vinegar dressing demands that you serve the salad warm.

6 medium potatoes (about 3 pounds)

1/4 cup finely chopped bacon

1 small onion, finely chopped

2 tablespoons all-purpose flour

1 teaspoon salt

4 teaspoons sugar

1/4 teaspoon freshly ground black pepper

2/3 cup cider vinegar

1/3 cup water

1/2 teaspoon celery seed

3 tablespoons chopped fresh parsley

1. Cook the potatoes, unpeeled, in boiling water until just barely tender, about 20 minutes. Drain.

2. Meanwhile, sauté the bacon in a large heavy skillet over medium heat until crisp. Add the onion; cook 1 minute. Stir in the flour, salt, sugar, and pepper. Cook, stirring constantly, 1 minute. Whisk in the vinegar and water. Cook, stirring frequently, 10 minutes. Keep warm over low heat.

3. Peel the potatoes and cut into thin slices. Combine with the celery seed and parsley in a large bowl. Pour the bacon dressing over the potato mixture. Gently toss to mix. Serve immediately.

Serves 6 to 8

HOT DRESSED POTATO SALAD,
YANKEE-STYLE

A little fire that warms is better than a big fire that burns.
—Irish proverb

KEEP THAT thought in mind when making the old New England hot dressing for the next recipe. Take care not to let the eggs curdle. This recipe is so rich, one small potato per person is just about right, but be more generous if you dare.

4 small baking potatoes (about 1 1/2 pounds)

2 tablespoons finely chopped green bell pepper

1/4 cup sliced radishes

1 shallot, minced

1 tablespoon lemon juice

3 large eggs

3 tablespoons water

3 tablespoons red wine vinegar

1/2 teaspoon salt

1/8 teaspoon freshly ground black pepper

Pinch of cayenne pepper

4 tablespoons (1/2 stick) unsalted butter

Chopped fresh parsley

1. Cook the potatoes, unpeeled, in boiling water until just barely tender, 15 to 20 minutes. Rinse under cold running water and drain. Allow to cool.

2. Peel the potatoes and cut each in half lengthwise. Cut each half into 1/4-inch-thick slices. Combine the potatoes with the bell pepper, radishes, and shallot in a large bowl. Sprinkle with lemon juice.

3. Beat the eggs with water, vinegar, salt, freshly ground pepper, and cayenne pepper in a medium bowl until light.

4. Melt the butter in a medium saucepan over medium-low heat. Remove from heat and whisk in the egg mixture. Return to low heat and cook, whisking constantly, until mixture thickens, about 3 minutes. Do not allow to boil. Pour over the potato mixture. Gently toss to mix. Sprinkle with parsley and serve immediately.

Serves 4

ORANGE COUNTY SALAD

FROM southern California, this unusual salad makes use of the local produce. Aside from being redolent of good tastes (oranges, smoky peppers, and cilantro), it is downright wholesome.

2 medium baking potatoes (about 1 pound)
1 jalapeño pepper
1 large seedless orange
1/2 medium red onion, thinly sliced
1 clove garlic, crushed
1/4 teaspoon salt

1 1/2 teaspoons Dijon mustard
2 tablespoons orange juice
1 teaspoon red wine vinegar
1/3 cup olive oil
Freshly ground black pepper
1 tablespoon chopped fresh cilantro (Chinese parsley)

1. Cook the potatoes, unpeeled, in boiling water until just barely tender, about 20 minutes. Rinse under cold running water and drain. Allow to cool.

2. Meanwhile, roast the pepper over a gas flame or under a broiler until

charred all over. Carefully wrap the pepper in paper towels. Place in a plastic bag. Cool slightly. Rub off the charred skin with paper towels. Seed, devein, and mince the pepper.

3. Peel the orange. Using a very sharp knife, remove all the pith. Slice across the orange, cutting into rounds about 1/4-inch thick. Cut each segment apart.

4. Peel the potatoes and cut each in half lengthwise. Cut each half into 1/4-inch-thick slices. Combine the potatoes with the minced pepper, the orange segments, and onion in a large bowl.

5. Mash the garlic with the salt in a small bowl until a paste is formed. Stir in the mustard, orange juice, and vinegar. Whisk in the oil. Pour over the potato mixture and sprinkle with pepper to taste and 2 teaspoons cilantro. Gently toss to mix. Sprinkle with remaining 1 teaspoon cilantro. Serve at room temperature.

Serves 4

TRUE BLUE IOWA POTATO SALAD

SOME OF THE finest blue cheese in the world is made in Iowa at Maytag Dairy Farms in Newton. No one will argue once they taste the creamy blue cheese dressing that coats the following potato and cucumber salad.

4 medium baking potatoes (about 2 pounds)

6 tablespoons olive oil

2 tablespoons finely chopped green scallion ends

2 tablespoons chopped fresh basil, or 1 teaspoon dried

2 tablespoons chopped fresh parsley

1 large clove garlic, crushed

1/2 teaspoon salt

1 teaspoon Dijon mustard

6 ounces creamy blue cheese (such as Maytag, Blue Castello, or Cambazola), at room temperature

2 tablespoons red wine vinegar

2/3 cup heavy or whipping cream

2 small cucumbers (about 4 ounces each), peeled, seeded, minced

1. Cook the potatoes, unpeeled, in boiling water until just barely tender, about 20 minutes. Rinse under cold running water and drain.

2. Peel the potatoes while warm. Cut in half lengthwise. Cut each half into 1/4-inch-thick slices. Combine with the oil, scallion, basil, and parsley in a large bowl. Let stand, covered, 1 hour.

3. Mash the garlic with the salt in a small bowl until a paste is formed. Whisk in the mustard. Remove any rind from the cheese and add to the garlic mixture in small pieces. Beat until smooth. Whisk in the vinegar and cream.

4. Sprinkle the minced cucumbers over the potato mixture. Pour the dressing over the top of the cucumbers. Gently toss to mix. Serve at room temperature.

Serves 4 to 6

NEW POTATOES AND PEAS
IN LEMON MAYONNAISE

What small potatoes we all are, compared with what we might be! We don't plow deep enough, any of us, for one thing.

WISE WORDS from the 1870 *My Summer in a Garden* by Charles Dudley Warner. But when it comes to small new potatoes, who cares, when they are tossed with peas and folded with a lemony mayonnaise.

20 small red new potatoes (about 2 1/2 pounds)

2 cups shelled fresh peas, or 1 package (10 ounces) frozen peas

2 shallots, minced

1 cup mayonnaise

2 tablespoons milk (approximately)

2 teaspoons tarragon wine vinegar

2 teaspoons Dijon mustard

Dash of hot pepper sauce

2 to 3 teaspoons finely slivered lemon peel

The juice of 1 lemon (about 3 tablespoons)

1/2 cup sour cream

Salt and freshly ground black pepper

Chopped fresh parsley

In *The Delectable Past,* Esther B. Aresty adapted Rev. Sydney Smith's famous poem for salad making for use in the kitchen. The only major change she made was slicing, rather than sieving, the cooked potatoes. The original poem goes like this:

> To make this condiment, your poet begs
> The pounded yellow of two hard-boil'd eggs;
> Two boil'd potatoes, pass'd through kitchen sieve,
> Smoothness and softness to the salad give.
> Let onion atoms lurk within the bowl,
> And, half suspected, animate the whole.
> Of mordant mustard add a single spoon,
> Distrust the condiment that bites so soon;
> But deem it not, thou man of herbs, a fault,
> To add a double quantity of salt;
> Four times the spoon with oil from Lucca Brown,
> And twice with vinegar procured from town;
> And, lastly, o'er the flavor'd compound toss
> A magic soupçon of anchovy sauce.
> Oh, green and glorious! Oh, herbaceous treat!
> 'Twould tempt the dying anchorite to eat;
> Back to the world he'd turn his fleeting soul,
> And plunge his fingers in the salad-bowl!
> Serenely full, the epicure would say,
> Fate cannot harm me, I have dined to-day.

1. Cook the potatoes, unpeeled, in boiling water until just barely tender, about 12 minutes. Rinse under cold running water and drain. Allow to cool.

2. Cook the peas in boiling salted water 30 seconds. (Or only until defrosted, if using frozen.) Rinse under cold running water and drain.

3. Cut the potatoes into 1/4-inch-thick slices. Combine the potatoes with the peas and shallots in a large bowl.

4. Whisk the mayonnaise with 2 tablespoons milk, the vinegar, and mustard in a medium bowl until smooth. Whisk in the hot pepper sauce, lemon peel, lemon juice, and sour cream. Add more milk if mixture seems too thick. Pour over the potato mixture. Gently toss to mix. Add salt and pepper to taste. Sprinkle with parsley and serve chilled.

Serves 6

TOSSED ZUCCHINI
AND POTATOES

ACCORDING to legend, zucchini seeds were given by the gods to the peoples of Abruzzi, Italy. They were told to protect the seeds from all other peoples, which they did until Christopher Columbus brought the seeds to America. But then it might have been Columbus who carried the potato back to Europe. One good turn deserves another, as they say, and both share honors in the next recipe.

16 small white potatoes (about 2 pounds)

2 medium zucchini (about 4 ounces each), cut into thin rounds

2 medium shallots, minced

1/4 cup finely slivered fresh basil leaves, or 1 teaspoon dried

1 large clove garlic, crushed

2 teaspoons anchovy paste

1/2 cup olive oil

6 tablespoons V-8 or Bloody Mary mix

2 teaspoons lemon juice

Salt and freshly ground black pepper

2 tablespoons chopped fresh parsley

1. Cook the potatoes, unpeeled, in boiling water until just barely tender, 12 to 15 minutes. Rinse under cold running water and drain. Allow to cool.

2. Peel the potatoes and cut into very thin rounds. Combine with the zucchini, shallot, and basil in a large bowl.

3. Mash the garlic with the anchovy paste in a small bowl until smooth. Whisk in the oil, V-8 juice, and lemon juice. Pour over the potato mixture. Gently toss to mix. Add salt and pepper to taste. Let stand, covered, at room temperature 2 hours. Sprinkle with parsley and serve at room temperature or slightly chilled.

Serves 4 to 6

BERT GREENE'S
COLD CURRIED SWEETS

THE FOLLOWING recipe is from Bert Greene's tome on vegetable cooking, *Greene On Greens* (Workman, 1984). I was fortunate to be one of the first to taste it—and have been making it ever since. Sweet potatoes stand in for the old white variety in this salad. You might call it "pure gold."

4 large yams (about 1 3/4 pounds)

1 medium red onion, finely chopped

1/2 green bell pepper, seeded, finely chopped

1/2 cup mayonnaise

1/2 cup sour cream

1/4 cup strong beef stock (see page 377), cooled

1 tablespoon curry powder

Salt and freshly ground black pepper

2 tablespoons chopped fresh parsley

1. Cook the yams, unpeeled, in boiling water until just barely tender, 20 to 25 minutes. Rinse under cold running water and drain. Allow to cool.

2. Peel the potatoes and cut in half lengthwise. Cut each half into 1/4-inch-thick slices. Combine the potatoes with the onion and bell pepper in a large bowl.

3. Whisk the mayonnaise with the sour cream in a medium bowl. Whisk in the stock, curry powder, and salt and pepper to taste. Pour over the potato mixture. Gently toss to mix. Sprinkle with parsley and serve at room temperature or slightly chilled.

Serves 4 to 6

WISCONSIN CREAMY
POTATO SALAD

Peace of mind and a comfortable income are predicted by a dream of eating potatoes in any form.

—*Your Horoscope and Dreams*

THE NEXT dreamy recipe from Wisconsin couples warm red potatoes with the shaved root ends of Pascal celery. The dressing is enriched with sour cream and should be tossed and served while the potatoes are still warm. Good fortunes are bound to follow.

10 medium red potatoes (about 2 1/2 pounds)

The root ends of 2 small Pascal celerys about 1/2 to 1 inch in thickness

1/4 cup freshly squeezed lemon juice

2 teaspoons sugar

1/2 teaspoon salt

1 teaspoon Dijon mustard

1/2 teaspoon freshly ground black pepper

1/4 cup red wine vinegar

6 tablespoons olive oil

2 shallots, minced

1 cup sour cream

1/4 cup chopped fresh parsley

1/4 teaspoon Hungarian hot paprika

1. Cook the potatoes, unpeeled, in boiling water until just barely tender, about 20 minutes. Rinse under cold water and drain.

2. Meanwhile, shave off the outer portion of the celery ends and discard. Shave the remaining ends with a vegetable peeler into strips. Sprinkle with lemon juice. Set aside.

3. Combine the sugar, salt, mustard, pepper, and vinegar in a large bowl. Whisk in the oil, shallot, and sour cream.

4. Cut the potatoes into 1/4-inch-thick slices while warm, and add to the sour cream mixture along with the reserved celery ends and 2 tablespoons parsley. Gently toss to mix. Sprinkle with paprika and the remaining 2 tablespoons parsley. Serve immediately.

Serves 6

POTATOES, ZITI-STYLE

THE STORE in Amagansett (New York) was famous for its ziti salad. A mixture of peppers, onions, pickles, tomatoes, and ziti-cut pasta, of course. However, it is equally delicious when potatoes act as a stand-in for the pasta.

3 medium baking potatoes (about 1 1/2 pounds)

1/2 small red onion, minced

1 medium tomato, seeded, chopped

4 small sweet gherkins, chopped

1/2 green bell pepper, finely chopped

1/4 cup sour cream

3/4 cup mayonnaise

1 tablespoon strong beef stock (see page 377)

1 1/2 teaspoons red wine vinegar

1 1/2 teaspoons pickle juice

Salt and freshly ground black pepper

2 tablespoons chopped fresh dill

1. Cook the potatoes, unpeeled, in boiling water until just barely tender, about 20 minutes. Rinse under cold running water and drain. Allow to cool.

2. Peel the potatoes and cut each in half lengthwise. Cut each half into 1/4-inch-thick slices. Combine the potatoes with the onion, tomato, gherkins, and bell pepper in a large bowl.

3. Whisk the sour cream with the mayonnaise in a medium bowl. Whisk

in the beef stock, vinegar, and pickle juice. Add salt and pepper to taste, and 1 tablespoon chopped dill. Pour over the potato mixture. Gently toss to mix. Sprinkle with the remaining 1 tablespoon dill and serve at room temperature or slightly chilled.

Serves 4

GRILLED POTATO WITH FRESH VEGETABLE SALAD

The discovery of a new dish does more for the happiness of mankind than the discovery of a star.

—Brillat-Savarin

THE FOLLOWING unique potato salad is an adaptation of a recipe from Greens restaurant in San Francisco as reported in *Women Chefs* by Jim Burns and Betty Ann Brown (Aris Books, 1987). The potatoes should be grilled briefly before mixing with the salad, but a stint under a broiler works almost as well.

8 small red and white potatoes (about 1 pound), unpeeled

4 1/2 tablespoons olive oil

Salt and freshly ground black pepper

2 cloves garlic, unpeeled, plus 1 clove, minced

1/4 pound tender young string beans, about 2 inches long

1/2 red bell pepper, cut into very thin strips, about 2 inches long

1/2 yellow bell pepper, cut into very thin strips, about 2 inches long

1/2 small red onion, sliced very thin

Finely grated peel of 1 lemon

1 tablespoon lemon juice

1 1/2 teaspoons sherry wine vinegar

2 tablespoons chopped fresh basil

1 tablespoon chopped fresh Italian parsley

1/4 cup sliced black olives

1. Preheat the oven to 400° F.

2. Place the potatoes in a heatproof baking dish and sprinkle with 1 1/2 tablespoons olive oil, 1/4 teaspoon salt and 1/8 teaspoon freshly ground pepper. Add the unpeeled garlic and toss well. Bake until potatoes are tender, about 30 minutes.

3. Meanwhile, cook the string beans in boiling salted water until just tender, about 2 minutes. Rinse under cold running water and drain. Set aside.

4. When the potatoes are tender, remove the garlic and set aside. Cut the potatoes in half and either place on a hot grill or under a preheated broiler until crisp on both sides. Allow to cool slightly.

5. Combine the potato halves with the string beans, red and yellow peppers, and onion in a large bowl. Toss well.

6. Peel the baked garlic and mash with the minced garlic in a small bowl until smooth. Stir in the lemon peel, lemon juice, sherry vinegar, the remaining 3 tablespoons oil, and the basil. Pour over the potato mixture. Gently toss to mix. Add salt and pepper to taste. Sprinkle with parsley and garnish with olive slices. Serve at room temperature.

Serves 4

NEW ORLEANS
SHRIMP AND POTATO SALAD

THE LAST recipe in this collection stems from New Orleans where the shrimp are fresh and the culinary notions even fresher. The zippy horseradish dressing is served on the side in this case. It is one potato salad that is a meal in itself.

4 medium baking potatoes (about
   2 pounds)
3 cups chicken broth (approximately)

1 tablespoon chopped fresh parsley
1 tablespoon chopped fresh basil, or
   1 teaspoon dried

(ingredients continued)

1/2 teaspoon salt

1/8 teaspoon freshly ground black
    pepper

4 teaspoons red wine vinegar

6 tablespoons olive oil

1/2 cup dry white wine

1/2 pound cooked, peeled and deveined
    medium shrimp, cut in half length-
    wise

2 tablespoons finely chopped green
    scallion ends

1/2 cup mayonnaise

1/4 cup sour cream

2 tablespoons lemon juice

1 teaspoon prepared white horseradish

1. Peel the potatoes and place in a medium saucepan. Add the chicken broth and water, if needed, to cover. Heat to boiling; reduce the heat. Simmer, uncovered, until the potatoes are just tender, about 20 minutes. Remove the potatoes from the broth, reserving the broth for use at another time.

2. Cut the potatoes in half lengthwise. Cut into thin slices and place in a large bowl. Sprinkle with the salt, pepper, vinegar, oil, and wine. Gently toss and let stand at room temperature 30 minutes.

3. Add the shrimp, parsley, basil, and 1 tablespoon chopped scallion to the potato mixture. Gently toss to mix. Sprinkle the remaining chopped scallion over the top.

4. Beat the mayonnaise with the sour cream, lemon juice, and horseradish in a small bowl. Serve the potato salad at room temperature. Pass the sauce on the side.

Serves 4 to 6

Pot Pies

$\mathscr{I}$N 1902, an English journalist, somewhat bemused by America's love of pies, suggested that Americans would be wise to eat them, whether sweet or savory, only twice a week. This, wrote the *New York Times* in reply, was

> . . . utterly insufficient . . . as anyone who knows the secret of our strength as a nation and the foundation of our industrial supremacy must admit. Pie is the American synonym of prosperity. . . . Pie is the food of the heroic. No pie-eating people can ever be permanently vanquished.

All of which is rather amusing since this nation inherited its love of pies from England in the first place.

As far back as the fourteenth century, London was chock-a-block with cookshops selling deep-dish meat pies laden with heavy (almost inedible) crusts fondly dubbed "coffins." What meat actually went into some of these pies was often questionable. Early Colonists brought the tradition with them but made their first meat pies in black iron kettles. They layered strips of dough over the bottom of the kettle. They spooned leftover stew with extra broth over the dough, the whole topped with more pastry or biscuit dough. They placed a weighted cover over the pie which was then cooked over hot coals for an hour's time. As the pioneer movement swept the country, supplies were often hard to come by in most of the new settlements that sprang forth everywhere. Frugal housewives quickly learned that it was much more economical to bake pies in their brick ovens in shallow dishes, rather than deep pots or kettles. This gave the meat pie a totally American stamp.

What is also American about the pot pie is its name. Food savants claim that tag stemmed from a native Pennsylvania Dutch dish called *bott-boi*. It was a thickish meat stew dappled with square noodles—probably delicious but hard to pronounce; so *bott-boi,* in time, became "pot-pie." By the Great Depression, pot pies had become a fairly common sight on American tables. It was a popularity born of necessity, as the dish was often composed of a week's leftovers—recycled. These pies were usually thick as glug and covered with a heavy pastry that not only stuck to the roof of the mouth but "lay in the belly like a lump."

The pot pie as a *treat* did not become a culinary option until twenty years later, when American dining became portable and moved into the living room. For pot pies were the very first TV dinners. Easy to eat—the filling always neatly clung to the fork and the gravy rarely dripped—this dish gave as much joy to family life as the inevitable happy endings they shared with Ricky and Lucy or Ozzie and Harriet.

Pot Pie Input Today's pot pies have a new look. For one thing, they usually have only a top crust and fewer calories. They are spicier, more aromatic, heightened with spirits, and lighter on the tongue. Moreover, they come with a great variety of crusts—everything from Mom's special pie pastry or biscuit dough to mashed potatoes. There are also no hard-and-fast rules for the containers they bake in. Oval, square, even shallow casseroles work in a pinch. And perhaps the most appealing aspect of pot pies is that, for the most part, they can be made ahead and even frozen. The fillings, thick stews or ragouts, inevitably taste better when made in advance. Pastry, though, even if made in advance, should not be rolled out until the day of baking for best results. If you wish to freeze the pie, however, place the pastry over the prepared (cooled) filling and stash it in the freezer, unbaked. Add about 15 minutes to the cooking times when ready to bake.

There is nothing better on a cold wintry day than a properly made pot pie . . .
—Craig Claiborne

GOOD WEATHER or bad, creative cooks all over the country are rediscovering this one-dish dinner, reinventing fillings under a surprising clutch of covers, and positioning pot pies in a prominent spot on their nightly menus. And why not? The pot pie's essential charm may be nostalgic, but it is the hearty flavor in the end that rings the dinner bell. Nothing was ever as warm, wonderful, or easy on the taste buds.

NANTUCKET SHORT-CRUSTED CLAM PIE

AN OLD-TIME New England staple with a borrowing from the new Southwest, this sensuous pie is dependent on sweet juicy fresh clams and dark roasted red pepper. The crust may be short, but the dish is long on flavor.

For the short-crust topping

1 1/2 cups all-purpose flour

1 teaspoon sugar

1/2 teaspoon salt

6 tablespoons vegetable shortening

1 large egg yolk

1 teaspoon red wine vinegar

2 to 3 tablespoons cold water

For the filling

1/4 cup dry white wine

3 sprigs parsley

1 small bay leaf

2 whole cloves

6 whole peppercorns

24 large clams, washed, scrubbed

1 large onion, finely chopped

1 small rib celery, finely chopped

1 large baking potato (1 1/4 pounds), peeled, diced

3 tablespoons all-purpose flour

1/4 cup heavy or whipping cream

(ingredients continued)

1 red bell pepper

2 strips bacon

5 tablespoons unsalted butter, plus
1 teaspoon, melted

1/8 teaspoon hot pepper sauce

1/8 teaspoon freshly grated nutmeg

Salt and freshly ground black pepper

1 large egg white, lightly beaten

1. To make the short-crust topping: Combine the flour with the sugar and salt in a medium bowl. Cut in the vegetable shortening with a knife. Blend with a pastry blender until the mixture has the texture of coarse crumbs. Lightly beat the egg yolk with the vinegar and water. Add the liquid, a tablespoon at a time, and mix gently with a fork to form a soft dough. Chill 1 hour before using.

2. To make the filling: Combine the wine, parsley, bay leaf, cloves, and peppercorns in a large heavy pot. Heat to boiling and add the clams. Reduce the heat to medium and cook, covered, 5 minutes. Remove from heat. Let stand, uncovered, 5 minutes. (The clams should be open just enough to insert a clam knife to pry them open.) Remove the clams from their shells over a bowl to catch the juices; discard the shells. Coarsely chop the clams. Add the clam cooking liquid to the juices in the bowl and strain through a fine sieve lined with cheesecloth. If you have more than 1 cup liquid, boil over high heat to reduce it to 1 cup.

3. Roast the pepper over a gas flame or under a broiler until charred all over. Carefully wrap in paper towels and place in a plastic bag. Let stand 5 minutes. Rub off the charred skin with paper towels. Core and chop the pepper. Set aside.

4. Sauté the bacon in a heavy skillet over medium heat until crisp. Drain on paper towels; crumble and set aside.

5. Pour off all the drippings from the skillet and melt 3 tablespoons butter in the skillet over medium heat. Add the onion; cook until golden, about 5 minutes. Stir in the celery and potato, scraping the bottom and sides of the pan with a wooden spoon. Cook, covered, over medium-low heat until softened, about 5 minutes. Transfer to a heatproof bowl.

6. Preheat the oven to 400° F.

7. Melt the remaining 2 tablespoons butter in the same skillet over medium-low heat. Whisk in the flour. Cook, stirring constantly, 2 minutes. Whisk in the reserved clam broth. Heat to boiling; boil until thick, about 2 minutes. Whisk in the cream, hot pepper sauce, and nutmeg. Continue to cook until very thick, about 2 minutes longer. Pour over the vegetables in the bowl. Stir in the roasted red pepper, the crumbled bacon, and the clams. Add salt and pepper to taste. Transfer to a lightly buttered 10-inch round or fluted glass or ceramic pie pan.

8. Roll out the pastry on a lightly floured board and use it to cover the dish. Trim and flute the edges. Brush with the beaten egg white. Cut a slash in the center of the pie. Bake until golden brown, about 25 minutes. Let stand a few minutes before serving.

Serves 4

NEW-FASHIONED CHICKEN POT PIE
WITH PHYLLO CRUST

What is a roofless cathedral compared to a well-built pie?
—William Maginn

THE FOLLOWING is definitely a well-built pie, but a chicken pie with a secret ingredient? Yes, jicama, that sweet super-crispy tuber usually found only in Mexican cuisine. Jicama's "crunch" holds up remarkably well even after long cooking and melds perfectly with just about every ingredient. You can make the pastry from scratch if you wish, but frankly the phyllo puff pastry, or strudel dough, now available frozen works just fine.

For the filling

1 whole chicken (about 3 1/2 pounds)
1 large yellow onion (unpeeled), halved
2 carrots, peeled; 1 sliced, 1 cut into
    1/4-inch cubes
1 rib celery, chopped
1 turnip, peeled, chopped
1 parsnip, peeled, chopped
4 sprigs parsley
1 quart chicken broth or stock (see
   page 378)
Water

1 teaspoon red wine vinegar
1 large leek, washed, chopped (about
   1 cup)
1 small jicama (1/2 pound), peeled, cut
   into 1/4-inch cubes (about 1/2 cup)
2 tablespoons unsalted butter
1 1/2 tablespoons all-purpose flour
1 cup heavy or whipping cream
Pinch of ground allspice
1/8 teaspoon freshly grated nutmeg
Salt and freshly ground black pepper

For the phyllo topping

8 sheets frozen phyllo or strudel dough,
   thawed, refrigerated

3 tablespoons unsalted butter, melted
   (approximately)
1 tablespoon fine fresh bread crumbs

1. To make the filling: Place the chicken in a large pot and add the onion, the sliced carrot, the celery, turnip, parsnip, parsley, chicken broth, and water to cover. Heat to boiling; reduce the heat. Simmer, partially covered, until the chicken is tender, about 50 minutes. Remove from heat, stir in the vinegar, and allow the chicken to cool in broth for about 30 minutes.

2. When the chicken is cool enough to handle, remove the skin and bones and cut the meat into bite-size pieces. Strain the stock and set aside.

3. Combine the leek with 1 1/2 cups of the reserved chicken stock in a medium saucepan. Heat to boiling. Stir in the carrot cubes and reduce the heat. Cook, uncovered, over medium-low heat 10 minutes. Add the jicama; cook 5 minutes longer. Strain the vegetables over a heatproof bowl. Set aside the vegetables. Add enough chicken stock to the vegetable juices to make 1 cup.

4. Melt the butter in a medium saucepan over medium-low heat. Whisk in the flour. Cook, stirring constantly, 2 minutes. Add the reserved 1 cup

vegetable juices. Heat to boiling; boil 3 minutes. Whisk in the cream, allspice, and nutmeg. Continue to cook, stirring frequently, until thick, about 8 minutes. Remove from heat and allow to cool, stirring occasionally, 10 minutes. Stir in the chicken and reserved vegetables. Add salt and pepper to taste. Transfer to a lightly buttered 1 1/2- to 2-inch deep, 10-inch round baking dish.

5. Preheat the oven to 375° F.

6. To prepare the phyllo topping: Cover a damp tea towel with wax paper. Remove the pastry from the refrigerator and place 2 sheets on the towel. Lightly brush with about 1 1/2 teaspoons butter and sprinkle with 1 teaspoon bread crumbs. Repeat twice more with phyllo, melted butter, and bread crumbs. Place the remaining 2 sheets of phyllo on top and brush with butter. Invert the pastry over the dish and trim all but 1/2 inch pastry from the sides. Brush the sides and top lightly with butter. Tuck in the sides and press firmly into the dish. Cut a small hole in the center of the pie. Bake until golden and crisp, about 30 minutes. Let stand a few minutes before serving. *Serves 4 to 6*

TURKEY AND FENNEL PIE
WITH OLD NEW ENGLAND PASTRY

PROBABLY the one pot pie in this whole collection that I make only when I have leftovers. Turkey that is. Actually, chicken stands in nicely, but this pie does make a wonderful change from turkey tetrazzini the weekend after Thanksgiving.

For the New England pastry

1 1/2 cups all-purpose flour

1/4 teaspoon salt

6 tablespoons (3/4 stick) unsalted
   butter, chilled

6 tablespoons lard, chilled

6 tablespoons ice water

1 medium potato (about 1/2 pound)

1 small fennel (about 1/2 pound)

1 1/4 cups chicken broth or stock (approximately)

2 tablespoons unsalted butter

1 small onion, finely chopped

1/2 teaspoon anise seeds

2 tablespoons all-purpose flour

1 cup heavy or whipping cream

1 tablespoon Pernod

3/4 cup cubed, cooked ham

1 1/2 cups cooked turkey, cut into bite-size pieces

Dash of hot pepper sauce

Salt and freshly ground black pepper

1 tablespoon milk

1. To make the New England pastry: Combine the flour with the salt in a large bowl. Cut in the butter and lard with a knife. Blend with a pastry blender until the mixture has the texture of coarse crumbs. Using the pastry blender, add the water to the flour mixture to form a soft, sticky dough. Transfer to a well-floured pastry board.

2. Pat the dough with floured hands and turn over, using a long metal spatula, if necessary. Gently roll the dough, using a well-floured rolling pin, to a rectangle about 15 inches long and 10 inches wide. The dough will still be fairly sticky at this point. With the use of the spatula, fold the left third of the dough over the middle. Then fold the right third over. Pick the dough up with the spatula and reflour the board. Continue to roll the dough and fold over in thirds nine more times, flouring the board, the pin, and your hands as you work. After the last folding, fold the dough over on itself. Chill 4 hours or overnight.

3. To make the filling: Peel the potatoes and cut into cubes. Cook in boiling salted water 8 minutes; drain.

4. Trim the fennel and remove and discard the core. Cut the fennel into cubes. Combine the fennel with the chicken broth in a medium saucepan. Heat to boiling; reduce the heat. Simmer, covered, 4 minutes. Drain the fennel, reserving the broth. Add more broth, if needed, to make 1 cup.

5. Preheat the oven to 400° F.

6. Melt the butter in a medium saucepan over medium-low heat. Add

the onion and sprinkle with anise seeds; cook 5 minutes. Whisk in the flour. Cook, stirring constantly, 2 minutes. Whisk in the 1 cup broth until smooth. Heat to boiling; boil 4 minutes. Whisk in the cream. Continue to cook until thickened, 5 to 6 minutes longer. Remove from heat and stir in the Pernod. Allow to cool, stirring occasionally, 10 minutes. Stir in the reserved fennel and potatoes, the ham, and turkey. Add the hot pepper sauce and salt and pepper to taste. Transfer to a lightly buttered 9- to 10-inch glass pie plate.

7. Roll out the pastry on a lightly floured board and use it to cover the dish. Trim and flute the edges. Brush with the milk. Cut a slash in the center of the pie. Bake until golden brown, about 25 minutes. Let stand a few minutes before serving.

Serves 4

ROCKY MOUNTAIN ORANGE-SCENTED LAMB PIE WITH ORANGE PASTRY

SOME OF THE world's best lamb is raised in this country, but it is still a relatively unappreciated meat. A dish of lamb everyone will appreciate is this redolent lamb stew from high in the Rockies, accented by orange, both in the stew and in the crust.

For the orange pastry

1 1/2 cups all-purpose flour

1/4 teaspoon salt

4 tablespoons (1/2 stick) unsalted butter, chilled

1/4 cup vegetable shortening, chilled

1/2 teaspoon finely grated orange peel

2 tablespoons orange juice

For the filling

3 pounds boneless lamb, cut into 1-inch cubes

3 1/2 tablespoons all-purpose flour

1/4 cup vegetable oil

1 large onion, chopped

1 large clove garlic, minced

Pinch of saffron

1/4 cup dry white wine

1 can (14 ounces) plum tomatoes with juice, crushed

1/2 cup chicken stock (see page 378)

1 teaspoon sugar

1/2 teaspoon salt

1/4 teaspoon freshly ground black pepper

1 tablespoon unsalted butter

1 tablespoon finely slivered orange peel

3 tablespoons cognac, warmed

1 cup shelled fresh peas, or 1 cup frozen peas, thawed

1 large egg white, lightly beaten

1. To make the orange pastry: Combine the flour with the salt in a large bowl. Cut in the butter and shortening with a knife. Blend with a pastry blender until the mixture has the texture of coarse crumbs. Add the orange peel and then the orange juice, a tablespoon at a time, and mix gently with a fork to form a soft dough. Chill 1 hour before using.

2. To make the filling: Pat the lamb cubes dry with paper towels. Sprinkle with the flour. Toss to coat.

3. Heat the oil in a large heavy pot or Dutch oven over medium heat. Sauté the lamb cubes, a few pieces at a time, until well browned on all sides. Transfer to a plate.

4. Add the onion to the pot; cook over medium heat 1 minute. Add the garlic; cook 3 minutes longer. Stir in the saffron and wine, scraping the bottom and sides of the pot with a wooden spoon. Add the tomatoes, chicken stock, sugar, salt, and pepper. Return the meat to the pot. Simmer, covered, 30 minutes.

5. Melt the butter in a small saucepan over medium-low heat. Add the orange peel; cook 4 minutes. Stir in the cognac and remove from heat. Set aflame and when the flame subsides pour over the meat. Continue to cook, partially covered, 30 minutes. Uncover and cook until the lamb is tender and the sauce is thickened, about 15 minutes longer.

6. Preheat the oven to 400° F.

7. Stir the peas into the stew. Remove from the heat and allow to cool, stirring occasionally, 10 minutes. Transfer to a lightly buttered 2-inch deep, 10-inch round baking dish.

8. Roll out the pastry on a lightly floured board and cover the dish. Trim and flute the edges. Brush with the beaten egg white. Cut a slash in the center of the pie. Bake until golden brown, about 25 minutes. Let stand a few minutes before serving.

Serves 6

NEW MEXICAN PORK PIE
WITH CRISP CRUST

THE CRISP in the crust is from cornmeal. The recipe hails from the Southwest. Although you may find versions topped with blue cornmeal in "uptown" dining spots, I'll take my cornmeal crust yellow, thank you all the same.

For the crisp crust

1 1/4 cups all-purpose flour

1/2 cup yellow cornmeal

1/2 teaspoon salt

1/2 cup vegetable shortening, chilled

5 to 6 tablespoons ice water

For the filling

1 1/4 pounds boneless pork shoulder, trimmed of excess fat, cut into 1/2-inch cubes

3 tablespoons all-purpose flour

4 tablespoons (1/2 stick) unsalted butter

1 tablespoon vegetable oil

1 medium onion, finely chopped

2 cloves garlic, minced

1 large tomato, peeled, seeded, chopped

1 1/2 cups beef broth

1 tablespoon chili powder

1 1/2 teaspoons ground cumin

1 teaspoon chopped fresh oregano, or 1/4 teaspoon dried

1 small green bell pepper, seeded, diced

1 small red bell pepper, seeded, diced

1 cup corn kernels (from 2 ears corn)

10 small pimiento-stuffed green olives, sliced

Salt and freshly ground black pepper

1 egg white, lightly beaten

Hot pepper sauce

1. To make the crisp crust: Combine the flour with the cornmeal and salt in a large bowl. Cut in the shortening with a knife. Blend with a pastry blender until the mixture has the texture of coarse crumbs. Add the water, a tablespoon at a time, and mix gently with a fork to form a dough. Chill 1 hour before using.

2. To make the filling: Pat the pork cubes dry with paper towels. Sprinkle with the flour. Toss to coat.

3. Heat 2 tablespoons butter with the oil in a large heavy pot or Dutch oven over medium heat. Sauté the pork pieces a few at a time until lightly browned. Transfer to a bowl.

4. Add the onion to the pot; cook over medium-low heat 1 minute. Add the garlic; cook 2 minutes longer. Stir in the tomato and beef broth, scraping the sides and bottom of pot with a wooden spoon. Return the meat to the pot and stir in the chili powder, cumin, and oregano. Simmer, covered, stirring occasionally, for 1 hour and 15 minutes. Uncover and cook, stirring occasionally, until the stew thickens, about 15 minutes longer. Remove from the heat and allow to cool, stirring occasionally, 10 minutes.

5. Meanwhile, melt the remaining 2 tablespoons butter in a medium saucepan over medium-low heat. Add the peppers and cook, covered, until softened, about 10 minutes. Remove from the heat.

6. Preheat the oven to 400° F.

7. Add the peppers, corn kernels, and olives to the stew. Add salt and pepper to taste. Transfer to a lightly buttered, shallow 4- to 6-cup oval or round baking dish.

8. Roll out the dough between sheets of wax paper. Peel off the top sheet of paper and invert the dough onto the dish. Carefully peel off wax paper. Trim and flute the edges. Brush with the beaten egg white. Cut a slash in the center of the pie. Bake until golden brown, about 25 minutes. Let stand a few minutes before serving. Serve with hot pepper sauce.

Serves 4 to 6

LITTLE SCALLOP PIES
UNDER BLANKETS

FIRST COURSE or brunch dish, this pot pie is definitely top drawer stuff devised of tangy scallops, seasoned with garlic and tomatoes, and tucked neatly under a thin crêpe crust. The crêpes are easy to make, calorie reduced, and can be prepared ahead.

For the blankets

1 large egg

6 tablespoons milk

3 tablespoons cornstarch

1 1/2 teaspoons vegetable oil

1/2 teaspoon baking powder

Pinch of salt

6 thin, long green scallion ends

For the filling

1 1/2 pounds bay scallops, or sea scallops, quartered

3 tablespoons all-purpose flour

3 tablespoons unsalted butter plus 2 tablespoons butter, melted

1 1/2 tablespoons olive oil

1 small yellow onion, finely chopped

2 large cloves garlic, minced

1 large ripe tomato, peeled, seeded, chopped (about 3/4 cup)

5 scallions, bulbs and green tops, chopped

1/8 teaspoon dried thyme, crushed

6 tablespoons dry white wine

1 teaspoon finely grated lemon peel

Salt and freshly ground black pepper

1. To make the blankets: Place the egg, milk, cornstarch, oil, baking powder, and salt in a blender container. Blend until smooth, scraping down the sides once.

2. Pour about 2 tablespoons batter into the center of a hot, greased 6-inch crêpe pan or nonstick skillet. Turn and twist the pan so that the bottom is evenly coated with the batter. Cook about 20 seconds over medium-high heat until the blanket is lightly browned and the top dries slightly around the edges. Turn the blanket over and cook 5 seconds. Transfer to a paper towel. Repeat with the remaining batter, stacking the blankets between paper towels

as they are done. Set aside.

3. Cook the long green scallion ends in boiling water until just wilted. Drain and reserve.

4. To make the filling: Rinse the scallops under cold running water; drain. Pat dry with paper towels. Sprinkle with flour.

5. Melt 3 tablespoons butter with the oil in a large heavy skillet over medium-high heat. Sauté the scallops, about half at a time, tossing gently until lightly browned, about 3 minutes. Transfer to a bowl.

6. Reduce the heat under the skillet to medium-low and add the onion; cook 1 minute. Add the garlic; cook 2 minutes longer. Stir in the tomato, chopped scallions, thyme, and wine. Cook over medium heat until very thick, about 5 minutes. Add to the scallop mixture. Add the lemon peel and salt and pepper to taste.

7. Preheat the oven to 350° F.

8. Evenly divide the scallop mixture among 6 ramekins. Place a "blanket" over the top of each ramekin and tie around the sides with a wilted scallion end. Trim the bottom edges of each blanket with a scissors.

9. Place the ramekins on a baking sheet and brush the top of each with melted butter. Bake in the preheated oven for 15 minutes. Serve immediately.
Serves 6

FLAGSTAFF TAMALE PIE

ONE OF THE traditional dishes of the Southwest, Tamale Pie has, over the years, become a favorite all over the country. I make this pie in a 9-inch cast-iron skillet for a "rustic" touch. Tamale Pie is one of those rare dishes that is almost as good reheated a day later.

For the filling

1/4 pound sausage meat
1 large onion, chopped
1 large clove garlic, minced

1 small hot red pepper, seeded, finely chopped
2 pickled jalapeño peppers, minced

2 tablespoons chili powder

1/4 teaspoon ground cumin

Pinch of dried thyme

1 teaspoon salt

1 pound ground beef chuck

1 medium rib celery, finely chopped

3 medium tomatoes, peeled, seeded, chopped (1 1/2 cups)

1 tablespoon yellow cornmeal

1 cup corn kernels

1/4 cup sliced black olives

1/4 cup currants

1/2 cup grated Monterey Jack cheese

3/4 cup grated cheddar cheese

For the topping

1 1/2 cups water

1/4 cup yellow cornmeal

1 tablespoon unsalted butter

The British often lay claim to having invented the meat pie, but truth be told, ancient Romans and Greeks have the nod from historians in that department. The British can make one claim, however. According to the Guinness Book of World Records, the largest meat pie ever baked was concocted in Denby Dale, in West Yorkshire. It weighed 12,880 pounds and measured 18-by-16 feet across and 18 inches deep. According to Guinness, the pie was baked on September 5, 1964 to celebrate four royal births. The tradition started back in 1788 to celebrate King George III's return to sanity. The fourth pie in the series, celebrating Queen Victoria's Jubilee in 1887, was "a bit off" and had to be buried in quicklime. There is no mention as to how many were fed by the prize-winning recipe.

1. To make the filling: Cook the sausage meat in a large heavy saucepan, breaking it up with a fork, over medium heat until it begins to lose its pink color. Drain all grease from the pan and add the onion; cook over low heat 1 minute. Add the garlic; cook 5 minutes. Stir in the chili powder, cumin, thyme, and salt. Add the ground beef and continue to cook, breaking the beef up with a fork, 5 minutes.

2. Add the celery, red pepper, jalapeño peppers, and tomatoes to the meat mixture. Stir in the cornmeal. Cook, skimming the surface as the fat rises, 10 minutes. Stir in the corn; cook 10 minutes longer. Remove from the heat and allow to cool, stirring occasionally, 10 minutes. Stir in the olives and currants. Transfer to a buttered 9-inch round cast-iron skillet. Sprinkle with both cheeses.

3. Meanwhile, to make the topping: Combine the water and the cornmeal in a medium saucepan. Heat to boiling, stirring constantly. Reduce the heat to low. Stir in the butter and cook, covered, stirring frequently, 30 minutes.

4. Preheat the oven to 350° F.

5. When the cornmeal mixture is ready, working quickly, spoon the mixture over the top of the meat mixture. The cornmeal will set as you work. Spread evenly with your fingers if necessary. Bake until golden brown, about 45 minutes. Let stand a few minutes before serving.

Serves 4 to 6

SAUSAGE AND PEPPER POT PIE
WITH LEMON CRUST

FROM NEW YORK City street food to gourmet extravaganza, the next recipe combines my favorite vender vittles—Italian sausages and peppers. Here, they are raised to culinary heights when tossed with tomato sauce and cheese and baked under a lemony pie pastry.

For the lemon crust

1 cup plus 2 tablespoons all-purpose
    flour
2 teaspoons baking powder
1/2 teaspoon salt

1/4 cup vegetable shortening, chilled
2 tablespoons lemon juice
3 tablespoons heavy or whipping cream

For the filling

2 tablespoons olive oil
1 large onion, chopped
1 large clove garlic, minced
1 small carrot, minced
2 medium tomatoes (about 1 pound),
    chopped
1 can (14 ounces) plum tomatoes with
    juices, chopped
1 teaspoon sugar
1 bay leaf
Pinch of dried oregano
1/8 teaspoon ground allspice

1/2 teaspoon salt
1/8 teaspoon freshly ground black
    pepper
6 sweet Italian sausages (1 1/4 pounds)
1 tablespoon unsalted butter
1 large green bell pepper, seeded, cut
    into 2-inch strips
1 large red bell pepper, seeded, cut into
    2-inch strips
1/2 cup grated Monterey Jack cheese
1 large egg white, lightly beaten

1. To make the lemon crust: Combine the flour with the baking powder
and salt in a medium bowl. Cut in the shortening with a knife. Blend with a
pastry blender until the mixture has the texture of coarse crumbs. Add the
lemon juice and then the cream, a tablespoon at a time, and mix gently with
a fork to form a soft dough. Chill 1 hour before using.

2. To make the filling: Heat the oil in a medium saucepan over medium-
low heat. Add the onion; cook 1 minute. Add the garlic; cook 4 minutes
longer. Stir in the carrot and tomatoes. Add the sugar, bay leaf, oregano,
allspice, salt and pepper. Heat to boiling; reduce the heat. Cook over medium-
low heat, stirring occasionally, until thick, about 45 minutes. Remove from
heat. Discard the bay leaf.

3. Sauté the sausages in an oil-rubbed heavy skillet until well browned
on all sides. Drain on paper towels. Cool slightly and cut into 1-inch pieces.

4. Discard all drippings from the skillet. Melt the butter in the skillet over medium-low heat. Stir in the peppers. Cook, scraping the bottom and sides of the pan with a wooden spoon, 2 minutes. Cover and continue to cook until the peppers are softened, about 5 minutes. Cool slightly.

5. Preheat the oven to 425° F.

6. Place half the tomato mixture over the bottom of a lightly buttered 9-inch round glass or ceramic pie pan, 1 1/2 to 2 inches deep. Spoon the peppers over the top. Place the sausages over the peppers. Sprinkle with cheese and cover with the remaining tomato mixture.

7. Roll out the pastry on a lightly floured board and use it to cover the dish. Trim and flute the edges. Brush with the beaten egg white. Cut a slash in the center of the pie. Bake on a foil-lined baking sheet until golden brown, about 25 minutes. Let stand a few minutes before serving.

Serves 6

NEW IBERIA BISCUIT-CLOAKED
SEAFOOD GUMBO PIE

THIS RECIPE was born in the heart of Cajun country. The gumbo, rich and dark, is an authentic bayou dispensation. The biscuit crust is pure Helen Johnson—whose restaurant of the same name was the culinary bright spot of the town when I stayed there back in 1979.

For the filling

3 tablespoons plus 1 teaspoon vegetable oil

3 tablespoons all-purpose flour

3 tablespoons unsalted butter

3/4 pound smoked sausage, sliced (andouille, if possible)

1/2 green bell pepper, seeded, chopped

1/2 red bell pepper, seeded, chopped

1 small rib celery, finely chopped

3 tablespoons long grain rice

2 cups chicken stock (see page 378)

3/4 pound cooked ham steak, cut into
strips 1/4-inch wide, about 2 inches
long

1 large onion, chopped

2 cloves garlic, minced

1/4 teaspoon cayenne pepper

Salt and freshly ground black pepper

3/4 pound raw medium shrimp, shelled,
deveined

1/2 pound okra, trimmed, sliced

For the biscuit topping

2 cups all-purpose flour

2 teaspoons sugar

1 tablespoon baking powder

1/2 teaspoon baking soda

1/2 teaspoon salt

1/3 cup cold unsalted butter plus
1 tablespoon melted butter

3/4 cup buttermilk

1. To make the filling: Make a roux by combining 3 tablespoons oil with the flour in a medium heavy skillet. Cook over medium-low heat, stirring about every 4 or 5 minutes, until dark mahogany in color, about 45 minutes to 1 hour. Do not allow the roux to burn.

2. Meanwhile, heat 2 tablespoons butter with the remaining 1 teaspoon oil in a medium heavy pot or Dutch oven over medium heat. Sauté the sausage slices until well browned on both sides. Transfer to a plate with a slotted spoon. Add the ham strips and sauté until lightly browned; transfer to the plate with the sausage slices.

3. Add the remaining butter to the pot and stir in the onion, scraping the bottom and sides of the pot with a wooden spoon. Cook over medium heat, stirring constantly, 2 minutes. Reduce the heat to medium-low and add the garlic, bell peppers, celery, and rice. Cook 5 minutes longer.

4. When the roux is cooked, add to the vegetable/rice mixture and stir in the chicken stock. Heat to boiling and add the reserved sausages and ham; reduce the heat. Cook, covered, over medium-low heat 25 minutes. Stir in the cayenne pepper, salt and black pepper to taste, the shrimp, and okra. Cook, stirring gently, 2 minutes. Remove from heat.

5. Meanwhile, preheat the oven to 450° F.

6. To make the biscuit topping: Combine the flour with the sugar, baking powder, baking soda, and salt in a large bowl. Cut in the cold butter with a

knife. Blend with a pastry blender until the mixture has the texture of coarse crumbs. Using a heavy wooden spoon, stir in the buttermilk and work into a soft dough. Roll out the dough about 1/2-inch thick on a floured board and cut into twelve 2 1/2-inch rounds.

7. Transfer the hot gumbo filling to a 2-inch deep, 9-inch round baking dish. Place the cut biscuit dough over the top. Brush the dough with the melted butter. Bake until the biscuits are puffed and golden brown, about 20 minutes. Serve immediately.

Serves 6

RATATOUILLE PIE
WITH HERBED TOPPING

ONE FOR THE vegetarian crowd to be sure, but not to be passed up in any case. A virtual veggie-cum-cheese pie covered with a basil-flecked short crust, it makes an exciting sidedish to grilled or broiled meats, if you must.

For the herbed crust

1 1/2 cups plus 1 teaspoon all-purpose
    flour

1 teaspoon sugar

1/2 teaspoon salt

6 tablespoons vegetable shortening,
    chilled

1 large egg yolk

1 teaspoon red wine vinegar

2 to 3 tablespoons cold water

2 tablespoons chopped fresh basil, or
    1 teaspoon dried

For the filling

1 large eggplant, about 1 1/2 pounds

Salt

1/2 cup olive oil (approximately)

2 small zucchini (about 1 pound),
    trimmed, sliced

2 medium tomatoes, peeled, cut into
    1/2-inch-thick wedges

1/4 teaspoon freshly ground black
    pepper

1/2 teaspoon Hungarian hot paprika

1 tablespoon unsalted butter plus
    1 teaspoon butter, melted

1 large onion, halved, sliced thin

2 large cloves garlic, minced

1 medium green bell pepper, seeded,
    sliced thin

1 medium red bell pepper, seeded,
    sliced thin

1/4 cup chopped fresh parsley

2 tablespoons chopped fresh basil, or
    1 teaspoon dried

2 cups grated Fontina cheese

1/2 cup freshly grated Parmesan cheese

1 large egg white, lightly beaten

1. To make the herbed crust: Combine the 1 1/2 cups flour with the sugar and salt in a medium bowl. Cut in the shortening with a knife. Blend with a pastry blender until the mixture has the texture of coarse crumbs. Lightly beat the egg yolk with the vinegar, water, and basil. Add the liquid, a tablespoon at a time, and mix gently with a fork to form a soft dough. Sprinkle the dough with 1 teaspoon flour. Chill 1 hour before using.

2. To make the filling: Trim the eggplant and halve it lengthwise. Cut into 1/4-inch-thick slices, place in a colander, and sprinkle with salt. Let stand 30 minutes. Brush the eggplant with damp paper towels to remove the salt. Pat dry.

3. Heat 2 tablespoons of the oil in a heavy skillet over medium heat. Sauté the eggplant slices, a few at a time, until golden on both sides. Add more oil as needed. Drain the slices on paper towels.

4. Add 2 teaspoons oil to the same pan and sauté the zucchini over high heat, tossing constantly, until golden. Reduce the heat and cook until the zucchini is soft, about 8 minutes. Drain well and transfer to a bowl. Add the drained eggplant to the bowl.

5. Wipe out the skillet. Melt the butter in the skillet over medium heat. Add the onion; cook 1 minute. Add the garlic and peppers. Cook, covered, 5 minutes. Stir in the tomatoes, 1/2 teaspoon salt, the pepper, and paprika. Raise the heat under the skillet and cook, uncovered, stirring frequently, until all the liquid has evaporated. Transfer to the bowl with the eggplant and zucchini. Toss in the parsley and basil.

6. Preheat the oven to 400° F.

7. Spoon one third of the ratatouille mixture into a buttered 10-inch

glass or ceramic quiche dish. Sprinkle with one third of each cheese. Continue to layer until all the ingredients are used, ending with the cheese.

8. Roll out the pastry on a lightly floured board and use it to cover the dish. Trim and flute the edges. Brush with the beaten egg white. Cut a slash in the center of the pie. Bake until golden brown, about 25 minutes. Let stand a few minutes before serving.

Serves 6

HEAVENLY BEEF PIE WITH DEVILISHLY RICH MASHED POTATO TOPPING

THE FOLLOWING dish is of mixed heritage. Not shepherd's pie, but a combination of two freely adapted Alice B. Toklas recipes that make an entirely new French connection. This one is a bit on the rich side, but worth every calorie.

For the filling

2 pounds trimmed boneless sirloin steak (1/2-inch thick), cut into 1-inch pieces

1/2 cup cognac

1/4 pound salt pork, diced

5 tablespoons unsalted butter

1 tablespoon vegetable oil

12 small white onions, peeled

1 tablespoon all-purpose flour

2 cups dry red wine

1/2 cup water

Herb bouquet: 3 sprigs Italian parsley, 1 sprig of thyme, 1 bay leaf, 5 whole peppercorns, and 1 crushed clove garlic, tied in cheesecloth

1 1/2 cups small mushroom caps

For the mashed potato topping

2 1/2 pounds baking potatoes

1/2 teaspoon salt

1/4 teaspoon freshly ground white pepper

1/8 teaspoon freshly grated nutmeg

4 tablespoons (1/2 stick) plus 1 teaspoon unsalted butter, melted

2 large egg yolks

3 tablespoons heavy or whipping cream

1. To make the filling: Place the meat in a shallow glass or ceramic dish. Pour 1/3 cup cognac over the top. Cover and let stand at room temperature for 3 hours. (Or refrigerate for 6 hours.)

2. Cook the salt pork in boiling water 4 minutes. Drain and set aside.

3. Heat 3 tablespoons of the butter with the oil in a heavy pot or Dutch oven over medium-high heat. Remove the meat from the cognac and pat dry with paper towels. Sauté the meat, about 4 pieces at a time, until well browned on both sides. Transfer to a plate.

4. Add the salt pork to the pot and sauté over medium heat until golden brown. Transfer with a slotted spoon to the plate with the meat.

5. Cut a cross in the root end of each onion. Sauté in the same pot until golden brown. Transfer to a bowl.

6. Drain all but 1 tablespoon drippings from the pot. Whisk in the flour. Cook, stirring constantly, 2 minutes. Whisk in the wine and the water. Heat to boiling, scraping the sides and bottom of the pan with a wooden spoon.

7. Return the meat to the pot and add the herb bouquet. Warm the remaining cognac in a small saucepan and ignite. When the flames subside, pour over the meat. Cover and cook over medium-low heat 1 hour. Add the onions to the pot and cook, partially covered, until the meat and onions are just tender, and the sauce is thickened, about 30 minutes longer.

8. Meanwhile, melt the remaining 2 tablespoons butter in a large skillet over medium-high heat. Add the mushrooms and sauté, turning once, until browned on both sides, about 5 minutes. Remove from the heat. When the meat and onions are tender, stir in the mushroom caps and remove from the heat. Discard the herb bouquet.

9. Preheat the oven to 400° F.

10. To make the topping: While the meat mixture is cooking, bake the potatoes until tender, about 1 hour. When tender, reheat the beef mixture, uncovered, over medium-low heat. Leave the oven on.

11. Split the potatoes in half and scoop out the insides. Rice the potatoes into a bowl and beat in the salt, white pepper, nutmeg, and 4 tablespoons melted butter. Beat in the egg yolks and cream.

12. Spoon the hot beef mixture into a 2-inch deep 1 1/2-quart baking

dish. Spread the mashed potatoes over the top. Drizzle on the remaining 1 teaspoon melted butter and bake 15 minutes. Run under a broiler for 1 to 2 minutes to brown the top. Serve immediately.

Serves 6

PROVIDENCE CORNED BEEF PIE
WITH PAPRIKA PASTRY

NO CABBAGE here, which corned beef, in my book at least, seems to cry out for. Still, healthy greens are not absent. Baby Brussels sprouts fill in nobly. This dish is so good, I make a corned beef specifically for this purpose. The leftover meat is reserved for sandwiches later in the week.

For the paprika pastry

1 1/2 cups all-purpose flour

1/4 teaspoon salt

1 teaspoon Hungarian sweet paprika

6 tablespoons (3/4 stick) unsalted butter, chilled

6 tablespoons lard, chilled

2 to 3 tablespoons cold water

For the filling

1 corned brisket of beef (3 1/2 to 4 pounds)

1 large carrot, peeled, halved

1 white turnip, peeled, halved

1 parsnip, peeled, halved

1 large onion, halved

4 whole cloves

2 tablespoons red wine vinegar

3 sprigs parsley

1 clove garlic

3 medium carrots (1/2-inch thick)

6 ounces (1 generous cup) small Brussels sprouts

2 tablespoons unsalted butter

2 tablespoons all-purpose flour

1 cup chicken or beef broth

1 tablespoon Dijon mustard

1 1/2 tablespoons prepared horseradish

1/2 cup heavy cream

1/4 teaspoon salt

10 whole peppercorns
1 1/2 teaspoons mustard seeds
2 medium baking potatoes (about
   1 pound)

1/4 teaspoon freshly ground black
   pepper
1 large egg white, lightly beaten

1. To make the pastry: Combine the flour with the salt and paprika in a large bowl. Cut in the butter and lard with a knife. Blend with a pastry blender until the mixture has the texture of coarse crumbs. Add the water, about a tablespoon at a time, and mix gently with a fork to form a soft dough. Chill until ready to use.

2. To make the filling: Place the corned beef in a large heavy pot and add the halved carrot, turnip, parsnip, onion, cloves, vinegar, parsley sprigs, garlic, peppercorns, and mustard seeds. Add water to cover. Heat to boiling; reduce the heat. Simmer, covered, until the meat is tender, 2 1/2 to 3 hours. Remove the meat from the liquid; cool. Cut enough meat into 1-inch cubes to make 2 1/2 cups. Set aside 1/2 cup cooking juices.

3. While the meat is cooking, peel the potatoes and cut into cubes. Cook in boiling salted water 8 minutes; drain. Peel the carrots and cut into 1/4-inch-thick slices. Cook in boiling salted water 12 minutes; drain. Trim the Brussels sprouts and cut a cross in the root ends. Cook in boiling salted water 4 minutes; drain and cut across into 1/4-inch-thick slices.

4. Preheat the oven to 375° F.

5. Melt the butter in a large heavy saucepan over medium-low heat. Add the flour. Cook, stirring constantly, 2 minutes. Whisk in the broth and reserved 1/2 cup cooking juices. Heat to boiling; reduce heat. Whisk in the mustard, horseradish, and cream. Cook until thickened, about 5 minutes. Add salt and pepper to taste. Remove from heat and cool.

6. Stir the vegetables and the meat into the cooled sauce. Transfer to a buttered 1 1/2- to 2-quart baking dish about 2 inches deep.

7. Roll out the pastry on a lightly floured board and use it to cover the dish. Trim and flute the edges. Brush with the beaten egg white. Cut a small hole in the center of the pie. Bake 30 minutes. Run under a preheated broiler to lightly brown the top before serving. Let stand a few minutes before serving.

Serves 6

Pot Roasts

Some hae meat and cannot eat,
Some can eat and hae not meat.
We hae meat and we can eat,
May the Lord be thanket.
—Scottish grace

POT ROAST is one of those signal foods that we can all give thanks for. And though no recipes appeared under that name in the earliest cookbooks, this style of cooking is very old indeed. It is, after all, just the French method of *braising*. Not to be confused with boiling, braising uses only a small amount of liquid during the cooking.

In olden times, French cooks nestled a heavy pot containing meat in hot coals and then placed more coals on top, in essence, creating an oven environment. Early Colonists hung their pots over low-banked coals in a fireplace, low enough for the heat to surround the entire pot. Incidentally, these heavy iron pots were known as Dutch ovens. Eventually, pot roasts were made in brick ovens in earthenware vessels, the edges sealed with pastry to compensate for the lack of a tight-fitting lid.

The English, Dutch, and French brought this style of cooking to our shores early on, though in those days the pot more than likely contained venison or bear. German immigrants settling in Pennsylvania came over with their sauerbraten recipes in hand. Others followed suit. While it is true that any meat can technically be "pot roasted," the term has become synonymous with beef. In eighteenth-century America, the beef was nowhere near as tender as the meat we find in butcher shops today. Therefore it was most often larded; the roast streaked with fat—a practice just about gone out of style in American households these days.

Some Potting Points For the record, pot roasting or braising is a style of cooking a large cut of meat in a small amount of liquid, covered in an oven environment, although many cooks these days lean toward cooking their roasts stovetop. It has long been believed that meat held its juices when cooked in this manner. But according to Harold McGee, author of *On Food and Cooking* (1984), just the opposite is true. Pot roasting, because this method speeds up the interior cooking, actually increases the fluid loss and can produce dry roasts if one uses tender cuts of beef. Oven roasting on a rack, on the other hand, while it cooks the exterior of the meat quickly, cooks the interior slowly, preserving the natural juices in the roast. Oven roasting is suitable *only* for tender cuts of beef.

Pot roasting is a natural tenderizing process, suitable for the lesser cuts of beef that contain hardy fiber that requires tenderization. Appropriate selections include blade, arm, rolled rump, eye of round, and flank, but by far the choicest cuts are chuck and brisket. Choose at *least* a 3 1/2- to 4-pound piece of boneless meat that is about three inches thick, as some shrinkage will occur.

There is such a mystique about making pot roast that it even had its fifteen minutes of fame on a Broadway stage a while back in a song from *Woman of the Year*. "First you brown an onion," is the way the lyrics start. Speaking of which, browning either onions or the meat is a matter of opinion. If the meat is good (streaked with fat for flavor), one needs only to place a layer of *raw* onions in the bottom of a pot and put the meat over the onions. Yes, the roast *and* onions will brown, even covered, in the oven. Browning meat beforehand does not seal in juices either. It does add flavor to the "drippings," however, so if you are one of those who make it stovetop (I do not), it is an essential step. Otherwise, it is at the discretion of the recipe giver.

POT ROAST, at least in my family, was most often served for Sunday dinner, the meal inevitably eaten at noon. It was, by the very nature of its cooking style, the perfect dish for such occasions. The roast slowly braised in the oven while we all attended church services. By the time the family gathered around the dining table, the roast was perfectly tender and juicy. Even long after one has left the intimacy of home, a good pot roast is always a reminder of "Mom's" cooking—no matter who is in charge of the pot these days. And for those who think there is only one way to pot a roast, the following dozen recipes will open up new horizons.

THE BASIC POT ROAST

I LEARNED to make pot roast from my mother, Mildred Schulz, who always made it in a covered roasting pan. There is an old saying that sometime during the cooking, a pot roast should "catch on" (stick to the pot) just enough to brown the meat, giving the gravy richness. Hence, no liquid is added here until after an hour's cooking time. If you wish, add whole peeled potatoes and carrots to the pan about 45 minutes to 1 hour before the meat is anticipated to be done.

1 large or 2 medium onions, chopped
1 beef chuck roast or brisket, 3 1/2
    to 4 pounds

1/2 cup beef broth (approximately)
Chopped fresh parsley

    1. Preheat the oven to 350° F.
    2. Place the onions over the bottom of a large heavy pot or Dutch oven. Place the meat on top of the onions. Bake, covered, 1 hour.
    3. Add the beef broth to the pot and continue to bake, covered, until meat is tender, 1 1/2 to 2 hours longer.
    4. Remove the meat and carve on a board into slices. Arrange on a serving platter. Sprinkle with parsley. Strain the juices and pass on the side.
Serves 4

MORAVIAN POT ROAST

It is very nice to think
The world is full of meat and drink,
With little children saying grace
In every Christian kind of place.
— Robert Louis Stevenson

THIS OLD recipe combines both meat and drink. The beef is marinated in seasonings and beer and then cooked in the marinade until the meat is rich and fork tender.

1 boneless beef chuck roast, 3 to 4 pounds
1 1/2 tablespoons sugar
2 teaspoons salt
1/2 teaspoon freshly ground black pepper
1/4 teaspoon ground cloves
Pinch of ground mace

1/8 teaspoon cayenne pepper
1 large onion, chopped
1 medium carrot, finely chopped
1 1/2 cups beer
1 large curl of orange peel
1 tablespoon unsalted butter
1 tablespoon vegetable oil
Chopped fresh parsley

1. Place the roast in a large glass or ceramic dish. Sprinkle the meat with sugar, salt, pepper, cloves, mace, cayenne pepper, onion, and carrot. Pour the beer over the top. Add the orange peel to the dish. Marinate, covered, several hours or overnight in the refrigerator.

2. Preheat the oven to 350° F.

3. Remove the meat from the marinade and pat dry. Discard the orange peel.

4. Heat the butter with the oil in a large heavy pot or Dutch oven over medium heat. Brown the meat well on all sides. Transfer to a plate. Add the marinade to the pot, scraping the bottom and sides of pot with a wooden spoon. Return the meat. Heat to boiling and bake, covered, in oven until tender, about 2 hours.

5. Remove the meat and carve on a board into slices. Arrange on a serving platter. Sprinkle with parsley. Strain the juices and pass on the side. *Serves 4 to 6*

MICHIGAN ROOT CELLAR
POT ROAST

THE NAME says it all. A wonderful hearty dish for a cold winter's night. And though few of us have root cellars anymore, this recipe brings back memories of the old days.

1 beef chuck roast, 4 pounds

1 clove garlic, bruised

1 tablespoon unsalted butter

1 tablespoon vegetable oil

2 small red onions, halved, sliced

1/4 cup chicken broth (approximately)

2 large baking potatoes (about 1 1/2 pounds), peeled, cubed

2 large carrots, peeled, sliced

2 medium turnips, peeled, cut into 1-inch strips about 1/4-inch thick

2 medium parsnips, peeled, sliced

1 cup sour cream, at room temperature

1/8 teaspoon hot pepper sauce

Salt and freshly ground black pepper

1/4 cup chopped fresh parsley

1. Preheat the oven to 350° F.

2. Rub the roast with the bruised garlic. Mince the garlic; set aside.

3. Heat the butter with the oil in a very large heavy pot or Dutch oven over medium-high heat. Brown the meat well on all sides. Transfer to a plate. Reduce the heat under the pot to medium-low.

4. Add the onions to the pot; cook 1 minute. Add the reserved garlic; cook 2 minutes longer. Stir in the chicken broth, scraping the bottom and sides of the pot with a wooden spoon. Return the meat to the pot. Heat to boiling and bake, covered, in oven 2 hours.

5. Stir the potatoes and carrots into the juices around the meat, scraping the sides of the pot with a wooden spoon as you stir. Bake, covered, 10

minutes. Stir in the turnips and parsnips. (Add more chicken broth if juices are drying out.) Bake, covered, 30 minutes longer.

6. Remove the meat and carve on a board into slices. Arrange in the center of a large serving platter. Remove the vegetables with a slotted spoon. Arrange around the meat. Keep warm in a low oven.

7. Whisk the sour cream into the meat juices (there should be about 1/2 cup). Stir over low heat until the sauce is warmed through. Do not allow to boil. Add hot pepper sauce and salt and pepper to taste.

8. Sprinkle the parsley around the edges of the meat. Spoon about 1/3 cup sauce over the meat. Pass the remaining sauce on the side.

Serves 6

POT ROAST WITH LENTILS

HIPPOCRATES regarded lentils (and beans) as:

> rough, creating gluey blood which stops up the liver, creates melancholia, fourth-day shivers, heavy dreams, and dulls the vision and strength of the brain.

Thankfully, he didn't have the last word. Other philosophers and doctors of the time claimed that to be a wise, healthy man, one had to learn, "To do all good, and to prepare lentils wisely." One such "wise" method follows.

2 tablespoons vegetable oil
1 beef chuck roast, with bone in, about
    4 pounds
1 large onion, chopped
2 cloves garlic, minced
2 pounds tomatoes (about 4 large),
    chopped

1 cup lentils, rinsed and picked over
1 green bell pepper, chopped
Salt and freshly ground black pepper
Chopped fresh parsley

1. Preheat the oven to 350° F.

2. Heat the oil in a large heavy pot or Dutch oven over medium-high heat. Brown the meat well on all sides. Transfer to a plate.

3. Add the onion to the pot; cook 1 minute. Add the garlic and tomatoes, stirring the bottom and sides of pot with a wooden spoon. Return the meat to the pan. Bake, covered, in oven until meat is almost tender, about 2 hours.

4. Meanwhile, cook the lentils in boiling salted water 15 minutes; drain.

5. When the meat is almost tender, stir the lentils and bell pepper into the juices. Cover and return to oven until the meat and lentils are tender, about 30 minutes.

6. Remove the meat and carve on a board into slices. Arrange on a serving platter. Add salt and pepper to taste to the lentil mixture and spoon mixture around the edges of the meat. Sprinkle with parsley.

Serves 4

SABINE RIVER ROAST

THE SABINE RIVER separates Texas from Louisiana, a geography that is apparent in the ingredient list in the next offering. Chili powder and hot green peppers give this Texas-style pot roast its character. The meat, in this instance, is floured and then browned to give it an extra-crisp exterior.

3 tablespoons all-purpose flour

1/2 teaspoon salt

1/4 teaspoon freshly ground black pepper

Pinch of ground allspice

1 boneless beef chuck, 3 1/2 to 4 pounds

2 tablespoons unsalted butter

1 tablespoon vegetable oil

2 jalapeño peppers, seeded, minced

1/3 cup red wine vinegar

1 rib celery, finely chopped

1 medium carrot, finely chopped

2 tablespoons chili powder

1/2 cup prepared chili sauce

2 tablespoons dark brown sugar

1 tablespoon Dijon mustard

(ingredients continued)

1 large onion, chopped   1 can (28 ounces) plum tomatoes
2 large cloves garlic, minced   Chopped fresh parsley

1. Preheat the oven to 350° F.

2. Combine the flour with the salt, pepper, and allspice on a plate. Roll the beef in the flour mixture, pounding the flour into the meat. Set aside excess flour.

3. Heat the butter with the oil in a large heavy pot or Dutch oven over medium heat. Brown the meat well on all sides. Transfer to a plate. Reduce the heat under the pot to medium-low. Add the onion; cook 1 minute. Add the garlic and jalapeño peppers; cook 4 minutes longer. Stir in the vinegar, scraping the bottom and sides of the pot with a wooden spoon. Stir in the celery and carrot. Sprinkle with chili powder and stir in the chili sauce, sugar, mustard, and tomatoes. Return the meat. Heat to boiling and bake, covered, in oven 2 hours. Partially remove cover and continue to bake until the meat is tender, about 45 minutes longer.

4. Remove the meat and carve on a board into slices. Arrange the meat on a serving platter. Spoon about half the sauce over the top. Sprinkle with parsley. Pass the remaining sauce on the side.

Serves 6

SOURED BEEF

Every sweet has its sour . . .
—Ralph Waldo Emerson

THIS next recipe, which is a version of sauerbraten, comes from Pennsylvania. The sour is in the marinade, the sweet, a touch of brown sugar in the pot.

1 beef brisket, 3 1/2 to 4 pounds   1/2 teaspoon dried thyme
1 cup red wine vinegar   1/4 teaspoon dried rosemary

1 cup water
1 onion, sliced
2 cloves garlic, minced
2 ribs celery, chopped
1 medium carrot, chopped
6 whole cloves
4 allspice berries
6 sprigs parsley plus chopped fresh parsley for garnish
2 bay leaves

1/4 cup diced salt pork
1 cup strong beef stock (see page 377)
2 cans (8 ounces each) tomato sauce
1 tablespoon dark brown sugar
1 tablespoon lemon juice
1 teaspoon finely slivered lemon peel
8 gingersnaps, crushed (3 1/2 to 4 tablespoons)
1 tablespoon Worcestershire sauce
Salt and freshly ground black pepper

1. Place the brisket in a large shallow glass or ceramic dish. Add the vinegar, water, onion, garlic, celery, carrot, cloves, allspice, parsley sprigs, bay leaves, thyme, and rosemary. Refrigerate, covered, turning the meat occasionally, at least 3 days.

2. Preheat the oven to 325° F.

3. Remove the meat from the marinade and pat dry.

4. Sauté the salt pork in a large heavy pot or Dutch oven over medium-low heat until golden, about 4 minutes. Transfer to a bowl with a slotted spoon.

5. Raise the heat under the pot to medium-high. Brown the meat well on all sides. Transfer to a plate.

6. Discard all but 1 tablespoon drippings from the pot. Return to medium heat and add the beef stock, scraping the bottom and sides of the pot with a wooden spoon. Return the meat to the pot and pour the marinade over the top. Add the tomato sauce, brown sugar, lemon juice, lemon peel, gingersnaps, and Worcestershire sauce. Heat to boiling and bake, covered, in oven until meat is tender, about 2 1/2 to 3 hours.

7. Remove the meat and carve on a board into slices. Arrange on a serving platter. Sprinkle with parsley. Add salt and pepper to taste to the cooking juices. Strain the juices and pass on the side.

Serves 6

A word on early American beef. Jane Carson writes in *Colonial Virginia Cookery* that in 1656, "Cattle and Hogs are every where." But she also points out that the cattle were raised just like the hogs. In other words, free to roam at will.

Epicures found Virginia beef somewhat inferior because cattles, raised like swine, were lean and tough after a winter in the woods, and even when they were penned and fed with grain before butchering, they never achieved the sleek fatness that made English beef so delicious. Beverly (Robert Beverly, the Virginia historian) deplored his countrymen's habit of starving young cattle and suggested that they drain the "noble marshes" and "make as fine Pastures as any in the world."

In time it came to pass, but Virginia never lived up to Robert Beverly's image of what could be.

GOLDEN BARBECUE POT ROAST

THE FOLLOWING is another of my Mother's pot roast recipes. I have good friends who make this dish just for the sauce and save the meat for sandwiches later! Not me. I like my sauce on my beef—with a mountain of mashed potatoes on the side to soak up all the juices.

1 small onion, chopped

1 boneless beef chuck roast, 3 1/2 to 4 pounds

1 small clove garlic, bruised

1/2 cup beef broth (approximately)

1 can (8 ounces) tomato sauce

2 tablespoons dark brown sugar

1/4 teaspoon Hungarian sweet paprika

1/2 teaspoon English dry mustard

1/4 cup lemon juice

1/4 cup ketchup

1/4 cup cider vinegar

1 tablespoon Worcestershire sauce

Chopped fresh parsley

1. Preheat the oven to 350° F.

2. Place the onion over the bottom of a large heavy pot or Dutch oven. Rub the meat well with the bruised garlic; discard the garlic. Place the meat on top of the onions. Bake, covered, 1 hour. Add some beef broth if the juices in the bottom of the pot dry up.

3. Combine the tomato sauce, sugar, paprika, mustard, lemon juice, ketchup, vinegar, and Worcestershire sauce in a medium bowl. Pour over the meat. Continue to bake, covered, basting the meat with the sauce every 20 minutes, until the meat is very tender, 1 1/2 to 2 hours.

4. Remove the meat and carve on a board into slices. Arrange on a serving platter. Spoon 1/4 cup sauce over the meat. Sprinkle with parsley. Pass the remaining sauce on the side.

Serves 4 to 6

NEW MEXICAN GREEN CHILE POT ROAST WITH POTATOES

Chilies—the soul of the sauce.

SO SAYS Huntley Dent, author of *The Feast of Santa Fe* (Simon and Schuster, 1985). The following recipe is highly inauthentic Southwestern fare. One could omit the potatoes and serve the meat chopped with tortillas to be more traditional, but in that case, don't forget to pass a fiery green salsa.

2 Italian frying peppers

2 tablespoons olive oil

1 beef brisket, 3 1/2 to 4 pounds

1 large onion, chopped

2 cloves garlic, minced

1/4 teaspoon ground coriander

1 can (4 ounces) chopped mild green chiles

3/4 cup chicken broth (approximately)

2 medium baking potatoes (about 1 pound)

Chopped fresh parsley

1. Preheat the oven to 350° F.

2. Roast the peppers over a gas flame or under a broiler until charred all over. Carefully wrap in paper towels and place in a plastic bag. Cool for 5 minutes. Rub off the skin with paper towels. Seed and chop the peppers.

3. Heat the oil in a large heavy pot over medium-high heat. Brown the meat well on both sides. Transfer to a plate. Reduce the heat to medium. Add the onion; cook 1 minute. Add the garlic; cook 4 minutes longer. Stir in the coriander, the roasted peppers, the mild chiles, and the chicken broth, scraping the sides and bottom of pot. Push the pepper/onion mixture to the sides of the pot. Return the meat to the pot and spoon some of the mixture over the top. Bake, covered, in the oven until the meat is almost tender, 2 to 2 1/2 hours.

4. Peel the potatoes and cut into sixths, lengthwise. Cut across into large cubes. Place around the meat, stirring to coat with juices. Continued to bake, covered, until the potatoes are tender, about 30 minutes.

5. Remove the meat and carve on a board into slices. Arrange on a serving platter. Spoon the potatoes around the meat. Pour the juices over the meat. Sprinkle with parsley.

Serves 4 to 6

DILLED POT ROAST

There is no love sincerer than the love of good food.
—George Bernard Shaw

THERE IS no better food than the following dish. The combination of beef and dill dates back at least to seventeenth-century England. This pot roast is definitely "uptown" material. The beef, best if brisket, is sliced and dappled with an egg-enriched dill sauce for an exceptional dining treat.

2 1/2 tablespoons unsalted butter
1 tablespoon vegetable oil
1 beef brisket, 3 1/2 to 4 pounds
Salt and freshly ground black pepper
1 medium onion, sliced
2 cups beef broth (approximately)
4 allspice berries, crushed
3 tablespoons chopped fresh dill

1/4 teaspoon minced fresh sage, or a pinch of dried
1 bay leaf
1 whole clove garlic
1 1/2 tablespoons all-purpose flour
1 1/2 tablespoons cider vinegar
1 1/2 teaspoons sugar
1 egg yolk

1. Preheat the oven to 350° F.

2. Heat 1 tablespoon butter with the oil in a large heavy pot or Dutch oven over medium-high heat. Sprinkle the brisket generously with salt and pepper. Brown the meat well on all sides. Transfer to a plate.

3. Add the onion to the pot and cook over medium-low heat 2 minutes. Add 1/2 cup beef broth, scraping the sides and bottom of pan with a wooden spoon. Return the meat to the pot. Add the remaining 1 1/2 cups broth, the allspice berries, 1 tablespoon dill, the sage, bay leaf, and garlic. Heat to boiling and bake, covered, in the oven until the meat is tender, 2 1/2 to 3 hours.

4. Transfer the meat to a platter and keep warm. Strain the cooking juices. You should have 1 1/2 cups. If you have more, boil down briefly. If you have less, add more broth.

5. Melt the remaining 1 1/2 tablespoons butter in a medium saucepan over medium-low heat. Add the flour. Cook, stirring constantly, 2 minutes. Whisk in the meat juices, the vinegar, sugar, and remaining 2 tablespoons dill. Cook 3 minutes. Remove from heat.

6. Lightly beat the egg yolk in a small bowl. Whisk in 1/2 cup sauce. Whisk this mixture back into the sauce. Cook over low heat 2 minutes. Do not allow to boil. Keep warm.

7. Carve the meat on a board into thin slices. Arrange on a serving

platter. Spoon some of the sauce over the meat. Pass the remaining sauce on the side.

Serves 6

SMOTHERED POT ROAST
WITH SAUSAGES AND SALAMI

I HAVE always wondered what to do with those large, thin chuck steaks found in supermarket meat counters. Here is one solution. I serve this dish over spaghetti and pass Parmesan cheese on the side.

1 tablespoon unsalted butter

1 tablespoon olive oil

1 large beef chuck steak (about 2 3/4 pounds), cut 1/2- to 3/4-inch thick

3 sweet Italian sausages (about 1/2 pound)

1 large onion, chopped

4 cloves garlic, minced

1/3 cup dry red wine

1 can (28 ounces) Italian plum tomatoes with juice, chopped

1/2 cup finely diced Italian salami (about 2 ounces sopresso, Milano, or pepperoni)

1 tablespoon chopped fresh basil, or 1 teaspoon dried

1/8 teaspoon dried thyme

2 tablespoons chopped fresh Italian (flat leaf) parsley

Salt and freshly ground black pepper

1. Preheat the oven to 350° F.

2. Heat the butter with the oil in a large heavy pot or Dutch oven over medium-high heat. Brown the meat well on both sides. Transfer to a plate. Reduce heat to medium and sauté the sausages until well browned. Add to the plate with the chuck steak.

3. Discard all but 2 tablespoons fat from the pot. Add the onion; cook 1 minute. Add the garlic; cook 4 minutes longer. Stir in the wine, scraping the bottom and sides of the pot with a wooden spoon. Add the tomatoes,

salami, basil, thyme, and 1 tablespoon parsley. Return the meat to the pot, pushing it down into the sauce. Add the sausages and bake, covered, in oven 1 hour. Remove cover and bake 30 minutes longer.

4. Transfer the meat and sausages to a carving board. Degrease the sauce and heat to boiling on the top of the stove until thickened, about 4 minutes.

5. Meanwhile, carve the sausages into slices and stir into the sauce. Pour the thickened sauce into a shallow serving dish. Carve the chuck steak into slices and arrange over the top. Sprinkle with the remaining 1 tablespoon parsley.

Serves 6

CHOLLENT

Full o' beans and benevolence.
—Robert Smith Surtees

SUCH IS the stuff chollent is made of. A pot roast with barley and beans, this dish is traditionally made over the Sabbath or Jewish holidays, as the dish originally cooked overnight in a very low oven. This version is adapted from *My Mother's Cookbook* (Carroll & Graff/Quicksilver Books, 1985).

1 cup dry pink beans

3 tablespoons vegetable oil

1 boneless beef chuck steak or brisket, 3 1/2 to 4 pounds

1 medium onion, finely chopped

1 clove garlic, minced

1 teaspoon salt

1/4 teaspoon freshly ground black pepper

2 teaspoons Hungarian hot paprika

1/2 teaspoon ground ginger

2 quarts beef broth

1 cup barley

Chopped fresh parsley

1. Soak the beans overnight in cold water to cover. Drain.
2. Preheat the oven to 250° F.

3. Heat the oil in a large heavy pot or Dutch oven over medium-high heat. Brown the meat well on all sides. Transfer to a plate. Reduce the heat under the pot to medium.

4. Add the onion to the pot, scraping the bottom and sides of the pot with a wooden spoon; cook 3 minutes. Add the garlic; cook 2 minutes longer. Stir in the salt, pepper, paprika, and ginger. Stir in the beef broth. Heat to boiling and stir in the beans and barley. Spread the beans and barley to the edges and return the meat to the pot. Bake, covered, in oven 2 1/2 hours. Stir the mixture and continue to bake, partially covered, until the meat and beans are very tender, about 1 1/2 hours longer. Remove cover completely if the mixture is too wet.

5. Remove the meat and carve on a board into slices. Spoon the bean and barley mixture into a large shallow serving dish. Arrange the meat slices over the top. Sprinkle with parsley.

Serves 6 to 8

GRAND POT ROAST

A POT ROAST that tastes almost like a Chinese stir-fry. Actually this is a twist on a recipe passed on to me a few years back, meant for the barbecue. A few adjustments made the sauce a surprisingly tantalizing addition for pot roast collections. Serve it over rice.

1 boneless chuck roast, about 3 pounds

3 tablespoons safflower oil

3 large cloves garlic, minced

1/2 cup tomato juice

1/2 cup dark brown sugar (lightly packed)

1/2 cup soy sauce

1/4 teaspoon freshly ground black pepper

1/4 teaspoon crushed dried hot red peppers

1 teaspoon unsalted butter

1/2 teaspoon all-purpose flour

2 tablespoons sour cream

Chopped fresh parsley

1. Place the roast in a large glass or ceramic dish. Combine 2 tablespoons of the oil with the garlic, tomato juice, sugar, soy sauce, freshly ground pepper, and hot peppers in a bowl. Pour over the meat. Refrigerate, covered, turning once, overnight. Let stand at room temperature about 1 hour before cooking.

2. Preheat the oven to 350° F.

3. Remove the meat from the marinade. Pat dry.

4. Heat the remaining 1 tablespoon oil in a large heavy pot or Dutch oven over medium heat. Brown the meat on all sides. Transfer the meat to a plate. Add the marinade to the pot, scraping the bottom and sides of the pot with a wooden spoon. Return the meat. Heat to boiling and bake, covered, in the oven, turning once, until tender, about 2 hours.

5. Transfer the meat to a heatproof platter. Cover and keep warm in a low oven. Degrease the pan juices.

6. Melt the butter in a small saucepan over medium-low heat. Add the flour. Cook, stirring constantly, 2 minutes. Whisk in the degreased juices. Heat to boiling; reduce the heat. Simmer 2 minutes.

7. Whisk the sour cream with 2 tablespoons sauce in a small bowl. Whisk this mixture back into the sauce. Cook over low heat 2 minutes. Do not allow to boil.

8. Carve the meat on a board into slices. Arrange on a serving platter. Sprinkle with parsley. Pass the sauce on the side.

Serves 6

Stews

. . . there are very few people who can resist, deep down, the earthy, sensual aroma and flavor of meat, poultry, or fish gently boiled with or without vegetables and flavored with herbs and spices . . . A lusty stew brings out the primitive in all of us . . .

—James Villas

IT HAS BEEN said that the ingredients of a stew, more than any other foods, reflect the personality of a nation. One look at the myriad stews being dished up from coast to coast in the United States reveals the melting pot that we are. American stews, like cioppino, burgoo, Brunswick stew, and fish muddles, all have roots in other lands, but the style is distinctively American. Most of our early recipes developed from what was on hand at the time. Game and fish played a major role. In fact, when the first Europeans arrived here, they found native American Indians eating stews of cod, venison, turkey, and bear, seasoned with dried plants and sweetened with honey. The berries of the sumac tree were the Iroquois' favorite seasoning. It was the Indians who first taught the early arrivals how to make stews in pumpkins nestled in hot coals.

Times change, however, and as civilization progressed, driving out wild game in the process, recipes evolved. Although one might be still able to find an old-fashioned venison stew in certain parts of the country, one is hard put to find a genuine Brunswick stew. The real thing, made with squirrel meat, that is. This is not to say that our stews are less tasty. America is blessed with an abundance of good things that, at one time or another, always wind up in a stew pot.

Not Stewing over Stews The technique for making a flavorful stew is almost as old as man, though what once was a hit-or-miss "kitchen sink" affair has become a sophisticated form of cooking. A stew involves more liquid than braising, but not enough liquid to turn it into a soup. Stews are generally classified as brown or white. In the brown variety, meat is sautéed first, giving the broth not only darkness in color but flavor as well. White stews are light in color, as the name implies, and this category includes various veal and fish stews. As with braising, lesser cuts of meats should be used in stews to ensure that the meat doesn't dry out during the long cooking process.

One of the most important ingredients of a stew is the stock. Though canned broth can be used successfully in long cooking dishes, fish and vegetable stews require homemade stock. It is always a good idea to freeze leftover gravies, soup stock, and fish poaching liquid whenever you have any on hand. When it comes to the amount of liquid to add, remember that the ingredients should not be "swimming." There is an old saying that goes: "A stew must smile, never laugh."

"COOKERY," said X. Marcel Boulestin in *Petits et grands plats,* "is not chemistry. It is an art. It requires instinct and taste rather than exact measurements." Stews are perfect examples of what he is talking about. Start by using prime ingredients, but be aware that ingredients change from area to area, even from pot to pot. Never be hesitant about adapting a recipe to your own taste, particularly when the dish is as open to interpretation as a stew.

NORTH CAROLINA FISH MUDDLE

A muddle is a stew made of various kinds of fish seasoned with fried fat meat, onions, potatoes, and peppers; at least it starts off that way.
—*The WPA North Carolina Guide* (1955)

ACTUALLY, the difference between a "muddle" and a "chowder" is slim, a muddle being slightly thinner in texture.

1 teaspoon vegetable oil

1/4 cup diced salt pork

2 medium leeks, white bulbs with 1-inch green stems, trimmed, washed, chopped (about 1/2 cup)

1/4 cup chopped green bell pepper

1 medium carrot, chopped

2 small baking potatoes, peeled (3/4 to 1 pound)

2 cups fish stock (see page 378)

1/2 pound sea scallops, halved

1/2 pound white fish (haddock, rock fish, cod), cut into pieces the size of the scallops

Good pinch freshly grated nutmeg

Dash hot pepper sauce

Salt and freshly ground black pepper

2 tablespoons heavy or whipping cream

2 tablespoons chopped fresh parsley

Lemon wedges

1. Rub a medium, heavy pot or Dutch oven with the oil. Cook the salt pork in the pot or Dutch oven over medium-low heat 1 minute. Raise heat slightly and continue to cook, stirring occasionally, until golden, about 4

minutes longer. Stir in the leeks, green pepper, and carrot. Cook, covered, stirring occasionally, over medium-low heat 15 minutes.

2. Add the potatoes and fish stock to the vegetable mixture. Heat to boiling; reduce the heat. Cook, covered, 12 minutes.

3. Add the scallops and fish to the stew. Sprinkle with nutmeg. Continue to cook, covered, until fish is tender, 4 to 5 minutes. Add the hot pepper sauce and salt and pepper to taste. Stir in the cream and parsley. Serve with lemon wedges.

Serves 4 to 6

COLORADO BEEF STEW

A PRIME example of changing times, this recipe is similar to what was known as Swiss steak when I grew up. However, way back in the 1800s and even early 1900s, venison, not beef, would have flavored the pot.

1/2 cup all-purpose flour

Salt and freshly ground black pepper

2 pounds 1/2-inch thick boneless beef steak (round or chuck), cut into 2-inch pieces

5 tablespoons unsalted butter

2 tablespoons vegetable oil

1 large onion, chopped

1 large clove garlic, minced

1/3 cup dry red wine

1 can (28 ounces) imported plum tomatoes

1 large fresh tomato, seeded, chopped

1 large carrot, finely chopped

1 stalk celery, finely chopped

1 tablespoon Worcestershire sauce

6 ounces mushrooms, sliced

Chopped fresh parsley

1. Preheat the oven to 325° F.

2. Combine the flour with 1 teaspoon salt and 1/2 teaspoon pepper on a large plate. Coat the beef pieces with the flour mixture, pounding the flour into the meat. Set aside excess flour.

3. Heat 2 tablespoons butter with the oil in a large heavy pot or Dutch

oven over medium-high heat. Sauté the meat, a few pieces at a time, until well browned on both sides. Transfer to a plate as they are done.

4. Discard all but 1 tablespoon fat from the pot. Add 1 tablespoon butter. Add the onion; cook over medium-low heat 1 minute. Add the garlic; cook until golden brown, about 5 minutes.

5. Sprinkle the onion mixture with 2 tablespoons of the reserved flour mixture. Stir in the wine, scraping the bottom and sides of the pot with a wooden spoon. Add the tomatoes, carrot, celery, and Worcestershire sauce. Return the meat and heat the mixture to boiling. Cover and bake in the oven until the meat is tender, about 1 1/2 hours.

6. Meanwhile, melt the remaining 2 tablespoons butter in a large skillet over medium high heat. Add the mushrooms and cook, tossing constantly, until golden, 4 to 5 minutes.

7. When the meat is tender, stir the mushrooms into the stew and return to oven. Bake, uncovered, 30 minutes. Add salt and pepper to taste. Sprinkle with parsley before serving with mashed potatoes (see note).

Serves 4 to 6

Note To make mashed potatoes for 4, cook 3 peeled and cubed, large potatoes (about 2 1/4 pounds) in boiling salted water until tender. Drain and force through a ricer. Return to the pot and place over low heat. Beat in 4 1/2 tablespoons softened unsalted butter and 6 tablespoons heavy or whipping cream. Add salt to taste.

OXTAIL STEW

I TASTED my first oxtail stew at the home of M.F.K. Fisher about ten years ago. I was in awe of her, but frankly less than enchanted with the idea of eating oxtails. (Which, of course, are not really *ox*tails, but beef tails.) I now consider Mrs. Fisher a close friend. And oxtail stew? A culinary delight.

2 tablespoons olive oil
1 tablespoon unsalted butter
2 1/2 to 3 pounds oxtails
12 small white onions, peeled with a cross cut in each root end
1 medium onion, finely chopped
1 large clove garlic, minced
1 medium rib celery, finely chopped
1 large carrot, finely chopped

1 tablespoon all-purpose flour
1 cup strong beef stock (see page 377)
1/2 cup dry red wine
1 can (14 ounces) plum tomatoes, drained and chopped
1/2 teaspoon sugar
1 tablespoon Madeira wine
Salt and freshly ground black pepper
Chopped fresh parsley

1. Heat the oil with the butter in a large heavy pot or Dutch oven over medium-high heat. Sauté the oxtails on all sides until well browned. Transfer to a plate.

2. Add the white onions to the saucepan and cook, stirring constantly, until golden. Transfer with a slotted spoon to a bowl. Set aside.

3. Discard all but 2 tablespoons drippings from the pot. Add the chopped onion and cook over medium heat 1 minute. Add the garlic; cook until well browned, 4 to 5 minutes longer.

4. Reduce the heat under the pot to medium-low and stir in the celery and carrot. Sprinkle with the flour and cook, stirring constantly, 2 minutes. Stir in the stock and wine. Heat to boiling, scraping the bottom and sides of the pot. Add the tomatoes and sprinkle with sugar. Boil 1 minute. Return the oxtails to the stew and reduce the heat to medium-low. Cook, covered, stirring occasionally, until the meat is almost tender, about 2 hours. Add the white onions and continue to cook, covered, 30 minutes longer.

5. Stir the Madeira into the stew. Cook, covered, 2 minutes. Add salt and pepper to taste. Sprinkle with parsley.

Serves 4

CHICKEN FRICASSEE
WITH CORNMEAL DUMPLINGS

Eating stew in a dream portends a reunion with old friends . . . Any kind of fowl seen in a dream are a sign of being able to hold up your head among the best people.

—*Your Horoscope and Dreams*

THE FOLLOWING recipe just happens to be a "company" dish that is sure to win you votes no matter who comes to dinner. A fricassee can be brown or white, but is much more aesthetically appealing when the chicken is first sautéed to a deep golden brown.

6 tablespoons (3/4 stick) plus 2 teaspoons unsalted butter

1 chicken (3 1/2 to 4 pounds), cut into pieces

2 leeks, washed, roughly chopped

1 onion, roughly chopped

1 whole clove garlic, crushed

1 large carrot, roughly chopped

2 pieces candied ginger (about 1 teaspoon)

2 cups chicken broth

2 cups water

2 sprigs parsley

1 bay leaf

1 sprig fresh thyme, or a pinch of dried

2 whole cloves

1/4 teaspoon ground mace

1/4 pound small white mushroom caps; caps whole, stems sliced

Cornmeal Dumpling Batter (recipe follows)

3 tablespoons all-purpose flour

Pinch of freshly grated nutmeg

1 tablespoon lemon juice

1/3 cup heavy or whipping cream

Salt and freshly ground black pepper

Chopped fresh parsley

1. Melt 3 tablespoons butter in a large heavy pot or Dutch oven over medium heat. Pat the chicken pieces dry with paper towels and sauté, half at a time, in the butter until the chicken is golden brown on both sides, about 15 minutes. Transfer the chicken to a plate.

2. Pour off all grease from the pot and stir in the leeks, onion, garlic, carrot, ginger, and broth, scraping the bottom and sides of pot with a wooden

spoon. Add the water, parsley sprigs, bay leaf, thyme, cloves, and mace. Heat to boiling, return the chicken pieces, and reduce the heat. Cook, covered, over medium-low heat 30 minutes.

3. Meanwhile, melt 2 teaspoons butter in a medium heavy skillet over medium-high heat. Add the mushrooms and cook, stirring constantly, until golden. Remove from heat. Make the cornmeal dumpling batter; set aside.

4. Transfer the chicken to an ovenproof dish and keep warm in a low oven. Raise the heat under the cooking liquid and boil the chicken stock until reduced by one third. Strain.

5. Wipe out the pot and return to medium-low heat. Add the remaining 3 tablespoons butter. When the butter foams, stir in the flour. Cook, stirring constantly, 2 minutes. Whisk in 2 1/2 cups chicken stock. Heat to boiling; reduce the heat. Simmer until thickened, about 4 minutes. Add the nutmeg, lemon juice, cream, and salt and pepper to taste. Return the chicken and sprinkle with mushrooms. Drop the dumpling batter by large tablespoonfuls over the chicken. Simmer, covered, until dumplings are firm, about 15 minutes. Sprinkle with parsley.

Serves 4

CORNMEAL DUMPLING BATTER

3/4 cup sifted all-purpose flour	3/4 teaspoon salt
3/4 cup yellow cornmeal	1 small egg
1 1/2 teaspoons baking powder	1/2 cup milk

Combine the flour, cornmeal, baking powder, and salt in a medium bowl. Beat in the egg and milk with a wooden spoon to form a soft dough. Keep covered until ready to use.

Serves 4

DAKOTA LAMB STEW

FROM Rapid City, just below the sheep belt in South Dakota, the next stew is smooth and rich—and deserves a place on the menu at even the most elegant dinner parties. A word of warning: Do not allow the stew to boil after you have stirred in the sour cream. Nothing is more unappetizing than a curdled pot of pottage.

4 pounds boneless lamb, cut into
   1 1/2-inch cubes

2 lamb bones (from your butcher)

Water

2 cups chicken broth

3 cups water

1 small white onion, peeled

1 rib celery, halved

2 carrots, peeled, quartered

1 parsnip, peeled, quartered

3 sprigs fresh dill plus 1/4 cup finely
   chopped fresh dill

6 sprigs parsley

2 sprigs fresh thyme

1 large bay leaf

10 black peppercorns

3 tablespoons unsalted butter

1 small yellow onion, finely chopped

Pinch of ground allspice

3 tablespoons all-purpose flour

2 teaspoons sugar

2 tablespoons lemon juice

Dash of hot pepper sauce

1 cup sour cream, at room temperature

Salt and freshly ground white pepper

1. Place the meat and the bones in a large heavy pot or Dutch oven and cover with cold water. Heat to a rolling boil; drain. Return meat and bones to the pot and rinse under cold running water until the water runs clear; drain. Wipe out pot.

2. Return the meat and bones to the clean pot. Add the chicken broth, water, onion, celery, carrots, and parsnip. Tie the dill sprigs with the parsley, thyme, bay leaf, and peppercorns in cheesecloth. Tuck into the meat. Heat to boiling; reduce the heat. Simmer partially covered, skimming the surface occasionally, until the meat is tender, about 1 hour.

3. Drain the meat, reserving the liquid. Discard the bones, vegetables, and herb bouquet. Cover the meat with foil and keep warm.

4. Melt the butter in a large heavy saucepan over medium-low heat. Add

the yellow onion; cook, covered, 5 minutes. Do not allow to brown. Add the allspice and flour. Cook, stirring constantly, 2 minutes. Whisk in the reserved cooking liquid, the sugar, lemon juice, hot pepper sauce, and 3 1/2 tablespoons of the chopped dill. Simmer until thickened, about 3 minutes. Remove from heat and stir in the meat and sour cream. Return to low heat until the stew is warmed through. Do not allow it to boil. Add salt and white pepper to taste. Sprinkle with the remaining 1/2 tablespoon chopped dill.

Serves 6

BOURBON-SCENTED PORK STEW

Gobble your food however you might,
Never eat a dish that is trite.

—Greek saying

THE NEXT stew, spiked with a touch of bourbon at the penultimate moment, is indeed worthy of gobbling. A hearty winter's dish, it's loaded with vegetables, and good taste.

1 tablespoon unsalted butter

1 tablespoon vegetable oil

1 large onion, chopped

1 clove garlic, minced

3-pound pork shoulder or butt, cut into 1-inch cubes

1 tablespoon sugar

2 tablespoons all-purpose flour

1/2 teaspoon salt

1/4 teaspoon freshly ground black pepper

1 can (16 ounces) imported tomato purée

1 bay leaf

1 medium turnip, peeled, quartered, sliced

3 medium carrots, peeled, sliced

2 medium parsnips, peeled, halved, sliced

3 medium red potatoes (about 12 ounces), peeled, quartered lengthwise

3 tablespoons bourbon

1/8 teaspoon ground allspice

1/8 teaspoon ground mace

1 cup beef broth

1 cup chicken broth

1/4 pound string beans, trimmed, cut into 1-inch pieces, blanched until just tender, 3 to 5 minutes

Chopped fresh parsley

1. Preheat the oven to 350° F.

2. Heat the butter with the oil in a large heavy pot or Dutch oven over medium heat. Add the onion; cook 1 minute. Add the garlic; cook until lightly browned, about 4 minutes longer.

3. Stir the meat into the onion mixture and sprinkle with the sugar. Cook, stirring constantly, 2 minutes. Sprinkle with the flour, salt, pepper, allspice, and mace. Continue to cook, stirring constantly, 2 minutes. Add the beef broth, scraping the bottom and sides of pot with a wooden spoon. Stir in the chicken broth, tomato purée, and bay leaf. Heat to boiling. Bake in oven with the lid slightly askew (about 2 1/2-inch opening) 1 hour and 15 minutes.

4. Remove stew from oven and skim off all grease. Add the turnip, carrots, parsnips, and potatoes. Return to oven with the lid slightly askew, 45 minutes.

5. Stir the bourbon into the stew. Return to oven 10 minutes. Stir in the beans and sprinkle with parsley.

Serves 6

BAKED BRUNSWICK STEW

NOWADAYS, chicken is used instead of squirrel, and lima beans, corn, and tomatoes have found their way into the pot as well. To add insult to injury, the next even-more-unorthodox recipe for Brunswick stew *layers* the ingredients in a casserole and then *bakes* the stew until "bubbles burst off." Not traditional perhaps, but delicious.

1 whole chicken (3 1/2 to 4 pounds)

1 carrot, chopped

1 rib celery with leaves, chopped

1 unpeeled onion, quartered, plus
    1 medium peeled onion, halved
    and sliced

4 sprigs parsley

10 whole peppercorns

6 cups chicken broth

2 cups water

1 large potato (about 10 ounces),
    unpeeled

5 tablespoons unsalted butter

1 clove garlic, minced

1/4 cup all-purpose flour

1/2 cup heavy or whipping cream

1 can (28 ounces) plum tomatoes,
    drained, chopped

1 cup frozen baby lima beans (thawed)

1 cup fresh corn kernels (from 2 large
    ears)

1/4 cup fresh bread crumbs

1. Place the chicken in a large pot. Add the carrot, celery, unpeeled onion, parsley, peppercorns, chicken broth, and water. Heat to boiling; reduce the heat. Simmer, covered, until the chicken is tender, about 1 hour. Remove the chicken from the stock and carefully cut away the skin and bones from the chicken meat. Return the bones and skin to the stock and boil until the stock is reduced to about 2 cups. Strain and set aside. Cut the chicken into bite-size pieces. Cover and set aside.

2. Meanwhile, peel and dice the potato. Cook in boiling salted water 5 minutes. Drain.

3. Preheat the oven to 350° F.

4. Melt 3 tablespoons butter in a medium skillet over medium heat. Add the quartered, sliced onion; cook 1 minute. Add the garlic; cook until it is lightly browned, about 3 minutes longer. Reduce the heat to low and stir in the flour. Cook, stirring constantly, 1 minute. Whisk in 2 cups reserved chicken stock and the cream. Cook over medium heat until thickened, about 8 minutes. Remove from heat.

5. Place half the tomatoes over the bottom of a lightly buttered casserole or shallow baking dish. Place half the chicken pieces over the top and sprinkle with half the lima beans, half the potatoes, and half the corn. Cover with half the sauce. Repeat the layers.

6. Melt the remaining 2 tablespoons butter in a small skillet over medium heat. Stir in the bread crumbs and cook, stirring constantly, until lightly browned, about 2 minutes. Spoon over the chicken mixture. Bake 35 minutes.

Serves 6

As legend has it, at least according to Raymond Sokolov in *Fading Feast* (E. P. Dutton, 1983), Brunswick stew was invented in Brunswick County, Virginia, in 1828 by a slave named Uncle Jimmy Matthews, while his masters were out hunting. They returned from the field to find him stirring up a batch in a big black kettle over an open fire. The original recipe, passed on by Uncle Jimmy's master to his descendants, goes like this:

> Parboil squirrels until they are stiff (half done), cut small pieces of bacon (middling), one for each squirrel; one small onion to each squirrel (if large, one to two squirrels), chopped up. Put in bacon and onions first to boil, while the squirrels are being cut up for the pot. Boil the above till half done, then put in butter to taste; then stale loaf bread, crumbled up. Cook then till it bubbles, then add pepper and salt to taste. Cook this until it bubbles and bubbles burst off. Time for stew to cook is four hours with steady heat.

Take note, there is not a vegetable (onions don't count) in sight.

LONG ISLAND MUSSEL
AND FISH STEW

The greatest dishes are very simple dishes.
—Escoffier

FROM MY PART of the country, this simple but masterful fish stew is on the thin side, thickened only with rice. It is a wonderful summer, as well as winter, offering—and can also be served as a first course, if you so desire.

4 dozen mussels

1 teaspoon cornstarch

2 tablespoons unsalted butter

6 medium scallions, white bulbs and green tops, chopped separately

1 large clove garlic, minced

1/8 teaspoon dried thyme

1 1/2 cups chicken broth

1 1/2 cups dry white wine

1/2 cup long grain rice

3/4 pound meaty fish (swordfish, monkfish, haddock), cut into 1-inch pieces

Chopped fresh parsley

1. Scrub the mussels well, pulling off the beards, under cold running water. Place in a bowl and cover with cold water. Stir in the cornstarch. Let stand 30 minutes. Drain; wash well under cold running water.

2. Melt the butter in a large heavy pot over medium-low heat. Add the scallion bulbs; cook 1 minute. Add the garlic; cook 3 minutes longer. Stir in the thyme, broth, and wine. Heat to boiling. Add the mussels and cook, covered, over medium heat until the mussels begin to open, about 2 to 4 minutes. Remove the mussels with a slotted spoon to a bowl. Cover with foil.

3. Stir the rice into the broth mixture. Heat to boiling; reduce the heat. Cook, covered, over medium-low heat 25 minutes. The mixture should be slightly wet.

4. Stir the fish into the rice mixture. Continue to cook, covered, 4 minutes. Add the mussels and cook, covered, 3 minutes longer. Sprinkle with green onion tops and parsley.

Serves 6 to 8

WISCONSIN-STYLE
BEEF STEW

THE NEXT recipe is for one of the best beef stews ever invented. Beer gives this German original its dark, rich taste. Take heed that the stew should cool down before the vegetables are added. In addition, a cooling-off period intensifies the flavors, so it is best to make the dish through step 4 the day before serving.

3 pounds boneless beef chuck, cut into
    1-inch cubes
Salt and freshly ground black pepper
3 tablespoons unsalted butter
1 tablespoon vegetable oil
1 large onion, chopped
1 large clove garlic, minced
2 tablespoons all-purpose flour
1 cup chicken stock (see page 378)

1 1/2 cups dark beer
4 teaspoons dark brown sugar
3 tablespoons red wine vinegar
1/4 teaspoon chopped fresh thyme, or a
    pinch of dried
1/2 cup beef stock (see page 377)
    (approximately)
2 medium potatoes (about 1 1/4
    pounds), unpeeled
1 cup frozen peas

1. Preheat the oven to 350° F.

2. Pat the beef cubes dry with paper towels. Sprinkle well with salt and pepper on both sides.

3. Heat 2 tablespoons butter with the oil in a large heavy pot or Dutch oven over medium-high heat. Sauté the meat, a few pieces at a time, until well browned on all sides. Transfer to a plate as they are done.

4. Add the remaining 1 tablespoon butter to the pot and reduce the heat to medium-low. Add the onion; cook 1 minute. Add the garlic; cook 4 minutes longer. Stir in the flour. Cook, stirring constantly, 2 minutes. Whisk in the chicken stock, scraping the sides and the bottom of the pot. Add the beer, brown sugar, vinegar, thyme, and meat. Bake, covered, until meat is tender, about 1 1/2 hours. Cool. Mixture should be very thick.

5. Before serving, reheat the stew on top of the stove over medium-low heat 15 minutes, adding just enough beef stock to thin to a stew-like consistency.

6. Meanwhile peel the potatoes and cut in half lengthwise. Cut across into 1/4-inch thick slices. Cook in boiling salted water 5 minutes; drain. Add to the stew along with the peas, tossing gently with two spatulas so as not to break the potatoes. Cook, covered, 5 minutes longer.

Serves 6

SAVANNAH-STYLE VEAL
AND MUSHROOM STEW

Show me the way people dine and I will tell you their rank among civilized beings.

—*Harper's New Monthly Magazine* (1868)

ANYONE who has ever visited Savannah, Georgia, knows that the city is among the most civilized and beautiful in the land. What could be more eloquent than a white creamy veal stew, dappled with mushrooms?

5 tablespoons unsalted butter

3 pounds boneless stewing veal, cut into 1-inch cubes

1 1/2 tablespoons all-purpose flour

1 medium onion, minced

1/2 cup chicken stock (see page 378)

1/2 cup dry white wine

Herb bouquet: 1 sprig thyme, 3 sprigs parsley, 1 bay leaf, 1 scallion, 1 crushed clove garlic, tied in cheesecloth

1/2 pound mushroom caps, cleaned

2 teaspoons vegetable oil

2 egg yolks

1/4 cup heavy or whipping cream

1/8 teaspoon freshly grated nutmeg

Dash of hot pepper sauce

1 tablespoon lemon juice

Salt and freshly ground black pepper

Chopped fresh parsley

1. Melt 4 tablespoons butter in a large saucepan over medium heat. Add the veal and cook, stirring frequently, until lightly browned, about 5 minutes. Sprinkle with the flour. Cook, stirring constantly, 2 minutes. Add the onion and continue to cook, stirring constantly, 2 minutes longer. Stir in the stock and wine. Heat to boiling; reduce the heat. Place the herb bouquet in the meat mixture. Cook, covered, stirring occasionally, over medium-low heat until the meat is tender, about 50 minutes.

2. Meanwhile, heat the remaining 1 tablespoon butter with the oil in a large skillet over medium-high heat. Sauté the mushroom caps until golden on both sides. Transfer with a slotted spoon to a bowl.

3. When the meat is tender, discard the herb bouquet and add the mushrooms. Reduce the heat under the pan to low.

4. Beat the egg yolks with the cream in a small bowl. Slowly whisk in about 2 tablespoons meat juices. Stir this mixture back into the stew. Cook over low heat until the sauce is just thick enough to coat a spoon, about 3 minutes. Do not allow the sauce to boil. Add the nutmeg, hot pepper sauce, lemon juice, and salt and pepper to taste. Sprinkle with parsley.

Serves 6

SOUTH CAROLINA
DRUMSTICK STEW

FOOD SERVED in seventeenth-century inns in the South did not always enjoy the greatest reputation. It seems that a Reverend Jones was once offered a very sorry looking dish that was noted as stewed chicken. He looked at his bowl and offered the following grace: "God bless the owl that ate the fowl and left the bones for Mr. Jones." A much more appetizing rendering is limned below.

4 whole chicken legs (about 3 pounds),
    cut apart
1 clove garlic, bruised
Hungarian hot paprika
Salt and freshly ground black pepper
1 tablespoon unsalted butter
1 tablespoon vegetable oil
2 medium onions, halved, sliced thin
1 medium rib celery, finely chopped

2 medium carrots, chopped
1/2 teaspoon chopped fresh thyme, or a
    pinch of dried
1/2 cup chicken broth
1 large red bell pepper, seeded, chopped
1/4 pound small okra, trimmed, cut
    into 1/2-inch thick slices
2 teaspoons all-purpose flour
1 egg yolk
Chopped fresh parsley

1. Rub the chicken legs well with the bruised garlic. Mince the garlic and set aside. Sprinkle the chicken pieces on both sides with paprika, salt, and pepper to taste.

2. Heat the butter with the oil in a large heavy skillet over medium heat. Sauté the chicken pieces, half at a time, until well browned on both sides. Transfer to a plate.

3. Reserve 2 teaspoons drippings in a small saucepan. Discard all but 1 tablespoon of the remaining drippings from the skillet. Add the onions to the skillet and sauté over medium heat 2 minutes. Add the reserved minced garlic, celery, carrots, and thyme. Stir in the chicken broth, scraping the bottom and the sides of the skillet with a wooden spoon. Return the chicken pieces to the skillet. Heat to boiling; reduce the heat. Cook, covered, over medium-low heat 25 minutes.

4. Add the bell pepper to the chicken. Continue to cook, covered, over medium-low heat 25 minutes.

5. Remove 1/4 cup chicken juices from the skillet. Stir the okra around the chicken. Cook, covered, 5 minutes.

6. Meanwhile, heat the reserved 2 teaspoons of the drippings over medium-low heat. Whisk in the flour. Cook, stirring constantly, 2 minutes. Whisk in the 1/4 cup chicken juices. Heat to boiling; remove from the heat. When the juices stop bubbling, whisk in the egg yolk until smooth.

7. Remove the skillet from the heat. Stir the egg mixture around the chicken. Place over low heat, stirring gently, until the juices are thickened,

about 2 minutes. Do not allow to boil. Add salt and pepper to taste. Sprinkle with parsley.

Serves 4

VEGETABLE STEW

There are many ways to love a vegetable. The most sensible way is to love it well-treated. Then you can eat it with the comfortable knowledge that you will be a better man for it, in your spirit and your body too . . .
—M.F.K. Fisher

MOST SENSIBLE words from a most sensible lady. The following was inspired by another Northern California friend, the very talented Jill Gardner. To turn it vegetarian, substitute strong vegetable stock for the chicken broth.

3 tablespoons unsalted butter

2 medium leeks, trimmed, washed well, thinly sliced

1 clove garlic, minced

1 small leafy rib celery, minced

1 tablespoon chopped fresh parsley

Pinch of dried thyme

1 bay leaf

1 1/4 cups chicken broth (approximately)

1 large red bell pepper, seeded, cut into 2-inch strips

1 medium green bell pepper, seeded, cut into 2-inch strips

1/4 cup brown rice

3 medium carrots (about 6 ounces), cut into 2-inch strips

1 small head cauliflower (about 1 pound), cut into florets

1/4 pound mushrooms, sliced

2 medium zucchini (about 10 ounces), halved lengthwise, sliced

20 snow peas, trimmed

Salt and freshly ground black pepper

1 tablespoon chopped fresh dill

1. Melt the butter in a large heavy saucepan over medium-low heat. Add the leeks; cook 2 minutes. Add the garlic, celery, parsley, thyme, bay leaf, and 3/4 cup chicken broth. Cook, covered, 3 minutes. Stir in the peppers and

rice. Continue to cook, covered, stirring occasionally, 30 minutes, adding more chicken stock as needed.

2. Meanwhile, cook the carrots in boiling salted water 4 minutes. Rinse under cold running water; drain. Cook the cauliflower in boiling salted water 3 minutes. Rinse under cold running water; drain.

3. Stir the carrots, cauliflower, and mushrooms into the stew. Cook, covered, 10 minutes. Stir in the zucchini and snowpeas. Cook, covered, 5 minutes longer. Add more chicken broth if mixture is too thick. Add salt and pepper to taste. Sprinkle with dill.

Serves 4 to 6

Waffles

ANOTHER mystery in the chronicles of food history is the waffle. The Dutch are generally credited with its invention. But then, the Germans lay claim as well—and the French aren't far behind. The word itself (according to Webster) is a variation of the Dutch *wafel*. If you are eating breakfast in Germany, however, you might be served a *waffel*, which is said to derive from the Old High German word for honeycomb, *wabe*. On the other hand, France has a long history of waffle making and, as far back as 1433, the French word for waffle iron, *fer a gaufres*, was in use. In fact, in the twelfth century, many a French ballad extolled the virtues of the *gaufre* (sometimes *gaufrette*). But to make things even more confusing, the words for wafers and waffles were often interchangeable at the time, so no one is quite certain when the waffle, as we know it, actually came into being.

In the Middle Ages, waffles (or were they wafers?) were associated with religious festivals. Waffle sellers set up stalls outside of churches and sold their wares on the street. The long-handled waffle irons they used were often stamped with religious motifs or the family's coat of arms. As time went by, the designs became less elaborate and waffles were eaten throughout the year, although in some countries, religious holidays are still celebrated with traditional waffle breakfasts. Mardi Gras is a prime example.

The Colonial Dutch are said to have introduced the waffle to America. It was custom, in the Dutch settlement of New Amsterdam, to give a bride a waffle iron with her initials and date of her wedding engraved in the iron. In those days, waffles were baked over hot coals in a fireplace and had to be turned during the cooking process. Waffles were made from yeast batters that remained the tradition until baking powder took the country by storm in the late 1800s.

Some Wisdom on Waffle Making Waffle irons were considered luxuries in the Colonies. For the most part, outside the Dutch community, only landed gentry could afford the irons well into the eighteenth century. Thomas Jefferson's love of waffles has long been bruited about, and his influence had much to do with the waffle's popularity in early America. Being the Francophile he was, the irons in his kitchen were all French made.

The electric waffle iron was introduced at the 1893 Columbian Exhibition as part of a presentation touting the world's first all-electric kitchen. But it would take a long time before the item became standard equipment in American households. Nowadays, with surfaces coated with Teflon or other nonstick material, waffle irons are inexpensive and easy to use. The only treatment a new iron needs is a quick rub with oil and a few practice heating exercises. Because electric waffle irons are available in different shapes and sizes, it will be necessary to adapt amounts of waffle batters to suit your own (or rather your iron's) needs.

Batters should be thin but not watery. The correct consistency resembles heavy cream as it used to be: pourable, but thick. Waffle batters are nothing more than liquid, eggs, flour, and a leavening agent—with variations. In most recipes, the egg whites are beaten until fairly stiff and folded into the main batter, producing a lighter waffle. Do not overwork waffle batter. The ultimate waffle is one that is light, but crisp—and since electric irons are thermostatically controlled, the degree of crispness is up to the cook. To ensure that the waffles remain crisp, unless you are serving them batch by batch, keep them warm in a single layer on a rack in a low oven. Cake racks placed over baking pans are best for this. Waffles freeze exceptionally well—and can be reheated in a toaster whenever the urge strikes.

*W*AFFLE traditions abound in America. Hash and gravy, fried chicken and gravy, kidney stew, chicken and oysters: all are served over waffles. Waffles are made with whole wheat, oats, cornmeal, grits; flavored with cinnamon, nutmeg, orange, or lemon. There are even chocolate waffles for dessert, topped with ice cream and rich, creamy chocolate sauce. Waffles aren't just for breakfast anymore, slathered with sweet butter, topped with Vermont maple syrup and served with a side of sausage. Though in truth, nothing is more satisfying.

OLD FASHIONED BUTTERMILKS

> Along the varying road of life,
> In calm content, in toil or strife,
> At morn or noon, by night or day,
> As time conducts him on his way,
> How oft doth man, by care oppressed,
> Find in an Inn a place of rest.
> —William Combe

THE FOLLOWING recipe is a version of what James Beard recalled eating at various inns around the country. It is actually a very standard recipe that has stood the test of time very well.

1 3/4 cups sifted all-purpose flour
1 teaspoon baking soda
1/2 teaspoon salt
2 tablespoons sugar

2 to 2 1/2 cups buttermilk
3 large eggs, separated
6 tablespoons unsalted butter, melted

1. Preheat the oven to 250° F.
2. Sift the flour with the baking soda, salt, and sugar in a large bowl.

Slowly whisk in 2 cups buttermilk, the egg yolks, and butter until smooth. Add more buttermilk if too thick.

3. Beat the egg whites until stiff. Fold into the waffle batter.

4. Heat a lightly greased waffle iron. Pour about 1/2 cup batter into the iron (depending on iron) and bake until the waffle is crisp. Transfer to a wire rack-lined baking sheet and place in the oven while baking the remaining waffles.

Makes about 10 large waffles

NASHVILLE'S BEST

IN THE SOUTH, cornmeal waffles are often served topped with fried ham and chicken and smothered in gravy. In more upscale homes, a creamy oyster and chicken stew blankets these crisp breads served only for Sunday brunch. I like 'em just fine with butter and maple syrup.

1/2 cup yellow cornmeal	2 large eggs, separated
1 tablespoon sugar	1 cup cake flour
1/2 teaspoon salt	2 teaspoons baking powder
1 cup very hot water	1/2 teaspoon baking soda
1 cup milk	4 tablespoons (1/2 stick) unsalted butter, melted

1. Preheat the oven to 250° F.

2. Combine the cornmeal, sugar, salt, and hot water in a medium saucepan. Cook, whisking constantly, over medium heat until the mixture starts to bubble. Remove from the heat and whisk in the milk.

3. Transfer the cornmeal mixture to a large bowl and whisk in the egg yolks, flour, baking powder, baking soda, and melted butter.

4. Beat the egg whites until stiff. Fold into the waffle batter.

5. Heat a lightly greased waffle iron. Pour about 1/2 cup batter into the

iron (depending on iron) and bake until the waffle is crisp. Transfer to a wire rack-lined baking sheet and place in the oven while baking the remaining waffles.

Makes about 7 large waffles

KANSAS CREAMY WHEATS

THE NEXT recipe from the wheat belt combines whole wheat flour with cake flour, which gives these waffles the texture of those served in times when not all our flour was as over-processed as it is today. Cream cheese and sour cream make these incredibly delicious, and a perfect foil for any of the aforementioned traditional accompaniments.

1 cup cake flour

1/2 cup whole wheat flour

1 teaspoon baking powder

1/2 teaspoon baking soda

1/2 teaspoon salt

2 tablespoons sugar

6 ounces cream cheese, softened

4 large eggs, separated

1 cup sour cream

1/2 cup milk

6 tablespoons (3/4 stick) unsalted butter, melted

1. Preheat the oven to 250° F.

2. Combine the flours, baking powder, baking soda, salt, and sugar in a bowl.

3. Beat the cream cheese with the egg yolks in a large bowl until smooth. Beat in the sour cream, milk, flour mixture, and melted butter.

4. Beat the egg whites until stiff. Fold into the waffle batter.

5. Heat a lightly greased waffle iron. Pour about 1/3 cup batter into the iron (depending on iron) and bake until the waffle is crisp. Transfer to a wire rack-lined baking sheet and place in the oven while baking the remaining waffles.

Makes about 10 large waffles

CINNAMON-ORANGE WAFFLES
WITH ORANGE SYRUP

Breakfast is a notoriously difficult meal to serve with a flourish.
—Clement Freud

NOT, HOWEVER, when you serve the following waffles devised of orange juice, cream, and a good splash of Grand Marnier liqueur. A drop of Grand Marnier wouldn't hurt the orange syrup either. On the other hand, these waffles make a stunning dessert dabbed with sweetened whipped cream. The syrup, by the way, is a fine stand-in for maple syrup anytime.

For the syrup

2 cups orange juice

1/2 cup sugar

3 tablespoons finely slivered orange peel

2 teaspoons vanilla

For the waffles

2 cups all-purpose flour

1/2 teaspoon salt

4 teaspoons baking powder

2 tablespoons sugar

1/2 teaspoon ground cinnamon

Pinch of freshly grated nutmeg

1 cup orange juice

1/4 cup heavy or whipping cream

2 tablespoons Grand Marnier liqueur (optional)

2 large eggs, lightly beaten

1/2 cup (1 stick) unsalted butter, melted

1. To make the orange syrup: Combine the orange juice, sugar, and orange peel in a medium saucepan. Heat to boiling; reduce the heat. Simmer, uncovered, until the syrup is reduced to about 1 1/4 cups, about 12 minutes. Stir in the vanilla. Keep warm.

2. Preheat the oven to 250° F.

3. To make the waffles: Combine the flour with the salt, baking powder, sugar, cinnamon, and nutmeg in a large bowl. Beat in the remaining ingredients.

4. Heat a lightly greased waffle iron. Pour about 1/2 cup batter into the

iron (depending on iron) and bake until the waffle is crisp. Transfer to a wire rack-lined baking sheet and place in the oven while baking the remaining waffles. Serve with the orange syrup.

Makes about 8 large waffles

MAINE POTATO CRISPS

IN MAINE, potatoes go into almost any dish. But mashed potatoes in a waffle? Why not? Some of the best pastries, cakes, and dumplings in the world are made with mashed potatoes. The potatoes in the batter produce very light, very crisp waffles.

1/2 cup leftover mashed potatoes, at room temperature

1/2 cup sour cream

2 tablespoons unsalted butter, melted

2 large eggs, separated

2 tablespoons sugar

2 teaspoons baking powder

Pinch of ground cinnamon

Pinch of freshly ground nutmeg

3/4 cup milk

1 cup all-purpose flour

1. Preheat the oven to 250° F.

2. Place the potatoes in a large bowl. Whisk in the sour cream, butter, egg yolks, sugar, baking powder, cinnamon, and nutmeg. Slowly whisk in the milk in two parts, alternating with two parts flour.

3. Beat the egg whites until stiff. Fold into the waffle batter.

4. Heat a lightly greased waffle iron. Pour about 1/2 cup batter into the iron (depending on iron) and bake until the waffle is crisp. Transfer to a wire rack-lined baking sheet and place in the oven while baking the remaining waffles.

Makes 7 or 8 large waffles

GEORGIAN BITS AND GRITS

A face on him as long as a late breakfast.
—James Joyce

LATE BREAKFAST or not, no one will have a long face after diving into these Southern specialties. Grits, served in one form or another at breakfast everywhere below the Mason-Dixon Line, are the foundation of the following recipe for hearty, flavorful waffles, speckled with bits of crisp fried bacon.

2 cups water

1/2 teaspoon salt

6 tablespoons stone-ground hominy grits

1/2 cup (1 stick) unsalted butter, cut into pieces

4 large eggs, separated

2 cups all-purpose flour

1 1/4 teaspoons baking powder

2 tablespoons sugar

1 1/4 cups milk

4 strips crisp fried bacon, drained, chopped

1. Preheat the oven to 250° F.

2. Heat the water with the salt in a medium saucepan to boiling. Whisk in the grits. Heat, whisking constantly, to boiling. Cover and reduce the heat to low. Cook, stirring occasionally, until thick, about 15 minutes. (If not thick, remove cover and cook a few minutes longer.) Stir in the butter until smooth. Transfer to a large bowl.

3. Beat the egg yolks, one at a time, into the grits mixture. Sift the flour with the baking powder and sugar. Stir into the batter along with the milk until smooth.

4. Beat the egg whites until stiff. Fold into the waffle batter. Fold in the chopped bacon.

5. Heat a lightly greased waffle iron. Pour about 1/2 cup batter into the iron (depending on iron) and bake until the waffle is crisp. Transfer to a wire rack-lined baking sheet and place in the oven while baking the remaining waffles.

Makes about 8 or 9 large waffles

Perhaps the true story of the first waffle is told in *Food Lore & Folk Cures* by Joan Wilen and Lydia Wilen (Irena Chalmers Books for Longmeadow Press, 1988). The authors write:

> Envision a 13th-century English kitchen. The lady of the house takes a tray of oat cakes out of the oven and places it on a surface to cool. Her husband, the crusader, comes home after a tough day at the crusade and—GULP—sits down on the oat cakes, flattening them and leaving imprints from his suit of armor. Undaunted, he puts butter on the cakes and eats them. His wife, pleased that the butter stays in the imprints, requests that he put on the armor once a week and be her 6 foot 2 inch waffle iron.

OAT SURPRISE WAFFLES

Oats. A grain, which in England is generally given to horses, but in Scotland supports the people.

—Samuel Johnson

NOT ONLY did oats support the people, in ancient Scotland, Robert Bruce attributed his armies' success to eating the grain. In fact, every man carried his own bag. And now nutritionists are telling us what Bruce knew all along. Oats are good for you! They taste good, too, particularly when folded into a waffle.

1 cup quick-cooking oats	1 teaspoon baking soda
2 cups buttermilk	3/4 cup all-purpose flour
1 tablespoon sugar	2 large eggs, lightly beaten

1. Combine the oats with the buttermilk in a large bowl. Let stand 10 minutes.

2. Preheat the oven to 250° F.

3. Whisk the remaining ingredients into the oat mixture. Let stand 15 minutes longer.

4. Heat a lightly greased waffle iron. Pour about 1/4 cup batter into the iron (depending on iron) and bake until the waffle is crisp. Transfer to a wire rack-lined baking sheet and place in the oven while baking the remaining waffles.

Makes about 8 large waffles

RISEN LEMONY WAFFLES

IN COLONIAL times, waffle batter was more akin to sourdough as the yeast sponge was left to stand overnight. Since the delicate flavor of lemon in the next recipe is overwhelmed by an overnight's stint, I let the batter rise for a mere hour and a half before baking—and serve them for lunch, instead of breakfast.

1 3/4 cups milk	1 package dry yeast
2 tablespoons sugar	2 cups all-purpose flour
1/2 teaspoon salt	2 large eggs, separated
2 tablespoons unsalted butter	Finely grated peel of 1 small lemon
1/4 cup lukewarm water	3 tablespoons lemon juice

1. Heat the milk in a small saucepan to scalding; remove from heat. Stir in the sugar, salt, and butter. Cool to lukewarm.

2. Place the water in a large bowl. Sprinkle the yeast over the top. Let stand 3 minutes. Whisk in the milk mixture and the flour until smooth. Cover and let stand in a warm place 1 1/2 hours.

3. Preheat the oven to 250° F.

4. Beat the dough down with a whisk. Whisk in the egg yolks, lemon peel, and lemon juice.

5. Beat the egg whites until stiff; fold into waffle batter.

6. Heat a lightly greased waffle iron. Pour about 1/2 cup batter into the iron (depending on iron) and bake until the waffle is crisp. (This batter does not run easily over the iron, so be sure to spread evenly toward the edges.) Transfer to a wire rack-lined baking sheet and place in the oven while baking the remaining waffles.

Makes about 8 large waffles

SWEET POTATO WAFFLES

THIS RECIPE is an adaptation of one invented by Jill Gardner. Jill's waffle is more delicate and requires infinite patience in removing it from a hot waffle iron, even a nonstick one. I have amended it for less adroit waffle makers, like myself. Caramel Syrup (see page 278) is the perfect topping.

1 1/2 pounds sweet potatoes (about 2 large)

2 large eggs, separated

2/3 cup sugar

3/4 cup (1 1/2 sticks) unsalted butter, melted

2 cups milk

1 cup plus 2 tablespoons all-purpose flour

1. Cook the potatoes, unpeeled, in boiling water until very tender, about 45 minutes. Cool slightly. Peel and transfer to the container of a food processor. Process until smooth. You should have 2 cups.

2. Preheat the oven to 250° F.

3. Place the puréed sweet potatoes in a large bowl. Beat in the egg yolks, sugar, butter, milk, and flour.

4. Beat the egg whites until stiff. Fold into the waffle batter.

5. Heat a lightly greased waffle iron. Pour about 1/2 cup batter into the iron (depending on iron) and bake until the waffle is nicely browned. (I use a dark setting.) Gently loosen one side of the waffle and fold over on itself to remove from iron. Unfold the waffle on a wire rack-lined baking sheet and place in the oven while baking the remaining waffles.

Makes 8 or 9 large waffles

HEAVENLY PECAN WAFFLES

My wife and I tried to breakfast together, but we had to stop or our marriage would have been wrecked.

—Winston Churchill

I GUARANTEE you that if Sir Winston Churchill had tried the following pecan studded waffles as détente, all would have been well on Downing Street. For breakfast or dessert, pecan waffles have been a long tradition in this country's Southern regions. This particular version, oddly enough, comes from Vermont where it is served with warm maple syrup laced with heavy cream.

1/3 cup unsalted butter (2/3 stick)
3 tablespoons light brown sugar
1/2 cup ground pecans (about 1 1/2 ounces)
1 1/4 cups all-purpose flour

4 teaspoons baking powder
1/2 teaspoon salt
1 1/2 cups buttermilk
2 large eggs, separated
1/2 teaspoon vanilla

1. Preheat the oven to 250° F.

2. Melt the butter with the sugar in a small saucepan over medium-low heat. Keep warm.

3. Combine the pecans with the flour, baking powder, and salt in a large bowl. Stir in the buttermilk. Beat in the egg yolks, vanilla, and butter/sugar mixture.

4. Beat the egg whites until stiff. Fold into the waffle batter.

5. Heat a lightly greased waffle iron. Pour about 1/2 cup batter into the iron (depending on iron) and bake until the waffle is crisp. Transfer to a wire rack-lined baking sheet and place in the oven while baking the remaining waffles.

Makes about 8 large waffles

GINGERBREAD FLATS

OUT OF THE "Blue Grass" country of Kentucky comes the following recipe for a gingery, honeycombed dessert that is so delicious, it is bound to become a favorite. These waffles are best when *not* baked until crisp. The texture should be slightly cakey. They can be made in advance and stacked between paper towels to keep them moist. Reheat them on a rack in a low oven. A dab of sweetened whipped cream flavored with vanilla is traditional.

1/2 cup plus 2 tablespoons milk	1 teaspoon ground ginger
1/4 cup sugar	1/2 teaspoon ground cinnamon
4 tablespoons (1/2 stick) unsalted butter	1/4 teaspoon ground cloves
1 1/4 cups all-purpose flour	1/2 cup molasses
3/4 teaspoon baking soda	1 large egg

1. Preheat the oven to 250° F.

2. Combine the milk, sugar, and butter in a small saucepan. Heat over medium-low heat until the sugar dissolves and the butter is melted. Remove from heat.

3. Combine the flour, baking soda, ginger, cinnamon, and cloves in a medium bowl. Mix well. Stir in the milk mixture and the molasses. Whisk in the egg until smooth.

4. Heat a lightly greased waffle iron. Pour about 1/3 cup batter into the iron (depending on iron) and bake until the waffle is golden brown, but not crisp. Transfer to a wire rack-lined baking sheet and place in a low oven while baking the remaining waffles. (Or stack on paper towels as directed above.)

Makes 5 or 6 large waffles

CHOCOLATE WAFFLE DESSERT

> For us the winds do blow,
> The earth resteth, heav'n moveth, fountains flow;
> Nothing we see but means our good,
> As our delight or as our treasure;
> The whole is either our cupboard of food
> Or cabinet of pleasure.
>
> —George Herbert

A GRACE NOTE to the last recipe in this celebration of American food. And a "cabinet of pleasure" it is. "Sinful" might be a more appropriate description. A chocolate lover's dream, this dessert of chocolatey malted waffles is topped with ice cream and drizzled with a rich gooey sauce. Amen.

2 ounces semi-sweet chocolate
2 1/2 tablespoons unsalted butter
1 extra-large egg, separated
1 tablespoon sugar
1 teaspoon chocolate or plain malted milk powder

1/2 teaspoon baking soda
1 cup milk
3/4 cup plus 2 tablespoons all-purpose flour
Confectioners' sugar
Vanilla ice cream
Chocolate Velvet Sauce (recipe follows)

1. Melt the chocolate with the butter in the top of a double boiler over hot water until smooth. Remove from heat.

2. Beat the egg yolk with the sugar in a large bowl until light. Whisk in the malted milk powder, baking soda, and chocolate mixture. Slowly whisk in the milk and the flour. Beat until smooth.

3. Beat the egg white until stiff. Fold into the waffle batter.

4. Heat a lightly greased waffle iron. Pour about 1/2 cup batter into the iron (depending on iron) and bake until the waffle is crisp. Transfer to a wire rack-lined baking sheet while baking the remaining waffles. You should get 6 large waffles.

5. Just before serving, preheat the oven to 450° F.

6. Place the waffles on the baking sheet in the oven for 2 minutes. Turn the waffles over and continue to bake until the waffles are very crisp, about 3 minutes longer. Do not allow to burn. Sprinkle the waffles with confectioners' sugar and serve immediately with a scoop of ice cream and Chocolate Velvet Sauce.

Serves 6

CHOCOLATE VELVET SAUCE

4 ounces semi-sweet chocolate, chopped
2 1/2 tablespoons unsalted butter, cut into bits

2 tablespoons milk
2 tablespoons heavy or whipping cream
1 tablespoon dark rum

Melt the chocolate in the top of a double boiler over hot water. Stir in the butter, bit by bit, until smooth. Stir in the milk, cream, and rum. Stir until smooth.

Makes about 1 cup

Addenda

THOUGH I, like everyone else, often resort to canned broth, a good stock makes good cookin' all the better. Stock is easy to make and can be left simmering away, while you're doing other tasks. Store stock, tightly covered, in the refrigerator for up to a week, or freeze indefinitely. Four basic stocks follow, including a vegetable stock that can turn many recipes in this book into total vegetarian fare.

BEEF STOCK

4 pounds raw beef bones, including some meat
3 large onions, peeled, chopped
3 carrots, peeled, chopped
3 ribs celery, chopped
2 cloves garlic
6 sprigs parsley

1 bay leaf
3 whole cloves
8 black peppercorns
1 teaspoon salt
3 quarts plus 2 cups water
2 tablespoons red wine vinegar

1. Preheat the oven to 475° F.
2. Place the bones in a large roasting pan, and bake them until brown, 15 minutes. Turn the bones over and reduce the temperature to 450° F. Continue to bake, another 15 minutes, until the second side is browned as well.
3. Meanwhile, combine the remaining ingredients, except the 2 cups water and the vinegar, in a large heavy pot. Heat to boiling over high heat; reduce the heat.
4. Add the browned meat bones to the stock. Pour off the grease in the roasting pan and stir in the 2 cups water, scraping the bottom and sides of

the pan with a wooden spoon. Add this liquid to the stock pot. Return stock to boiling; reduce heat to low. Simmer, partially covered, skimming occasionally, for 3 hours. Stir in the vinegar and simmer until the stock is reduced to 1 1/2 quarts, about 2 hours longer. Strain.

Makes about 1 1/2 quarts

CHICKEN STOCK

4 pounds chicken pieces (backs, wings, necks)

4 quarts water (approximately)

2 yellow onions, unpeeled

1 leek, cleaned, chopped

2 cloves garlic

2 carrots, peeled, roughly chopped

2 ribs celery with leaves, chopped

2 turnips, peeled, roughly chopped

2 parsnips, peeled, roughly chopped

8 parsley sprigs

4 whole cloves

8 black peppercorns

1 teaspoon salt

1 small bay leaf

1/2 teaspoon chopped dried thyme

2 tablespoons red wine vinegar

1. Place the chicken pieces in a large pot and add the water. The chicken should be totally covered, so add more water if necessary. Heat to boiling; boil 5 minutes, skimming the surface as the scum rises to the top.

2. Add the remaining ingredients with enough water to cover the chicken by 3 inches (about 4 quarts altogether). Return to boiling; reduce the heat to low. Simmer, partially covered, skimming occasionally, until reduced to 1 1/2 quarts, about 2 hours. Strain.

Makes about 1 1/2 quarts

FISH STOCK

2 1/2 to 3 pounds fish bones, including heads

4 cups water

6 sprigs parsley

1 bay leaf

2 cups dry white wine

3 cups clam juice

2 onions, chopped

2 ribs celery with leaves, chopped

4 whole cloves

8 black peppercorns

1 teaspoon salt

1 lemon, halved

Combine all the ingredients in a large pot. Heat to boiling; reduce the heat to medium-low. Simmer, partially covered, until reduced to about 6 cups, about 30 minutes. Strain.

Makes about 1 1/2 quarts

VEGETABLE STOCK

4 tablespoons (1/2 stick) unsalted butter

5 onions, chopped

2 cloves garlic

4 ribs celery with leaves, chopped

4 carrots, peeled, roughly chopped

1/2 ounce dried mushrooms

1 bunch parsley

1/2 teaspoon dried thyme

Pinch of dried sage

1 bay leaf

1 teaspoon salt

8 black peppercorns

6 allspice berries, lightly crushed

Pinch of ground allspice

4 quarts water

1 tablespoon red wine vinegar

Melt the butter in a large heavy pot over medium heat. Stir in the onions; cook 5 minutes. Add the remaining ingredients except the vinegar. Heat to boiling; reduce the heat to low. Simmer, partially covered, until reduced to about 2 1/2 quarts, about 2 hours. Add the vinegar and simmer, uncovered, until reduced to 1 1/2 quarts, about 30 minutes longer. Strain, gently pressing the liquid out of the vegetables with the back of a spoon.

Makes about 1 1/2 quarts

METRIC CONVERSION CHART

Liquid and Dry Measure Equivalencies

Customary	Metric
1/4 teaspoon	1.25 milliliters
1/2 teaspoon	2.5 milliliters
1 teaspoon	5 milliliters
1 tablespoon	15 milliliters
1 fluid ounce	30 milliliters
1/4 cup	60 milliliters
1/3 cup	80 milliliters
1/2 cup	120 milliliters
1 cup	240 milliliters
1 pint (2 cups)	480 milliliters
1 quart (4 cups, 32 ounces)	960 milliliters (.96 liters)
1 gallon (4 quarts)	3.84 liters
1 ounce (by weight)	28 grams
1/4 pound (4 ounces)	114 grams
1 pound (16 ounces)	454 grams
2.2 pounds	1 kilogram (1000 grams)

Oven Temperature Equivalencies

Description	°Fahrenheit	°Celsius
Cool	200	90
Very slow	250	120
Slow	300–325	150–160
Moderately slow	325–350	160–180
Moderate	350–375	180–190
Moderately hot	375–400	190–200
Hot	400–450	200–230
Very hot	450–500	230–260

Noted Quotables

Athenaeus—Greek anecdotist c. 200 A.D.

Beard, James—American food writer, author 1903–1985

Beecher, Henry Ward—American clergyman, editor 1813–1887

Bierce, Ambrose—American short-story writer 1842–1914?

Bossidy, John Collins—English poet 1860–1928

Boulestin, X. Marcel—French chef, writer 1878–1943

Brillat-Savarin, Anthelme—French politician, gourmet 1755–1826

Carroll, Lewis—English author, mathematician 1832–1898

Carson, "Kit"—American frontiersman, trapper, guide 1809–1868

Chaucer, Geoffrey—English poet 1340?–1400

Churchill, Sir Winston—British Prime Minister 1874–1965

Claiborne, Craig—American food writer, author 1920–

Combe, William—English poet 1741–1823

Curnonsky (Maurice Edmond Sailland)—French writer, editor,
    "gastronome" 1873–1956

de Coquet, James—French food writer, journalist 1898–

Emerson, Ralph Waldo—American poet, essayist 1803–1882

Escoffier, Auguste—French chef, author 1846–1935

Field, Eugene—American poet, journalist 1850–1895

Fisher, M.F.K.—American writer, author 1908–

Freud, Clement—British politician 1924–

Goethe, Johann Wolfgang von—German poet, dramatist 1749–1832

Haines, John—American poet 1924–

Herbert, Alan Patrick—English writer 1890–1971

Herbert, George—English poet 1593–1632

Heywood, John—English dramatist, aphorist 1497?–1580?

Hippocrates—Greek physician 460?–377? B.C.

Holmes, Oliver Wendell—American poet, essayist, novelist 1809–1894

Hugo, Victor—French dramatist, novelist, poet 1802–1885

Hunt, Leigh—English poet, essayist 1784–1859

Irwin, Wallace—American journalist, humorist 1875–1959

Johnson, Samuel—English lexicographer, critic, author 1709–1784

Joyce, James—Irish novelist 1882–1941

Lampton, William G.—American journalist 1920–

Lin Yutang—Chinese philosopher, novelist, editor 1895–1976

Maginn, William—Irish writer, wit 1793–1842

Martial (Martialis), Marcus—Roman poet, epigrammatist 40?–104? A.D.

Mission, Francoise Maximilien—French writer 16th Century

Ousley, Clarence—American poet, editor 1863–1948

Parloa, Maria—American cooking teacher, author 1843–1909

Publilius Syrus—Roman writer c. 1st Century B.C.

Root, Waverley—American journalist, author 1903–

Sandburg, Carl—American poet, biographer 1878–1967

Sangster, Margaret E.—American writer, essayist 1838–1912

Shakespeare, William—English dramatist, poet 1564–1616

Shaw, George Bernard—Irish-born English dramatist, essayist, critic 1856–1950

Smith, Sydney—English clergyman, writer, wit 1771–1845

Sokolov, Raymond—American journalist, author 1941–

Steinbeck, John—American novelist 1902–1968

Stevenson, Robert Louis—Scottish poet, novelist 1850–1894

Surtees, Robert Smith—English novelist 1805–1864

Swift, Jonathan—English satirist 1667–1745

Taylor, Bert Leston—American writer 1866–1921

Trillin, Calvin—American author, satirist 1935–

Twain, Mark (Clemens, Samuel)—American author, humorist 1835–1910
Untermeyer, Louis—American poet, anthologist 1885–1977
Villas, James—American journalist, author 1938–
Warner, Charles Dudly—American writer 1829–1900
White, William Allen—American politician, editor 1868–1944
Wilder, Laura Ingalls—American novelist 1867–1957

Selected Bibliography

America's Favorites, Kay and Marshall Lee, G. P. Putnam's Sons, New York, 1980

The American Heritage Cookbook, The Editors of American Heritage, American Heritage Publishing, New York, 1964

American Taste, James Villas, Arbor House, New York, 1982

The Anthology of Puddings, Irene Veal, John Gifford, Ltd., London, 1942

Apple Kitchen Cookbook, Demetria Taylor, International Apple Institute, Washington, DC, 1971

Back-To-Basics American Cooking, Anita Prichard, G. P. Putnam's Sons, New York, 1983

Beeton's Book of Household Management, (first edition facsimile), edited by Mrs. Isabella Beeton, Farrar, Straus, and Giroux, New York, 1969

The Benevolent Bean, Margaret and Ancel Keys, Farrar, Straus & Giroux, New York, 1972

The Best of De Gustibus, Marion Burros, Simon & Schuster, New York, 1988

The Brilliant Bean, Sally and Martin Stone, Bantam Books, New York, 1988

Bull Cook and Authentic Historical Recipes and Practices, George Leonard Herter and Berthe E. Herter, Herter's, Waseca, MN, 1969

The Cake Bible, Rose Levy Beranbaum, William Morrow & Co., New York, 1988

Campbell's Great American Cookbook, Edited by Flora Szatkowski, Random House, New York, 1984

Colonial Virginia Cookery, Jane Carson, The Colonial Williamsburg Foundation, Williamsburg, VA, 1985

The Complete Bean Cookbook, Victor Bennett, Prentice-Hall, New Jersey, 1967

Consuming Passions, Edited by Jonathon Green, Fawcett Columbine, New York, 1985

The Cook's Encyclopedia, Tom Stobart, Harper & Row, New York, 1981

Cooks, Gluttons & Gourmets, Betty Wason, Doubleday, New York, 1962

The Cook's Quotation Book, Edited by Maria Polushkin Robbins, Pushcart Press, Wainscott, NY, 1985

The Delectable Past, Esther B. Aresty, Simon & Schuster, New York, 1964

The Dictionary of American Food & Drink, John F. Mariani, Ticknor & Fields, New Haven and New York, 1983

Dictionary of American Regional English, Frederic G. Cassidy, Chief Editor, Volume 1, The Belknap Press of Harvard University Press, Cambridge, MA, 1985

Dictionary of Gastronomy, Andre L. Simon and Robin Howe, McGraw-Hill, New York, 1970

Eating in America, Waverley Root and Richard de Rochemont, William Morrow & Co., New York, 1976

Fading Feast, Raymond Sokolov, E. P. Dutton, New York, 1983

Familiar Quotations, (thirteenth Centennial edition), John Bartlett, Little, Brown & Co., Boston, 1955

Food for Thought, Edited by Joan and John Digby, William Morrow & Co., New York, 1987

Food In History, Reay Tannahill, Stein And Day, New York, 1973

The Food Lover's Book of Lists, Patricia Altobello and Deirdre Pierce, New American Library, New York, 1979

Guinness Book of World Records, (1987 Special Edition), Sterling Publishing, New York, 1987

The Horizon Cookbook and Illustrated History of Eating and Drinking through the Ages, William Harlan Hale and the Editors of Horizon Magazine, American Heritage Publishing, New York, 1968

The International Chili Society Official Chili Cookbook, Martina and William Neely, St. Martin's Press, New York, 1981

The Joy of Cookies, Sharon Tyler Herbst, Barron's, New York, 1987

Lang's Compendium of Culinary Nonsense and Trivia, George Lang, Clarkson N. Potter, New York, 1980

The Little House Cookbook, Barbara M. Walker, Harper & Row, New York, 1979

Magill's Quotations In Context, Edited by Frank N. Magill, Harper & Row, New York, 1965

Malachi McCormick's Irish Country Cooking, Malachi McCormick, Clarkson N. Potter, New York, 1988

Mary Margaret McBride's Harvest of American Cooking, Mary Margaret McBride, G. P. Putnam's Sons, New York, 1956

Mrs. Allen on Cooking, Menus, Service, Ida C. Bailey Allen, Doubleday, Doran & Company, Inc., New York, 1929

Mrs. Rorer's Cook Book, Arnold and Co., Philadelphia, 1886

Mythology and Meatballs, Daniel Spoerri, translated by Emmett Williams, Aris Books, Berkeley, 1982

The Oxford Book of Aphorisms, Chosen by John Gross, Oxford University Press, Oxford, England, 1983

The Oxford Dictionary of Quotations, (Second Edition), Oxford University Press, Oxford, England, 1955

Pancakes, Dorian Leigh Parker, Clarkson N. Potter, New York, 1987

The Potato Cookbook, Gwen Robyns, Stemmer House Publishers, Owings Mills, MD, 1976

Simple Cooking, John Thorne, Viking, New York, 1987

Southern Food, John Egerton, Alfred A. Knopf, 1987

The Taste of America, John L. Hess and Karen Hess, Grossman Publishers, New York, 1977

Tastings, Jenifer Harvey Lang, Crown Publishers, New York, 1986

Third Helpings, Calvin Trillin, Ticknor & Fields, New York, 1983

Tropic Cooking, Joyce LaFray Young, 10-Speed Press, Berkeley, 1987

20,000 Quips & Quotes, Evan Esar, Doubleday, New York, 1968

"Unabashed Passion for Brownies," Diane Stoneback, *The Morning Call,* Allentown, PA, April 3, 1988

The Viking Book of Aphorisms, A personal selection by W. H. Auden and Louis Kronenberger, Viking Press, 1981

Woman's Day Encyclopedia, Volumes 1–12, Editors of Woman's Day, Fawcett Publications, New York, 1966

The Yankee Cook Book, Imogene Wolcott, Ives Washburn, New York, 1963

Your Horoscope and Dreams, Ned Ballantyne and Stella Coeli, Books, Inc., New York, 1966

Index

fish (*cont.*)
  see also scallop(s); seafood; shrimp
Fisher, M.F.K., 172, 345, 359
Flagstaff tamale pie, 310–12
flannels, spinach stuffed, 274–75
Florida Keys bread pudding with rum sauce, 93–95
flour, 68–69, 135
Freud, Clement, 87, 366
fricassees, 203
  chicken, with cornmeal dumplings, 347–48
fried chicken, *see* chicken, fried
frosted Baltimore brunettes, 110–11
frostings:
  burnt sugar, 149–50
  caramel nut, 146–47
  chocolate-coke buttercream, 142–43
  classic boiled, 145–46
  Colorado snow, 151–53
  fudge, 136–37
  fudge and marshmallow, 141–42
  milk chocolate buttercream, 138–40
fudge:
  chocolate cake with milk chocolate buttercream, Rose Levy Beranbaum's, 138–40
  frosting, old-fashioned layer cake with, 136–37
  and marshmallow frosting, 141–42
Fusco, Pat, 61

Gardner, Jill, 125, 126, 359, 371
Georgian:
  bits and grits, 368
  coke, 60
  "greens and beans," 47–48
  moppin' sauce, 61

Germantown iced apple and raisin pie, 23–24
ginger:
  barbecue sauce, 65
  chocolate chips, 160
gingerbread flats, 373–74
glazed meat loaf, 248–49
Gloucester fish hash, 231–233
Goethe, Johann Wolfgang von, 243
golden barbecue pot roast, 332–33
grandmotherly cole slaw, 190–91
grand pot roast, 338–39
gravy:
  cream, Old Dominion fried chicken with, 207–8
  lemon, honey and bacon fried chicken with, 210–12
  over fried chicken, 206
  red-eye, fried chicken and ham with, 213–14
Great Lakes corn chowder, 185–86
green chile pot roast with potatoes, New Mexican, 333–34
green chilied pork with polenta, 126–27
Greene, Bert, 85, 118, 190, 291
Greens (San Francisco), 294
"greens and beans," Georgian, 47–48
Greenwich Village "Brownstone" brownies, 103
grilled potato with fresh vegetable salad, 294–95
grits, Georgian bits and, 368
guava, in Hawaiian pork sauce, 63–64
Gulfport seafood chili, 128–129

Haines, John, 200
ham:

and apple hash, Corinth, 230–31
baked sweet billy beans, 51–52
and cheese biscuits, Alabama, 77
fried chicken and, with red-eye gravy, 213–14
loaf, Clara Armstrong's, 254
Lushington chili, 121–22
road to Galveston hash, 241–42
Hampton, Sister Cora, 97
happily ever after shrimp and scallop hash, 243–244
hard sauce, bread pudding with, 83–84
hash, 225–44
  black olive and minted lamb, 242–43
  chicken, ultimate, 236–37
  Chinese-American, 239–240
  fiftieth state, 234–35
  fish, Gloucester, 231–33
  ham and apple, Corinth, 230–31
  history of, 225–26
  molded lamb, with egg sauce, 233–34
  red flannel, Woonsocket, 229–30
  road to Galveston, 241–242
  roast beef, 227–28
  sheepherder's, 238–39
  shrimp and scallop, happily ever after, 243–244
  tips for, 226–27
Hawaiian pork sauce, 63–64
Hawkins, Sir John, 281
Heath Bars, in dastardly hash, 164
Heatter, Maida, 99–100, 106
heavenly beef pie with devil-

ishly rich mashed potato topping, 318–20
heavenly pecan waffles, 372–73
Helen's buttermilk skyscrapers, 72
Henderson, Ruth, 192
herbed:
  and crusted turkey loaf, 261–62
  topping, ratatouille pie with, 316–18
Herbert, George, 374
Herbert, Sir Alan Patrick, 266
Herbst, Sharon Tyler, 70, 160
Herter, George and Berthe, 236
Heywood, John, 140
Hippocrates, 328
Holmes, Oliver Wendell, 69
hominy, sombrero fried chicken with salsa ranchera and, 220–22
honey and bacon fried chicken with lemon gravy, 210–12
Hoppin' John, baked, 48–49
hot dressed potato salad, Yankee-style, 285–86
Hotel Touraine (Boston), 99
Hugo, Victor, 273
Hunt, Leigh, 76

ice box pudding, chocolate malted, 91–92
icings, see frostings
Indians, 35, 52, 74, 115–16, 123, 169–70, 185, 264, 341
Iowa potato salad, true blue, 287–88
Irwin, Wallace, 231

James, Frank and Jesse, 115
Jeanette's bars, 111–12
Jefferson, Thomas, 362

Jersey pudding with Amaretto sauce, 95
Johnson, Helen, 314
Johnson, Samuel, 369
Jones, Reverend, 357
Joyce, James, 368

Kansas creamy wheats, 365
Kate's biscuits, 71
Knuehman, John, 120

lace cakes, 270–72
lamb:
  baked beans Cassie's way, 46–47
  and black olive minted hash, 242–43
  molded hash with egg sauce, 233–34
  pie with orange pastry, Rocky Mountain orange-scented, 305–7
  stew, Dakota, 349–50
Lampton, William James, 278–79
Lang, Jennifer Harvey, 155
leek and potato seafood slurp, 175–76
lemon:
  crust, sausage and pepper pot pie with, 312–14
  gravy, honey and bacon fried chicken with, 210–12
  mayonnaise, new potatoes and peas in, 288–90
  waffles, risen, 370–71
lentils, pot roast with, 328–329
Leslie, Eliza, 187–88
Lewis, Edna, 204
Lewis, Nelly Custis, 226
lima beans, in Bleecker Street veggie chili, 129–131
Lin Yutang, 157
little scallop pies under blankets, 309–10
Long Island mussel and fish stew, 354
Lucas, "Chicken Betty," 208

Lundberg, Donald E., 135
Lushington chili, 121–22

McLaughlin, Michael, 129–130
McQueary, Pat, 72
Madeline's red hot slaw, 194–95
Magavern, Jane, 59
Maginn, William, 301
Maine potato crisps, 367
malted ice box pudding, chocolate, 91–92
malties, Chicago chocolate, 107–8
Manhattan Chili Company (New York City), 129–130
Manhattan clam chowder, 179
marbled wonder brownies, 109
Marin County chocolate chippers, 160–61
marshmallow(s):
  brotherly love bars, 104–105
  and fudge frosting, 141–142
Mary of Agreda, Sister, 123
Mary Surina's San Pedro baked beans, 39–40
Mary Surina's wilted slaw, 199
Matthews, Uncle Jimmy, 353
mayonnaise:
  cocoa cake with burnt sugar frosting, 149–50
  lemon, new potatoes and peas in, 288–90
meat loaves, 245–62
  bran and mushroom, 258–59
  with crisped potatoes, 249–50
  glazed, 248–49
  ham, Clara Armstrong's, 254
  history of, 245–46

INDEX

About the Author

PHILLIP SCHULZ is a food writer and the author of several other cookbooks, including *Vodka 'n' Vittles* and the ever popular *Cooking With Fire and Smoke*. He lives in New York City and Amagansett, Long Island.